STOLEN FROM MY ARMS

STOLEN
FROM
MY ARMS

*A young mother crosses international boundaries,
risking everything, to get her child back . . . a true story*

Katherine Sapienza

with Zach Taylor

Lighthouse Trails Publishing
Eureka, Montana

Stolen From My Arms
© 2011 Katherine Sapienza

Published in Eureka, Montana by
Lighthouse Trails Publishing, LLC
www.lighthousetrails.com

Scripture quotations are taken from the *King James Version*.

Cover design and book layout by Lighthouse Trails Publishing. Cover photo: Peeter Viisimaa; used with permission from istockphoto.com.

Library of Congress Cataloging-in-Publication Data

Sapienza, Katherine.
  Stolen from my arms : a young mother crosses international boundaries, risking everything, to get her child back : a true story / Katherine Sapienza ; with Zach Taylor.
      p. cm.
  ISBN 978-0-9846366-0-0 (softbound : alk. paper)
  1. Conti, Alex–Kidnapping, 1992- 2. Kidnapping–Italy. 3. Absentee fathers–Italy. 4. Custody of children–Italy. 5. Mothers–Italy. I. Taylor, Zach. II. Title.
  HV6604.I82S27 2011
  362.82'97092–dc23
  [B]
                                        2011020112

Note: Most Lighthouse Trails books are available at special quantity discounts. Contact information for publisher in back of book.

Printed in the United States of America

To my loving parents Apuka and Mamuka

Contents

Note to the Reader from Author

Some aspects of this book may appear denigrating to the whole of Sicilian culture and the Sicilian people. Such is definitely not the case. As in every culture on earth, there is a generous mixture of good and bad, and the chronicling of my experiences in Sicily bear this out. It must be remembered that this book was written through a lens of captivity, wherein my son was stolen from me and where the whole of the Italian legal system was arrayed against me. The understandable stress of living in a foreign country and being portrayed as an "uninterested" mother contributed greatly to the way I saw both my situation in particular and Sicily in general. Had I remained there as a vacationing tourist or even an expat* with a good home life, this book would never have been written. So, I ask the reader to bear with me, in grace, and perhaps consider if my feelings, though graphic, were also understandable.

On the up side, much of Sicilian culture was and is a blessing on my life. While there, I made some wonderful Sicilian friends, some of whom remain friends today. I rave about the cuisine (with the exception of cow spleen sandwiches~see Chapter 7) and the country's incredible beauty and rich history. Having become somewhat fluent in Italian while there, I still speak that lovely language when the opportunity arises. And, no mention of the country would be complete without touching on the people themselves. Sicilians, for all their faults, are the most wildly enthusiastic people I've ever met. They carelessly embrace each day as it comes, and their boundless optimism is contagious.

With all my heart, I thank them for what they have taught me.

Katherine (Katie) Sapienza

* Short for expatriate; a person who resides in another country other than the one in which he or she grew up in or has legal residency in.

Publisher Note: Some names in this book have been changed out of respect for the privacy of certain individuals involved. The story itself is factual and true in every sense.

Prologue

Chi nasconde quel che fa,
Vuol dire che male fa.
Who hides what he is doing,
means he is doing something bad.

It would be nice if, like that old cliché, life really was like a highway—a broad, well-paved avenue flatlining to a distant horizon. It is instead a seemingly untended crust of broken asphalt, fraught with potholes, agonizingly narrow at spots, clogged with fellow travelers who haven't got a clue where they're headed but want to get there in a hurry. Finally, it is a roadway marred with flashing light detours that force the vehicle of the soul onto some shadowed, tufted-over jeep trail whose terminus may be a forgotten emotional backwater.

No young mother wakes up one fine morning and thinks, *Today my child will cave in to peer pressure and try drugs for the first time* or *tonight, after my daughter's prom, she will be fatally struck by a drunk driver.* Nor does she awake thinking, *This is the last day for many years that I'll be able to kiss my son's face, stroke his hair, or feel his nearness. This is the day he'll be torn from my side without my notice, that he'll be removed to a foreign country, told his mother is a bad person, and held against his will by those claiming to love him. This is the day he'll be kidnapped.*

For me, it was a time of many other things as well: the beginning of walking through an empty house haunted by the quiet, touching his toys, going to sleep at night hugging his clothes. Oh, and the tears, always the tears. Coming unbidden at every inconvenient moment of every hellish day, this protracted grief became prison bars through which I saw the world. It was the catalyst for a long, waking nightmare, of unyielding anguish and finally of the unreasoning rage of a momma bear deprived of her cub.

This momma would fight. Had I known beforehand just how long the battle would go on or how many emotional breakdowns I'd have to experience, I wonder if I could have held to my sanity. Just the thought of facing so many looming obstacles, while uncertain of the outcome, could have knocked the fight out of me. The detour down this dark, weed-strewn road led to places I hope never to see again. And to one that changed my life.

How can a person prepare herself for the unthinkable? During the Holocaust, when the deportation of European Jews to the death camps was in full swing, when the horrors of Auschwitz, Dachau, and Treblinka were beginning to be known to their prospective victims, even then many refused to believe. For more than a millennium, Europe hosted a small but strong Jewish community. Often derision, pogroms, and slander would come with the territory. But the Jews could no more contemplate their planned eradication than they could believe the moon would be whisked from the night sky. As a group, they were an integral part of the European scene, and as such, were needed. Their philosophy of bending in the strong winds of change instead of being broken by them had kept their communities intact through war and societal abuse. They just could not fathom such a mass atrocity as their own intricately planned extermination. "We have always suffered persecution," they said, "and this will pass, as all the other times. Things will return as they once were."

Even when shuttled into cattle cars and brutalized by sadistic guards, many refused to look reality square in the face. It was not that they were naïve; it was simply that such a monstrous plan directed at them was beyond the scope of anything they—or indeed the civilized world—had ever dealt with. There were simply no parallels to it in their collective experience.

As a mother whose child is abducted, you find yourself thinking over and over—*This isn't happening, not really. This is the stuff* of Grade B movies or trashy novels. At the very least it should be happening to someone else. You keep waiting for the alarm clock to go off so you can open your eyes and breathe an exhausted, heartfelt prayer of thanks that it was only a horrific dream. But you don't waken. There's no merciful escape for even a moment, and with every tick of the clock, you're left with that unrelenting fear that balls its fist in your stomach. It reminds you this is life, baby, and just like what the Bard said, you're just an actor playing out your part, completely at the mercy of another's script. Everything is outside your control.

Yet, before the first act starts, before the first incident sets off the unraveling of your well-ordered world, that first twenty-four hour span kicks it off and leaves it cemented in your mind forever . . . that first day . . .

Ode to Alex

There's a place in my heart that you hold,
It's a space so large—*that* you've been told
Time after time, day after day,
I care for you in a special way.
The moment I saw you when you were born,
A love light around you, and now that's been torn.
I'm convinced you're so special,
I'm sure that I'm right,
It goes on forever, this continuous light.
My son, my son, I love you so much;
The wish that I feel and cannot yet touch—
A chance to be with you, day after day,
Just a moment, a glance to see when you play.
The years are running out; I'm so afraid!
So often I've prayed, "Oh, God, please help me!"
I've done so much, not in vain,
To endure this horrible pain.
The most wonderful thing in my life has been you;
There's so much more for us to do.
Do what I must in this never-ending strain,
The torture, the torment, and the endless pain.
I lay awake nights thinking how it was and could be;
It's useless now and we'll never see.
A kiss and a hug, it's the end of the night;
You are my joy and my forever delight.

Katherine

1

The Twist of the Knife

Chi nasce tondo non muore quadrato.
Who is born round doesn't die square.

The day was gorgeous, a California classic of brilliant sunshine and startlingly blue skies, with the scent of the ocean in the gentle breeze. The summer was fixing to be a hot one and of the endless variety from my standpoint. A few brief moments more, a couple tight hugs and hurried endearments, and the focus of my life would be removed for six interminable weeks.

I sat in the midst of a crowd of other parents, most of them beaming, pointing, snapping photos of the little scholars all lined up in the courtyard of Meadow Brook Elementary School. It was June 10, 1992. Alex had turned six the week before, and he'd been gearing up for the ceremony. The children's excitement was palpable, manifested in nervous grins and sporadic chattering, and although not quite understanding all that was going on, they were happy to be at the center of such attention and excitement. They reveled in their self-importance, parading past in their homemade paper hats, and shuffling forward one slow step at a time to receive a diploma that would usher them into the next phase of their education—from kindergarten to first grade. Immensely proud, I waved to Alex, giving my best fake happy face so I wouldn't ruin the moment for him. Through the smiles I could feel the tears wanting to come. *Later,* I told myself, choking them back. *Plenty of time for that tonight.*

It was embarrassing—borderline outrageous, really—that his dad hadn't the interest to even show up for the ceremony. Massimo had dropped off Alex at school and left without so much as a word of greeting to me or praise for his son. For all the fanciful talk about the importance of "family," which I'd heard ad infinitum during my three years in Sicily, I'd found that Massimo ably modeled the opposite. I wondered if it even crossed his mind that he'd be missed at a gathering like this and that his absence would raise uncomfortable questions that I'd have to answer, when every other child there was represented by both doting parents. He had played his part so convincingly in the courtroom a week earlier that, with a smile, the judge ruled in his favor.

Massimo had been all humility then. Love for his son was written all over him. It was utterly disturbing, really, because I knew him for what he was. Three years of a tormenting marriage had convinced me of his true nature, and only leaving him and Sicily for the United States had been the saving of my sanity. But for those outside his immediate circle of relationships, his masterful charade offered up a character at once to be pitied and admired. He was misunderstood, after all, and now he was a foreigner in a strange country, having come all the way from his distant homeland to prove his father's love. Yes, he'd made his mistakes but that was all in the past, and now he was eager to make up for time misspent. All he wanted to do was make sure Alex had the opportunity to re-connect with his Italian heritage and spend some time with the grandparents he might never see again. The judge wholeheartedly agreed. It would be a shame to let such devotion be for naught.

Although outraged, I couldn't fault the judge personally. Massimo's performance was flawless. He'd had a lifetime to perfect it, and a courtroom was simply another stage to make it work.

And so this perfect, misunderstood father didn't even show enough respect for his son to stay a half-hour and tell him "Good job!"

What hypocrisy, I thought to myself.

On top of that, when Alex had been dropped off, he looked like he'd been up half the night. His eyes were puffy and ringed underneath, and his thick dark hair, which I always took special care of, was in shoddy disarray. I was concerned and a little angry. I didn't hide it well from Alex.

"What did you do last night?"

"I don't know. We watched TV, and Papa made me macaroni and cheese."

I smiled. "You're kidding."

"No, really. It was great."

He said the last part with a child's flair for the dramatic. Alex loved mac and cheese, and Massimo hated the idea of it. He thought it a corruption of Italian cuisine. That Alex had talked him into making the meal for him was quite an accomplishment, and one I secretly enjoyed. The knowledge helped lighten my mood a bit.

During the ceremony, a young Christian woman approached me. She was the wife of a long-time friend, a mother with two of her own little ones standing in the graduation line. We chatted briefly, and when I told her Alex was going with his dad back to Sicily for part of the summer, she grew suddenly very serious. In a quiet voice she asked, "Katie, aren't you concerned about Alex being taken so far away?"

The question took me by surprise. Well, of course I was concerned; inwardly I was frantic. Alex and I had never before been separated, and the thought of him being taken some 6,000 miles by a man who detested me was almost more than I could bear. She had no idea how much self-control it took to keep from falling apart right in front of her. I was sick about the situation. Added to this was the creeping suspicion I'd had all along that something was not quite right. Fear had been nagging at me

Alex on graduation day

since the judge had rendered his decision. I dismissed the growing anxiety as the product of my own mind, but still . . .

And then this kindly woman voices the same things I'd been feeling. What is it about mothers when their babies are threatened secretly? So much of the time, they know. Although unable to pin it down in exact terms, the heart instinct tells them when a setup is in progress. But I didn't want to entertain her fears as well as my own. To preserve my sanity I couldn't consider the implications.

I hunched my shoulders in a gesture of helplessness and looked away. "Sure I'm concerned, but what can I do? The judge said it was okay for Alex to go with his dad. How can I fight that . . .?"

We talked a bit more. Then as the ceremony ended, I reluctantly led Alex to the car for the trip back home. The time had come. His suitcase was already packed, and all that was left to do was grab it then go pick up Massimo who was staying at the house of an Italian acquaintance. And on the drive back to the house, with Alex sitting happily on the seat beside me, I kept hearing those words echo in an endless refrain: "Aren't you concerned . . . ?"

Massimo was ready to go, eager, and on the drive to the airport he and Alex chatted nonstop. Inside, I was dying, but didn't want to spoil it for Alex, so I remained for the most part very quiet and tried to concentrate on maneuvering through California traffic. We had gone about halfway when Massimo asked for Alex's passport. I nearly slammed on the brakes. The passport! I'd completely forgotten it in the maelstrom of emotion. Massimo was livid. "How could you possibly have forgotten such an important document? We're almost to the airport! Katie, I know what you're trying to do and it won't work . . ."

He went on and on while I located a place for a turnaround, my stomach grinding. All this was doing was prolonging the inevitable. We got back to the house, grabbed the passport and lit out the door at a dead run.

We made it to the airport in good time, cleared security, and waited together in the departure lounge. By this time I was bawling like a baby. I pressed Massimo into photographer's service, and he grudgingly snapped a last photo of Alex and me before boarding. Alex held me tight at the waist, and we both faced the camera. The photo of me was absolutely awful, and it was a prelude to the rest of the night's crying. I barely slept at all.

I phoned Alex the very next day and told him all the motherly things that both he and I needed to hear, then I asked him if he liked some of the things I'd packed in his luggage. One was a hand-made calendar, prominently marked on the date he was to return.

"What calendar?" he asked innocently.

That's strange, I thought. "What about the picture of the two of us?"

Again, Alex hadn't seen it. Something passed over me briefly, like a breath of cold wind from an open window. I quickly dismissed

Worst day of my life—saying goodbye to Alex before his trip to Italy

17

the suggestion and thought that perhaps it was absurd. Massimo wouldn't dare pull anything, not after the court appearance and the papers that lawfully restrained him from taking custodial liberties. No, he hadn't wasted any time getting in his digs now that he was out of the country, but I forced myself to rack up the incident as only borne of his contempt for me. I refused to let myself emotionally pursue it. But, like the proverb says, "Who is born round doesn't die square." How could I expect the round Massimo to change into the square good guy, on the order of a judge? Hadn't I filed papers with the California court system stating that I had felt threatened by Massimo, had been the victim of psychological and emotional abuse by him, and that, if I tried to divorce him in Sicily, he would likely have succeeded, in that convoluted court system, in taking Alex from me, permanently? But now I willed myself to believe that, since the California judge had given Massimo direct instructions regarding his returning Alex to me after his "vacation," that that was the end of it. I had yet to understand what many battered wives stalked by ex-husbands came to learn the hard way—that a court document, however official-looking, could never prevent the actions of a person intent on accomplishing the evil of his own heart.

Six weeks is a long wait when you're separated from the most important person in your life. For me, time seemed reduced to the barest increments. I learned not to think in terms of weeks, but in days, one tumultuous sunrise-to-sunset cycle after another. Although it never got easier, per se, I did find things to take up the slack. Foremost, I threw myself into my work. As a medical assistant, I put in a lot of clinical hours. A satellite for a larger facility, it provided a lot of distraction from counting the hours. I also went for bike rides and a lot of walks, and occasionally did dinner with friends. My most pressing need was to be around people, consistently. That interpersonal contact was the best medicine, and one person in particular stands out during that time—my apartment manager, of all people. He was so very kind. A perceptive man some years older than me, he'd make opportunities to come see me, not with any romantic intentions, but because he was just a nice guy who knew I desperately missed my son. Sometimes he'd even bring a stack of paperwork to my apartment, so he could sit and do figures while I enjoyed his just being there.

Five weeks crawled by, and the excitement about Alex's return began to build. I went through all the favorite things he'd like to do when he got home, what meals I could prepare, what little adventures we could go on as a kind of welcoming-home present. The apartment had been empty without him; my heart ached the entire time, and I still felt like crying whenever I'd imagine holding him, being near him again. Still, there remained that disconcerting something way back in my mind, that consistent little jabbing that would never quite let up but that I'd never admit. It was exacerbated by some then-inexplicable incidents. I'd called Sicily, trying to speak with Alex, but always there were excuses—"Oh, he's out playing with friends." "He's taking a nap." "He's somewhere with his father." There was always something that kept him from speaking with me directly. So, a week before his vacation was due to end, it was a relief to actually get him on the phone. We chatted only briefly, and after I told him excitedly, "Just one more week, honey, and you'll be back home again," Massimo bulled his way into the conversation.

"He's not coming back," he said matter-of-factly.

I felt like I'd been slapped but managed to stutter out, "W . . . what?"

I couldn't have heard correctly.

Massimo's hard voice slid into me like a knife. "He's staying here, Katie. This was planned the whole time. I had no intention of letting my son go back to the United States. He's Italian, not American. He never should have left Italy."

The vague fear I'd felt all along rose up and leered at me. My voice screeched, cracked. "You can't do that!"

Massimo flaunted his power over me, not even trying to soften the blow. "Oh, I can do it, all right. I've already got custody."

"But the courts . . . !"

He fairly sneered. "Those documents I gave to the judge in California didn't mean anything. The courts have granted me custody in Italy, and there's not a thing you can do about it."

At this point, I was in tears, pleading. "Oh, please, Massimo, please don't do this. Not Alex. You can't . . . *pleeeaaase* . . ."

The line went silent as I sat there, begging, crying into a dead phone.

I went completely hysterical, panicking alone in the apartment that now mocked me with its emptiness. "This can't be," I said aloud, over and over. "This isn't happening." Walking in tight circles, pulling my hair, I was hearing from a distance my voice as unintelligible screeches. In a panic, I grabbed the phone and, trembling violently, called my good friend Michael Constantine. Between sobs, I told him what had just occurred. He raced over; when he saw my condition, he wrapped his arms around me and held me. He spoke impotent soothing words, and geared into his own man emotions—seething about Massimo's outrageousness. This was no longer a disagreeable custody battle. It was kidnapping. Mike's take-charge personality kicked into overdrive. When I finally calmed enough to actually respond to him, he said determinedly, "Okay, we have to make a plan."

I phoned several others, including my lawyer, James Finegold. He was furious, as was Massimo's American attorney. From a professional standpoint it made him look foolish. He had no idea that Massimo had planned this entire fiasco. He realized he had been taken in by this smooth operator. "We should have asked for a bond," he fumed.

Fat lot of good it did to suggest that now.

I went to work the next day in a fog of grief and rage, informed my boss of the kidnapping and somewhat tried to function. I'd take in a patient, go to the bathroom to cry, and then take in another one. Over and over, I portrayed a merry-go-round of stone-faced professionalism followed by a descent into the pit of anguish. The ache in my heart was almost more than I could bear, and having to hold it in even part of the time took great effort. In the privacy of the clinic bathroom, I hugged myself and doubled over, wanting to wail out loud but forced by protocol to keep the sobs within discreet boundaries. When needed in the office, I'd gather myself, attempt to dry my eyes and make myself moderately presentable until I could escape behind the bathroom door once again. My coworkers were very sympathetic but completely helpless. How do you comfort a mother whose young son has been stolen? What words will make it all better, retrieve the only child from a world away and render appropriate justice to the criminal who inflicted the torment?

In the following days a thought occurred to me, a remembrance of something that I'd been told (from Alex?), that in the next few weeks Massimo would be going to Malta for a hunt, and would likely take Alex along. When I relayed this to Mike Constantine, a "Bingo!" light went on in his eyes, and he got me a plane ticket to Malta. A fairly well-off man, he also purchased some call card minutes for me and told me to get on the phone to Malta and set up something.

At the same time, my lawyer followed up with another piece of the haphazard plan. "I've got a connection for you in Malta," he said, and excitedly told me of a new ally in the fight to regain Alex. An American, this contact co-owned a popular restaurant in Santa Cruz, and his business partner's brother managed a large industrial plant in Malta. This kind man signaled his eagerness to help me as soon as he was told the story. He requested that my lawyer send him recent photos of both Massimo and me. I prepared to leave Santa Cruz. In the meantime, Michael Finegold gave my story to a Santa Cruz newspaper in the hope that media exposure would result in some kind of America-Italy negotiations on my behalf. The paper hopped on the story and wanted to send over a reporter for an interview, but I dismissed the idea. I didn't have the time, and I wasn't really interested in anything other than shooting across the sea one day and coming back with my son the next.

At work the day before I left for Malta, I became engaged in conversation with a man whose infant son was a patient at the clinic. As he waited for the clinic to fill his prescription, and since it was also my lunch break (in the same building, one floor down), we both had time on our hands. We chatted idly for a few moments until the incident with Alex began spilling out. The man was fascinated. When I mentioned that a Santa Cruz newspaper wanted to do a story, he jumped up and said, "Stay right there!," and made for the nearest telephone. The man turned out to be the newspaper's photographer; he phoned the main office to send a reporter down there to get the whole story. That same day the photographer showed up at my apartment, and the deal was done. I still remember the photographer's face, his look of genuine sorrow, and his efforts at consolation over the kidnapping. He was deeply moved by the whole rotten affair.

The next day I was at the airport. I had no real idea how we were going to get Alex away from Massimo, but this impromptu rescue team was a lifeline. After what had seemed like a forever of grief, here was a glimmer of hope. I wasn't fooling myself. There was no plan, really; just board a plane to an exotic island, wait for Massimo to show, and somehow—somehow—get my son back. I was scared, but I was also really, really ticked off. Massimo may have thought he'd seen the end of it; he was used to having his way with me. But I thought it fitting that we'd face off while he was preparing for a hunt. As far as I was concerned, he'd better come armed to the teeth.

Mamma bear was about to show her fangs.

2

Beginnings

A goccia a goccia si scava la pietra.
Drop by drop the water shapes the rock.

"*Mamuka*, leave that! You know better. You shouldn't play around with your health."

I didn't have to correct Mom often—she was a great patient, all around—but she had a cleaning streak a yard wide and was used to managing her own household.

She sighed tiredly, "I'm sorry, Kati. I just want to do things again. It's frustrating, sometimes. You know . . ."

I smiled. After all these years, she still called me Kati*, the Hungarian rendering of my name. I guess some things aren't meant to change, even with age. Today, when thinking of my own grown son, I figure it's good that there are some "unalterables."

New Jersey itself didn't much agree with me anymore—I was a confirmed California girl by that time—but the urgency to return to my parents' house in New Brunswick, New Jersey was something I couldn't downplay. Mother was on her sickbed, or rather, in the beginning stages of mending after a grueling operation. Recovering from the first of what would prove to be two brain surgeries in which some benign tumors had been successfully removed, she still had great difficulty getting around and

* Pronounced as "Cutty."

23

performing everyday functions. She slept a lot and couldn't do any real lifting, so a live-in nurse was just what she needed, and it helped that it was her daughter.

As a medical assistant for a cardiologist in Santa Cruz, I was quite familiar with nursing techniques. As a Licensed Practical Nurse (LPN) in California, I had enough experience to assist her in the recuperative stage. Strange that my professional residency had been shuttled from an office setting with the latest medical equipment to a home environment where basic, hands-on know-how was the primary requirement. Even stranger was that I had been a fixture in this same house for many years while growing up.

It was somehow an otherworldly experience, traveling back to my geographical roots after a long absence. Having seen so much of the world, sampled different lifestyles, and interacted with people with whom I'd had absolutely nothing in common, then going back to the residence of my childhood was maybe my attempt to cross a bridge that had long since burned away. Everything appeared different: the old familiarity didn't rouse the same feelings as during my younger years.

They say that to one's parents you're always a little boy or girl, and their tendency to treat you as such regularly manifests. At that particular time, though, Mom was generally too tired to play that part, and in fact, she leaned on me a lot so that in some ways our roles were reversed. It was I who took charge, and she was grateful for it.

For me, "going home" was always an experience in cultural transition, a shifting of gears from one country to the next simply by crossing the threshold of a lovely New Brunswick home. Although Dad and Mom were solid Americans, their DNA was woven together in the Old Country; they were solid Hungarian stock whose own parents had brought to their adopted homeland all the language, customs, cooking, and cultural appendices they could carry in their luggage and hearts. Always addressed at home in the affectionate *Apuka* and *Mamuka*, they were very passionate about their ancestry. To them it was a living heritage that flowed through their veins and manifested itself in a love for all things Hungarian. None of us spoke anything but Hungarian in the home; indeed, it was so by parental decree. English was the language of "out there" on the street, in the business and educational worlds, but the mother tongue ruled family life. It was so much more than a means of communication. To my parents, it was the breath of where they had come from and of who they were. At least, that's how they looked at it.

For an American kid who wanted desperately to fit in with her peers, however, it was sometimes an embarrassment. Growing up bilingual had its definite benefits, but in the company of my friends, English was all I pretended to know. I grew so good at hiding it that most of my friends never had a clue that I could understand the spoken exchanges of my own parents. On the occasions I allowed other kids into the kitchen or whatever other room while Mom or Dad was present, I always kept one eye on the nearest escape route. When the folks would initiate a rapid-fire conversation, my friends' eyes would bug out, and they'd stammer in fascination, "Wow! What is that? What are your mom and Dad saying to each other? Katie . . ."

I rarely allowed them to finish the sentence. While literally pushing them out the door, I'd mutter distractedly, "Yeah, yeah, I don't know. Let's get out of here."

We were, unfortunately, not a close family in those days. Dad, the distinguished August Molnar, was way too busy—at first with his professorship at Rutgers University, then with his presidential duties at the American Hungarian Foundation that he founded. Our household was a strict one, likely in keeping with the ascetics of Hungarian family life, and as a child I never could quite bridge the gap between our generations. With one foot in the Old World, the other in the good old USA, the tensions during my early days laid the groundwork for adolescent upheaval.

I was a terrible teenager. Although my school grades were always on the high side, I ditched whenever the weather was conveniently nice. I purposely hung out with a rough crowd, smoked and drank, frequented rock concerts, and the lot of us regularly patronized a local bar whose management didn't believe in checking ID cards. Drugs were also part of the rebellion routine. Ironically, when I'd come home reeking of cigarette smoke and alcohol, Mom always attributed it to "those other kids." Once, while getting ready for Saturday grocery shopping, she found one of my baggies of pot, and I foisted the blame onto one of my friends, saying she'd dropped it out of her jacket pocket. Incredibly, Mom always bought into the deception. Because like any normal parent, she simply couldn't fathom her Kati would be willingly involved with such shameless behavior.

God was merciful, even in those years I spurned Him. The gang often went swimming in the local reservoir, a dangerous place that was off limits. We once even put together a makeshift raft and floated it way out. The cops were kept pretty busy shooing us from the property, and my legs got strong from the constant exercise of running away—while laughing, of course. I've wondered if maybe I had forged such a close relationship with my friends because I hadn't really felt loved at home. It seemed best to trade one traditional family for a ragtag one. In the group, there was complete acceptance, and I demonstrated my close emotional ties by being as wild as the rest. By the time I hit nineteen and had finished nursing school, I was chomping at the bit to head west. California seemed like the other side of the world, so I settled there.

Oh, but there were good times at home, too. One of the side benefits of Dad's position at Rutgers University was the yearly Christmas party at our house. He'd show up with a crowd of university students, and we'd all be divvied up into little clans, sent to different rooms, and instructed on the arts of handcrafted tree ornaments. One group strung popcorn, another garlanded walnuts, others decorated Christmas cookies made from an old Hungarian recipe. Everything was edible. When everyone was finished, the groups would gather at the Christmas tree and commence positioning their handiwork. What a wonderful time!

And then there were the meals, made with Hungarian expertise. One of my favorite earlier memories was of my brother and I helping Dad make Hungarian pancakes called "almás palacsinta." These were apple fritters fried in oil and sprinkled, while hot, with confectioner's sugar or spread with jam. We'd help him get all the ingredients together, slice the apples on the grater, and stand as close as we could to the saucepan while the apples cooked. Browning took only a moment each side, then out of the popping oil, onto a bed of paper towels for blotting, then into our by then watering mouths. Delectable! They were wonderful times when Dad was less pressured and had more opportunity to simply love on us.

And, oh, the chicken soup! I can smell it yet. If I close my eyes even now, I'm again in that most favorite part of home— the kitchen—leaning over the bubbling pot and inhaling deeply. How I miss those terrific Hungarian noodles made the old way with the spices that went into the broth. It was the one meal I craved above all the others when I'd come for a visit. No matter if we were in the middle of a sweltering summer day when I'd arrive, Mom always expected, "Mamuka, would you pleeease make that soup?"

Yet in that late winter of 1985, the laughter and the freewheeling times were on hold. And the rift between Mom and I was beginning to heal. Funny how time, removing yourself from a place of turmoil, and taking your licks and dishing it out in life all have a tendency to smooth over some of the rough places in our hearts. Now, I was the one being sought after for help. Dad was still so very busy—quite in demand, actually—and he really didn't know how to handle the situation of sickbeds, changing dressings, and reassuring a recuperating patient, even if she was his wife. This was all very much out of his league. And to give him a little defense, it really demanded a woman's touch. Mamuka was glad to have me there, a nurse who knew the emotional ropes, could act as confidante, and help coax her back to good health.

Dear, precious Mom was afraid to even look at the surgical wound. A headscarf concealed from view a ghastly, ear-to-ear scar over the top of her scalp, shot through with dozens of staple marks, and it unnerved her to do the necessary daily examinations to make sure the area was clear of infection. Naturally, like any woman, her shaved head affected her view of herself; the mirror became her enemy. She eventually broke down, and I drove her to a local hair shop for a wig. A kindly salesgirl helped her make the selection, taking her into the back area to try it on. It was purely cosmetic, but it was a pick-me-up for her on some exceptionally hard days. Also, it made going out of the house less of a chore.

Mom bore this horrible period of her life with an admirable stoicism. I'm not sure I'd have done so well. A go-getter and impulsive adventurer at that time, I would likely have proved a more difficult patient, hating the confinement and the temporary disability. I would have felt like a prisoner in my own home. Cabin fever, they call it in places like Alaska, where being shut in by weather (or in this case illness) grates on the nerves like the slow dragging of fingernails against a dry blackboard. Not Mom. Her inborn determination forced strength back into her traumatized body, and when she was well enough, she gave me the boot.

I kept to myself that I'd quit my job as a medical assistant in Santa Cruz in order to go nurse her. Mom didn't need the guilt of that on top of everything else she had to deal with. And I'd only hinted at the trip that "I might be taking" but was in reality determined to accomplish. Besides, at twenty-five, I had the world by the tail, and a temporary unemployment wouldn't be more than an inconvenience. I'd been looking forward to that European trip with a couple of new friends, and I'd soon be boarding a plane for a whirlwind adventure of different foods, languages, and cultures.

After returning to California from New Brunswick, an added incentive turned up by way of an incoming phone call. I smiled, as I recognized the voice on the other end—Thomas Wittinger, former employer, cardiologist extraordinaire, and all-around great guy.

"Katie, are you doing anything special this weekend?"

"Not that I can think of." My itinerary was completely blank, one of the dubious side benefits of unemployment.

"How would you like to go to dinner, then? Chinese. There's someone I'd like you to meet. He's an Italian doctor, and I think you'd find him interesting. How about it?"

Sounded great. I'd had nothing special to do that night anyway, and I loved Chinese food. Plus, someone else would pick up the tab.

Dinner that night seemed a bit like a surgeon's convention. The medical talk around the table was rampant. The physicians were there along with their wives, and I was one of only two people who arrived unaccompanied—and who do you think the other was? That explained Tom's enthusiasm for my presence there. What a sneak.

I really didn't mind being paired off with the Italian physician. It wasn't actually a date, and besides he was kind and interesting. He had been the guest speaker at a local chapter of the Rotary Club, was just finishing up his week-long stay in the States, and wanted to meet some Americans more his age. I assumed that since he'd come to Santa Cruz, he had spent most of his time with the older generation of surgeons, and although he was five or so years older than me, he still craved some socializing with his own age group.

I honestly don't know what I found more interesting about Paolo—his Mediterranean demeanor or his obvious wealth. He didn't flaunt it, not aggressively. But he carried himself like a guy accustomed to the feel of a lot of lire and used to getting his way because of it. His English was OK, and we talked for several hours. He was looking forward to getting back home to Palermo, Sicily, and when I mentioned to him that I'd been planning a European trip with some friends, he was delighted. Gesturing expansively with both hands, he threw out a personal invite.

"I have a house in the city," he said, "and one in the country. Come stay with us, all of you! I have plenty of room. I'll show you around, and you'll have a great time."

I was floored, flattered, and a little hesitant. I thought American men were fast movers! They'd be eating this guy's dust. Actually, I wasn't quite sure if the offer was a pass at me or an innocent invitation, but I have to admit it played in my mind. I'd never been to Italy, and even as he continued to speak,

I drifted away to an exotic land that I'd only read about so far. *Wow*, I thought, *opportunities like this don't just get dropped into your lap. Staying rent-free at the fancy home of a rich Italian, who'd also be a built-in tour guide . . . it just doesn't get any better . . .*

Enter the irony.

Paolo—wealthy, self-confident Paolo—was to be the catalyst that would turn my life into shambles for years to come. Had he only known. It was he, you understand, who introduced me to his good friend, an electrical engineer named Massimo Conti.

Funny that the most innocuous of incidents can transform an otherwise stable world into a wildly spinning melee.

So it was that day I met Paolo. It was only supposed to be a vacation, a carefree, six-month getaway with some acquaintances whose adventurous spirit matched my own. How simple that sounds; the thought is positively disarming—go, have a good time, come back. Pick up where I left off in the real world.

If I'd been listening closely, I would have heard a sound, subtle but with a warning finality—the sound of a single domino falling.

The trip itself was fantastic. It felt as if I'd gotten caught up in a traveling hurricane, whisked through foreign lands at breakneck speed, and made continually giddy with excitement. The three of us traveling together did not exactly make the best of friends, though. The fact is, I barely knew Sherri and Angela. We'd been introduced almost at the last moment by a mutual friend, found out we were heading in the same general direction at vacation time, and somehow we just went as a team. I liked the other girls well enough, but to be honest, they were even wilder than I was. It was unnerving at times, the loose way they approached life, and it seemed that as tourists, they felt all the stops could be pulled out. They thought nothing of going off with strange men to see the sights or pick up and leave on a moment's notice to visit someplace they'd heard about or got a sudden craving for.

We flew into Geneva, took in part of northern Europe, caught a ferry to Greece, and from there sailed to Italy. Heading south by train, we hit Venice, Florence, and finally Rome where we caught another train that would take us into the tip of "the boot" before the jump over to Sicily and on to Paulo's place. The trip across the Strait of Messina was incredible. At the historic port village of Villa San Giovanni, the tracks ended at the pier, and the whole kit and caboodle was loaded onto a ferry for the twenty-minute crossing; who'd have thought I'd be looking out a train window at cobalt blue sea waters and feeling the heave and sway of a ship underneath! When we arrived at land, they docked at the railhead, and we continued on. It was absolutely amazing!

Paolo's home in Palermo was all I'd imagined it to be. Extravagantly decorated and spacious, it gave the impression of a five star hotel. The guy fussed over us, and we drank it in. We were catered to, ushered around town in style, and whirled through the tourist bit with scarcely time for drawing breath.

I'd been there only a few days when I met Massimo Conti. We were both on Paolo's invite list and (perhaps deliberately) seated next to each other at an outdoor restaurant that Paolo had commandeered for one of his parties. "This is my good friend," Paolo said with his characteristic smile. "We went to undergraduate school together. Enjoy!"

Massimo took the cue and struck up a conversation.

I have to say that there was no real attraction, "chemistry," or whatever you want to call it. By that time, I had met several Mediterranean guys, so the mystique was a bit worn, and although we chatted easily enough, to me he was just another new face. About five years older than me, his looks were typically Italian and average; not bad but not devastatingly attractive either. Swarthy, with thick dark hair and a somewhat rugged face, he wasn't Romeo epitomized, but I guess it was his sense of humor that won the day for him. He was witty—I'll give him that—and the life of the party. Always cracking jokes and smiling like he owned the world. His English was passable, but I had to be careful not to speak too quickly, and often things got lost in the translation. Americanisms he simply didn't understand, and with a laugh he'd bid me to take it one slow step at a time and stick to the basics in communication.

As we were both staying at Paulo's home, he and I became something of an item, if only in the casual sense. The lack of romantic involvement didn't seem to bother him, at least not at first. He made lots of time for me and took me all over the city, showing me places of interest and giving me personal insights into Sicilian living that I couldn't have gleaned through professional tourist agencies. However, his demeanor when we were alone, I at first found somewhat repugnant. He was haughty, almost arrogant, and his conversation lacked the decorum I thought should be fitting for two people who were almost strangers to each other.

"See that woman?" he'd say, pointing out the car window as we zoomed along Palermo's twisting streets. "What do you think of her?"

I stammered something, caught completely off guard.

He'd continue without batting an eye. "She's really something, huh? Maybe I'll go make a date with her . . ."

Cathedral of Palermo

How bizarre, I thought. In hindsight, I wonder if it was either some kind of Sicilian machismo manifesting or if he was testing the waters in preparation for a hit on me.

Later, though, after a few more outings, he seemed to soften up, and my natural inclination was simply to disregard his earlier behavior. After all, I was a stranger here, under the care of strangers who had been in some respects very kind to me, and I reasoned that there was so much I simply didn't understand about this culture. Besides, I'd be leaving soon, so I was determined to soak up as much adventure as I could without making a big deal about one guy's strange fantasies.

My two friends skipped over to Greece, and I was due to meet them for a week's review of the country. We'd been there before and loved it. From there, I'd say goodbye to Italy and reluctantly catch a flight back to California. The stash of American travelers' checks was rapidly dwindling, and it was time to tie it up and head home.

The day before I was to leave, Massimo determinedly approached me. "Look," he said with some persuasion, "I know you're going to Greece, but if you'll come back here for a couple more weeks, I'll buy you a round-trip ticket."

His proposition knocked the wind out of me. "Um, well, I don't know," I began, but really, it was only a half-hearted protest, as my mind was even then clicking off how many extra days I could squeeze out of this trip.

Massimo was persistent, as I'd secretly hoped he'd be. "Oh, come on. You *have* to come back. There's so much I want to show you. And . . ." He paused for effect. "There is an island. Such a place—the most beautiful! If you come back from Greece, we'll go, and I'll take care of everything."

With just the right amount of fake reluctance, I let him talk me into it.

It wasn't that I thought, "Wow, this guy is really wonderful!" No, it was more like, "Terrific! Someplace else to see. With all expenses paid yet!"

And another domino fell.

Greece was wonderful, and it was there I said farewell to my traveling companions. In all honesty, I was looking forward to some time on my own and savoring a new adventure crafted just for me.

Ustica in the first week of September was a paradise. This tiny speck of land (only a few miles across) has long been a favorite getaway for Sicilians, and I immediately understood why. The teal blue waters of the Tyrrhenian Sea roll against beaches of both luxurious sand and volcanic outcroppings. Cliffs hang over portions of the little village, and a coastal trail tops ridges that run most of the length of the island. The coastline is dotted with magnificent grottos, which make it a haunt for scuba divers and swimmers alike.

The town square is a portal into the past. Wonderful historic buildings line the streets, and with its bakeries, cafes, and a few small restaurants, it is the quintessential Italian village. The whole of it is situated quite high above the port where the ferries and other boats come in, and the sweep of sky and sea is breathtaking.

Ustica Port

Massimo and I stayed in the apartment of one of his friends and spent a large part of our days walking the island, swimming, or just lying on the sandy beach and letting the hours slip quietly away. We took a boat around the island, and he and his friend caught some small fish, which we ate for dinner that night. We ate every meal with Massimo's friends, which was a good thing because he, too, was on a limited budget.

We did adhere to the Italian custom of leisurely meals. It was an inviolable, unspoken rule. You simply didn't rush through it. A meal was more than just the food—it was atmosphere, conversation, enjoying your companion's presence. Fish and pasta dishes were a mainstay. Italians eat what is called primo piatto and then secondo piatto (first and second dishes). The first is pasta, which is followed by a fish or meat dish. There were two main meals, the bigger one at lunchtime and a smaller, lighter sampling in the evening.

As Massimo sometimes went rabbit hunting with his island friends, I had some time to myself. I was only beginning to learn some Italian words, so I hadn't even the basics of conversation down pat. I was especially grateful for the company of a Swedish, English-speaking couple and their small son with whom I spent many happy hours. The island people themselves were simple in their lifestyles, warm and very giving.

All of this gave Ustica a somewhat illusory quality, a Robinson Crusoe veneer that made it seem like real life didn't apply, that you could fling caution to the wind in this Mediterranean idyll and come away with no consequences whatsoever.

Real life doesn't work that way.

In the seductive atmosphere that played all around this enraptured American, I realized one day I was pregnant.

Massimo didn't know. I wasn't really sure until a few weeks after I got back to the States, and when I called him in Palermo he got good and mad.

"Well, you know what to do. You have to have an abortion. That's all there is to that."

I was horrified. "What are you saying? I'm not going to kill my baby."

"Katie, I'm telling you . . ."

"No. No, Massimo. If you don't want to have anything to do with it, that's fine. I just thought you'd want to know and maybe get involved. But I'm not going to kill my baby. Forget it."

He was livid, but I wouldn't consider having an abortion. I knew that would be wrong.

I hung up from talking to Massimo and braced myself for a confrontation with Mom. Oh, boy, this was going to be hard. So hard that I couldn't even make the phone call myself. At the last minute, I chickened out and had a friend do it for me. The patient, uncomplaining Mamuka I had nursed back to health suddenly took a powder. She wrote me a long, stinging letter accusing me of all manner of foolishness. At one point she wrote, "How could you do this?," and I really sensed what she meant was, "How could you do this *to me?*"

I could understand. She was a marvelous Christian lady, and an unplanned pregnancy went counter to all the beliefs she held about my character and all the aspirations she'd long nursed for me. For a long time, she would not speak to me, and perhaps it was just as well, since our words would necessarily become crossed swords. Dad, on the other hand, seemed to take the whole thing in stride. His acceptance of the situation was startling, since we hadn't gotten along when I lived at home. But his reaction was somewhat reassuring. At least I didn't have to wage a two-front war.

To support myself during the pregnancy, I did in-home care for convalescents or the bedridden. The pay would be enough to see "us" through. Alex was born in California, and the bond I'd had for him while he was in the womb increased by leaps and bounds. What a beautiful, precious child! My life took on new meaning, as motherhood, the single kind, began to occupy my entire view of the world. In the meantime, Mom was suggesting that I should try to complement the birth with a marriage. She periodically brought up the idea in conversation, and I felt myself slowly being squeezed into the position of doing something that, in my spirit, I knew to be dead wrong. Massimo, on the opposite end of the world, was being encouraged to pursue a relationship with me for family's sake—if not marriage, exactly, at least to step up to the plate and take responsibility for Alex's welfare.

After some major indecision on my part, we both agreed to give a deeper relationship a try. Mom was elated, while I felt myself grow cold inside, despite my desire to make it work, for her sake. Let's face it—I didn't even know this guy. I tried to talk myself into thinking I loved him, but I was simply swimming upstream on that one.

Seven weeks after Alex was born I returned to Palermo.

Massimo wasn't overjoyed, but as he'd also been consistently nudged by his parents, he agreed to make the best of what he considered an undesirable situation. I never did have to get a visa; I can't remember why exactly, only that it was part of my flying under the radar. Nobody gave me a hard time about not having the necessary paperwork for Italian residency, so I relaxed after awhile. After only a couple of months in our own apartment, we moved in with his parents to save money. Massimo was finishing up his stint at graduate school and the unanticipated financial burden was cutting into his funds.

A year later, we tied the knot. Mom was finally happy that we "did the right thing."

The "marriage" was doomed from the beginning.

I'd known all along that it wasn't going to work. Massimo revealed himself to be an egocentric, very opinionated and a classic blame-shifter. He never missed an opportunity to remind me that he'd have a swollen bank account by then if I hadn't requisitioned his life. His resentment came easily over the smallest of incidents, and his verbal tirades came with predictable regularity. He eventually grew to love Alex over the years, but at first he had little to do with him. I learned firsthand the macho Italian attitude of sequestering the woman in the home to raise the child until a more convenient age for the father.

His open disdain for me was not only exercised in private; later in the marriage more than one friend took me aside to whisper things that chilled my blood:

"Do you know what Massimo said about you when you left the room?"

I shouldn't have been surprised. His remarks were merely variants of things he'd said to my face:

"I can't stand her."

"Katie? Hah! She's ruined my life . . ."

"I'd have all kinds of money if it hadn't been for her."

Then there were the trysts, the many liaisons that captured his fancy. I'll probably never know the half. To make ends meet and get in a little socializing (since Massimo would never want to go out as a couple), I'd give English lessons to the locals. I'd take a call to plan a meeting with this or that student, then Massimo would get hold of the number and during afternoon rest times, when he thought I was sleeping, he'd phone the girls and literally try to pick them up over the phone. I'd listen outside the door and stand aghast. I know

Me and Alex, more than three years before the abduction while living in Palermo with Massimo.

for certain he had an affair with a secretary in his office, and amazingly he didn't care that I knew. One day I stormed into the kitchen, where his mother was busy preparing a meal.

"Mamma, do you know that Massimo is fooling around on me?"

She didn't seem very interested. "What are you talking about, dear?"

"Massimo. He's cheating on me," I sputtered. "He was on the phone, coming on to some of my students. I know there are others."

Mamma smiled, almost to herself. Her voice was meant to be reassuring. "It's nothing, Katie. Men, well, they do things like that all the time. We just give them a little room. He'll come around . . ."

I stood there, stunned, then turned and left, speechless.

On top of everything, I knew only a smidgen of Italian, and Massimo, cheapskate that he was, refused to hire a tutor to help me learn the language. He'd criticize, all right, mocking my grammar or pronunciation, but he never offered to help. I did eventually gain a working knowledge of Italian, being cooped up in that apartment with only Mamma for company, and her knowing not a word of English. Language immersion, they call it, a tool of missionaries . . . and prisoners in a foreign land. It works.

All this time Alex learned Italian and English growing up with both. I was careful to teach him correctly, and we always spoke English when we were together. He was my one bright spot in a deepening darkness. We went for walks, played together, read books—anything to share—and grew closer. He had no idea of the turmoil in my heart, and I did my best to keep it from him. Through all of it, I still wanted this crazy situation to turn out good. It seems borderline insanity now, but back then in the mornings I'd wake up and think, "Today is going to be different. I'll be the best wife and mother, and Massimo will respect me, maybe even fall in love with me."

But there was no magic pill to take, no formula that would ("Poof!") make everything all right.

It was eerie, in a way. I'd often wake in the middle of the night, listen to his measured breathing, and think, "Who is this guy sleeping next to me? What am I *doing* here? None of this makes any sense."

The man who had taken me to Ustica and romanced me was gone. I was beginning to believe he'd never existed.

Three years of constant abuse had frayed my nerves to the breaking point. I was growing more depressed, suffering severe anxiety attacks and insomnia, and was losing weight. I often thought of the situation as a painting and that I had been painted onto the canvas by mistake. Looking back, I can see I was right on the edge of a total crackup.

A year before I left Massimo for good, an incident occurred that was to be eerily prophetic. I'd regularly meet with an English-speaking women's group in Palermo. The whole yakking mob of us would exchange news from our respective countries, shore up the faltering spirits of expats missing their homelands and just enjoy a break from the machine-gun chatter of the locals. Through this group, I had befriended a young English woman who'd invite me to her home so that her own two small children could play with Alex. Her Sicilian husband worked during the day and her kids were Alex's age, so it worked out well. I commented on her spotless house and couldn't help noticing the seeming fetish she had for cleaning up immediately. Even the children seemed well-versed in cleanup; she was nearly obsessive about it and seemed like a frightened woman.

She called a few days after my second visit and opened her heart. Living in constant fear of her physically and emotionally abusive husband, she pleaded for my help to get her and her frightened kids back to the safety of her home in England. I was floored and didn't really know what to say. Unfortunately, I couldn't help her personally, as I was leaving the next day for a summer visit with Alex to my parents' home in New Jersey. I did, however, put her in touch with an American missionary woman who'd witnessed to me earlier (bless her heart, she tried, but I just wasn't ready at that time). This godly woman hid the whole family until they could safely evade the husband and return to England.

In the years after Alex had been torn from me, I was to remember this incident and think, "Now it's my turn."

Out of the blue, Massimo announced we'd try living in the United States. I was overjoyed. *Maybe things will get better back on my own soil,* I thought; and the three of us headed for California. I quickly found out that though you could take Massimo out of Italy, you couldn't take the Italy out of the man. He grew morose, the verbal abuse continued, and I'd often hear him talking to his little escapade—the Italian secretary—over the phone. He didn't even care that I knew of the affair. Four months was all he could handle of it, and one day he just hit me with—"I don't like it here. Work's not happening, and I'm going home. Come if you want to."

I loved California, but the battered wife syndrome never rested, and like a crazy woman I followed him back to Palermo. A year later, the tables turned. Something must have snapped because I'd finally had enough. I packed up Alex and went home, stopping off at my parents' house in New Jersey. I was an emotional wreck, and I sat my parents both down and took a deep breath before telling them I wasn't going back to Massimo. I ended with, "I need help. A psychiatrist, something."

Mom started to protest but I waved her off. "No, no. I'm really, really not right in the head. I have to speak to somebody who can do something . . ."

Then I spilled it: the constant put downs, the mockery, the adulteries, all of it. Their expressions were a sad mix of horror and regret. Mom, especially, felt terrible, having basically shoved me into the relationship. I couldn't actually call it "marriage," because the word simply didn't apply. Marriage meant love, two people building their lives together, always faithful . . . No, what I had with Massimo was a waking nightmare.

Mom hugged me. "Oh, Kati, I'm so sorry."

I let her hold me as I cried and murmured. "Somebody, please help me."

❋

Reestablishing myself in Santa Cruz was like treading quick-sand. That whole time period was a merry-go-round of psychiatrists, sociologists, even family practitioners. One woman shrink, who squeezed me into her schedule, listened attentively till the "ding" of her one-hour timer signaled the interview's termination. "Wow," she told me, "You're really going to need a lot of counseling. Come back when you have insurance, and we'll fit you in."

I felt like a shock victim. Who knew they'd only give you sixty lousy minutes to spill your whole life and then send you out the door to fend for yourself? I figured that maybe they'd recommend a hospital or something, anything other than turn me loose hoping I'd come back with an insurance payment. As I left the building in a daze and stepped out onto the busy sidewalks of Santa Cruz, I eyed the heavy flow of traffic in the street just a few feet away. The thoughts zinged. *It's a good thing I'm not suicidal. One step off the curb would end this . . .*

Even the meds they cycled through me proved a waste of good money. I was a genuine basket case, a mental bag lady making the rounds of one medical dumpster after another, desperately hoping to find the bare remains of something that would make life a bit more livable.

Amazingly, I managed to land a job as a nurse, but I wasn't half there. Looking back, I feel bad for everything my boss and coworkers had to deal with. Seems about all I was good for was watering the plants! I couldn't focus, the panic attacks went on unabated, and restful sleep eluded me. Oh, that was the worst part. Never was there a respite with closing my eyes for the night. I'd lie awake and stare into the dark, simply exhausted but unable to drift off. During the day, every day, I was on a continuous caffeine buzz because it was the only way I could get the energy to function.

Along about this time, I discovered the soothing effects of tranquilizers. Valium, especially, seemed to help, so I laid in a supply (legally) and popped a little every other day, alternating them with alcohol. I still had enough presence of mind to know you never mix the two. It wasn't as if I was in a drug-induced fog, either; the calming down actually enabled me to function day-to-day. For the first time in ages, I got some relief from the anxiety attacks, I was able to sleep, and I put on some much-needed weight. The lady in the mirror started to look like me again. It was only a stop gap. It was wrong, and I knew it, but it felt necessary for my survival. I had literally been emptied of other alternatives. It is shameful to admit that for years, carefully measured doses of drugs and alcohol were as necessary to me as breakfast.

Finally, I filed for divorce in Santa Cruz, and when I called Massimo to clue him in he did an abrupt about-face.

His voice was pleading, completely out of character. "Oh, please, Katie, don't do this. Come back. We'll make it work. I don't want to lose you."

My, who was he kidding? This is the same guy who repeatedly told me to my face that he couldn't stand me, who did everything in his power to reduce me to . . . well, the state I now found myself in. *No, not this time, buster,* I thought to myself. Actually, I knew the only reason he acted this way was because I'd finally gotten one up on him, and his easily bruised ego cried out for vengeance.

Making two trips to Santa Cruz for custodial court appearances, he was all politeness, fawning over the judge with stories of his separation grief. Represented by paid counsel, whenever he personally addressed the court, he did so with feeling. "Please, your honor," he pleaded. "Don't take my son from me. I've come all this way. I know I've made mistakes, but I'm willing to make it all up. I want my son to know his Italian heritage."

Massimo performed well, and it outraged me that no one in that courtroom could recognize his schmooze for what it was.

On the surface, it did seem unlikely that Massimo would travel six thousand miles, twice, if he hadn't experienced a genuine change of heart. The judge was swayed and granted joint custody of Alex. Massimo could take him to Sicily for six weeks; I would have him the rest of the year.

How could any of us have known that there was another courtroom drama being played out behind our backs, half a world away? Even Massimo's American lawyer was kept in the dark, because all this time Massimo had been petitioning the Italian courts for full custody. He'd sent me paperwork sometime earlier—documents which turned out to be a summons for a custodial hearing in Palermo—but I'd never gone because I rightly thought, *Hey, Alex is my son, and he's an American citizen. I'm not going all that way to prove he should stay with me. There's nothing they can do to us in the States.* For sure, not in the States. But in Sicily, the court had ruled in Massimo's favor, ironically on the very day, April 7, 1992, that the California court had ruled in my favor. As I'd never shown up for the hearing in Palermo, the powers that be declared me an uninterested mother and handed Alex over fully to my ex-husband. The only thing Massimo had to do was somehow bring the boy back to Sicily. Once there, no one could touch him . . . or Alex.

With Massimo's prideful admission that he would not return Alex, I informed both lawyers about his subterfuge. They were incensed. As he was already out of U.S. legal reach, the best the Santa Cruz court could come up with was an arrest warrant for Massimo, on the charge of kidnapping.

Okay, that was something, and I figured it was a pretty heavy bargaining chip. Let Alex leave with me, Massimo, and I won't make trouble. Fight me and you'll spend the next fifteen years in prison. I didn't want to do it, but I also wouldn't hesitate. I was getting my son back, one way or the other. I was frightened and angry, but I anticipated an easy victory in Malta.

3

Disappointment in Malta

**Chi lascia la strada vecchia per la nuova sa quel
che lascia, ma non sa quel che trova.
Who leaves the old street for the new one,
knows what he left but not what he'll find.**

I've read that our lives are like a tapestry, with multi-layered threads interwoven so intricately that we cannot tell where one ends and another one begins. It is a masterwork, but often it is seen as a grand pattern only after a life has been lived and pondered from the viewpoint of the aged, though at the time it seems like when we're in the middle of it and when circumstances or emotions barrel out of control, we see the tapestry from the reverse side. Knots, frayed ends, a maze of colored strands all form a startlingly garish mockery, and in fear, we wonder if that's how the rest of life is going to be. It's all we can see at that point . . .

The flight from San Jose to Malta was uneventful, with one brief stopover in London, but the entire time in transit was marked by a jumble of feelings. I can't even recall the trip clearly, not exact incidents, anyway, because my whole focus was internal. It had been a mere three weeks since I'd spoken to Alex over the phone, but it seemed an eternity. I was lost in a whir of thoughts, memories, and self-remonstrance: *Stupid, stupid, stupid! How could I have been so blind? Did I really think that Massimo would just roll*

over without a fight? I lived with him how long? And I didn't know what he'd do . . . ?!

Then there were all the other thoughts, ricocheting from one corner of my mind to the other: *What in the world am I doing here? Am I crazy? I don't even know this man who's waiting for me at the airport. Can he really help me? Where will I stay? How am I going to survive? I don't have much money . . .*

I'd spoken with Philip Cantwell several times over the phone, prior to my leaving for Malta, listening both in fear and hope as he comforted and gently, unrelentingly prodded me to go see him. There was much he could do, he insisted; he was ready to help, and if I'd go he'd open it up full throttle. There was something in his voice, too, wrapping round our conversation and drawing me in—he was mad clean through. The gentleman in him would not allow him to stand idly by while a mother was forcibly separated from her only child. He didn't even know Massimo, and yet he already had nursed a huge dislike for him. I had to smile at that. Philip didn't know me either, but made me feel I really did have an ally in all this, one who maybe had the personal and professional connections to effect a rescue.

One piece of the otherwise unformulated plan to retake Alex was the sheaf of legal documents I had brought with me. I had papers showing that as an American citizen I had been granted by the California court system full and legal custody of Alex and an arrest warrant for Massimo on the charge of violating the court custody decree. I was confident that if nothing else worked, this would be the end-all to any restraint on my taking my son back home with me. If I couldn't reason with Massimo, then surely the Maltese and/or Italian authorities would assist in Alex's recovery. I didn't want to bring in the law; Massimo would no doubt be looking at a long stretch in prison if I did. But he'd better get out of my way, because I was mad enough to lock his cell door myself.

My plane landed in Malta under a faultless blue sky and with a hot wind blowing in from the sea. I had only left the deplaning area when I was approached by three rather serious and formidable young men in casual wear. "Katie?"

Philip smiled warmly. Shaking hands with him, I was sure he could feel the jangling of my nerves. My heartbeat pounded in my temples, I was so nervous, and now again unsure of myself. Philip introduced me to his companions, subordinate business associates, and the meeting took on an immediately serious air. One of them, laden with photographic equipment, took shots of the pictures I'd brought with me, of Massimo and Alex. I collected my luggage, and the two other men left on the first part of "the mission."

Philip and I exited the airport as he escorted me to his car in the parking area. While he loaded my luggage into the vehicle, he began explaining his strategy.

"Okay. Here's what we're going to do. Tomorrow, you and I go to the American embassy and see what they can do on their end. Alex is an American citizen, so I'm hopeful we can at least get the gears moving. You up for that?"

I nodded, grateful that someone was taking charge. He put the car into gear and eased into traffic. Contrary to the U.S., Malta's vehicles take the left-hand side of the road with the driver on the car's right side. I watched with fascination as Philip effort-lessly worked the stick shift with his left hand.

"Meanwhile," he continued, "We're going to get you situated outside of town."

He smiled, shooting me a quick look. "Way out. I hope you like solitude. You've got a room booked for an indefinite stay at a hotel that's kind of back in the sticks. I'll let you know when we get a line on your ex so we can figure our next move from there."

"So . . . what will you be doing . . . exactly?"

He gave a short laugh. "Well, it's not just me and those two guys you met back there. We've got help. A lot of guys from the plant want in on this, and they'll be stationed, in shifts, at the harbor, watching for Massimo and Alex getting off one of the boats. We'll be in constant communication, so if they're spotted, we'll know right away."

"You think there'll be trouble?"

Philip shrugged. "Depends on Massimo. My guess is he'll be

a little wary of causing any kind of scene away from his home turf. Going anywhere with Alex outside the protection of the Italian authorities is a calculated risk for him. He likely won't chance getting himself into a legal jam. All this is just guessing, of course . . .'"

I felt the tension building, but in a good way for a change. "Is there anything I can do?"

Philip shook his head. "Not just yet. What we really need you to do at this point is keep a low profile. That's why we're having you stay outside town. Massimo spots you and there goes all our preparations. He'll head right back to Sicily, and we're back at square one."

The hotel was a study in contrasts. It was a lovely old place, but spooky in that I was the only guest. The proprietor was an older German man (his accent gave him away) who politely took my money, showed me my room, and most of the time simply left me alone. Every morning we'd share the breakfast table and engage in curt, civil conversation about nothing in particular, which, when exhausted, left us surrounded by the disturbing quiet of a building completely devoid of other lodgers. As we ate, the clink of silverware on plates was uncomfortably loud. The hotel seemed at times more a mausoleum, and I felt almost apologetic for the unwarranted intrusion of the normal sounds of human life. The proprietor/clerk/bellhop/custodian was ever the gentleman, though maintaining the classic German personal distance, and although I ached to ask him the whys of this huge, empty guest house and his particular place in it, I never did.

He, on the other hand, regarded me with a well-mannered suspicion that never conveyed itself in words but disposition. During the week that I stayed there, I'd catch him eyeing me from time to time, and though he never commented directly, I could see the wheels turning. He'd watch as, every day like clockwork, Philip showed up as escort to one place or another, and he'd be there when I returned after an all-day's absence. I'm sure that the things particularly striking to him were the getups I'd be decked out in, with sunglasses to hide my eyes and oversized ladies' hats to cover my giveaway blonde hair. As the only person in the hotel after I'd leave every morning, he had plenty of time to think. Looking back on it, I like to imagine that his thoughts ran toward my being involved in an international escapade of some kind, a spy-vs.-spy scenario that gave him the jitters yet spiked the kind of adrenaline rush he'd likely not experienced for years. I wonder if he thinks of me after so long, and if the remembrance encourages just a little smile.

My first day in Malta, Philip took me to the United States Embassy in Valletta and introduced me to the staff. He'd already laid out for them the story in detail, so by the time I entered the office they were already up to speed. Unfortunately, it wasn't but a few seconds into the interview that my hope was considerably deflated. The woman at the desk was sympathetic—a mother herself, no doubt—but her authority was severely limited. Her eyes were kind, but her voice firm. "I'm sorry, Mrs. Molnar. You have to understand our position in this. We are on foreign soil here,

City of Valletta, Malta

representing a government friendly to Malta, and we try hard to restrict our diplomatic activities in government-to-government matters. What you're describing might be considered by our Maltese associates to be more on the line of a domestic dispute."

I was aghast, and on the verge of tears. "But he kidnapped my son!" I hurried to show her the arrest warrant and the California custody papers. "See? He took my son! You *have* to help . . ."

"I wish I could do more." She reached over to touch my hand. "What I'd suggest is that you take whatever legal avenues are available, and that would mean getting in touch with a lawyer. I could do that for you, if you like—set something up?"

I nodded, dumbfounded. This whole thing was insane. I'd felt sure that representatives of my own country would pull some strings, muster a show of force, anything. What could be more intimidating than being stared down by an agent of the United States? Besides, I was in the right. All my paperwork was in order, and I'd pursued the kidnapper of my son halfway across the world. Yet, if I understood this sympathetic embassy worker, I was pretty much on my own in all this.

One good outcome of this visit was that I managed to secure a passport for Alex, which I'd need for his return to the States. It was simple enough, and they were glad to help at least in this way. I had a small photo of Alex with me, and in a few minutes his smiling little face graced the opening pages of a brand new American passport.

Actually, it wasn't a passport photo I'd given them, but I kept that part to myself. You see, when Massimo had left California, he had naturally taken Alex's passport, and I had no official photo of him. What I did have was a school photo, one of those neat little professional jobs with the colorful background, which I'd gotten in Santa Cruz. During the few weeks prior to my Malta sojourn, I'd been walking around with a jumble of ideas in my head about how to get my son back. I knew I'd need a passport for him, and to get that required that I'd have an acceptable photograph. On the spur of the moment I wandered into a camera shop and presented that little school picture.

"What do I need to get a passport photo?"

The clerk glanced at the picture, then back up at me. "Can't use this. This is a school shot. It's not acceptable because of the colored background."

Undaunted, I asked, "Can you white out the background?"

"Well, sure, but . . ."

"Okay. How long will it take?"

He stumbled over his response, a subdued, "Uh, not long," looking almost cross-eyed at the loon who came in from the cold, but he went into the back room to get the job done. When he came out, I had a nice "passport photo" of the son I was going to be bringing back to the U.S.

Meanwhile, at his own expense, Philip had outfitted all his work crew—those who were involved in this hide-and-seek caper—with the fairly new cell phone. They were huge, more like walkie-talkies, and with an antenna protruding from the top. His people worked in shifts, keeping a close eye on the ferry coming from Sicily. Each employee was given photos of Massimo and Alex, and instructed to call Philip should the pair arrive. We were all being a bit premature when Alex had informed me of the actual date of their arrival in Malta, but we wanted to keep the odds in our favor. If for some reason, a change in their schedule landed them in Malta a day or so early, we would be waiting.

The day following my visit to the American embassy, I met with two Maltese lawyers who spoke perfect English. What they explained to me made the situation appear even bleaker. Even the local police wouldn't want to get involved, I was told. In a country where divorce is illegal, I might actually be looked upon as the aggressor, since I was the one who filed the papers. Another facet of this whole fiasco was that, if I retook Alex and ran with him, the tables could be turned because Malta at that time had very good relations with Italy. Incredibly, I could be the one to land in jail. I thanked them and terminated the meeting.

On the day Massimo and Alex were due to arrive, I sat just outside the ferry disembarking area and peered through the gate for a glimpse of either my ex-husband or Alex. Behind the façade of a big hat and sunglasses, I knew I wouldn't be recognized, but my system was on overload regardless. At each ferry docking, I craned my neck to get a view of the incoming passengers, while at the same time trying not to expose myself to someone else's view. Massimo never showed, and I was crushed. Philip did his best to encourage me, but the disappointment was evident on his face as well. Perhaps Massimo thought better of the trip, as it was still a bit early in his kidnapping game, and maybe he thought he was overplaying his hand.

While Philip continued to post his workers at the dock for the next week, I left the hotel and transferred residence to that of a wonderful American family who lived in Malta and worked at the firm's compound. They made it clear that their home was mine, to the extent that they gave me their eldest daughter's bedroom. They refused payment of any kind, and treated me like one of the family. Stressed as I was, I was deeply moved by their kindness.

Another week passed without event. The job was a bust and we all knew it. The surveillance was called off. Philip was especially apologetic, as by this time he felt he had a personal stake in this. He tried to be encouraging, but really didn't have any definite direction for me. Yet, ever since Massimo's no-show, I'd been doing some serious thinking. I hadn't come all this way to turn around and go back home, pouting and feeling sorry for myself. I was only a short ferry ride away from Sicily. I still had friends there. It wasn't exactly a "Plan B," but it would have to do.

My American host family grieved at the way things turned out for me, but they were in complete agreement on my pulling up stakes for Sicily. It's funny how you can get attached to a place you've lived in just a short time. Malta had been a base of operations, the first place I'd have hope restored in some measure and where I was surrounded by people who didn't even know me but showered me with their affection. Here, I was not alone, as I had been in Santa Cruz those horrible weeks after Alex's kidnapping; here on this hot, sun-blasted island, I'd taken part in a clandestine operation to retake my son. Where I was going there was no Philip Cantwell, no group of impromptu commandos eager to lay a sting on the scorpion himself. Once on board that ferry, I'd be on my own.

My Malta family had gathered at the dock and waved to me as the stevedores cast lines, waving still as the ferry eased into the calm Mediterranean waters. I watched their figures recede with distance, seeing them finally turn away. I thought of the home they would return to, of their family eating dinner that night, and of all the simple things they enjoy by simply being together. How poignant those simple things were to me then; how my heart broke with the need to just experience them again for myself, with Alex.

I turned and walked to the bow, facing into the wind, toward Sicily and my uncertain future.

I stood alone on the dock at Pozzallo. All the others, the whole crowd of ferry passengers, who came across the strait with me, were all gone; it seemed only a few moments and they had all been picked up by waiting relatives or disappeared down the nearest streets. They'd been smiling, joshing one another, talking non-stop with partners . . . and they'd melted suddenly away, leaving me on the hot pavement with a suitcase at my feet, sweating in the stifling humidity of late August. It was ironic. I felt almost betrayed, as if they should have done the decent thing and hung around until I was safely on my way to . . . Palermo.

My, that was a long way from here. Pozzallo was in the southernmost part of Sicily, and I had to get clear over to the northeast coast. I waited for some time, hoping for a cab, a bus, some kind of transportation to the nearest railway station, but nothing materialized.

So, I walked.

The town appeared deserted. This was the siesta hour; plus, Sicilians in general take this time of year to go on holiday to cooler climates. There was literally nobody around. The suitcase felt like lead in my hand, and the early afternoon sun beat down with an intensity that threatened to steal the breath right out of me. My footsteps on the sweltering asphalt were the only sound. I still had the hat and sunglasses, but they did little to moderate the temperature or my mood. Sicily can be nearly unbearable in August. The suffocating "sirocco winds" blow in from the North African desert, giving one the impression of standing before a very hot oven with a fan blowing from the inside. Sometimes the winds are accompanied by red sand from the coast. Living

in Palermo with Massimo for those four years, I had ample opportunity to see the mess it made of cars, the streets, and if you
had one, your balcony. Some of my more unpleasant memories of
that time revolve around continually sweeping my tile floor, trying
to keep the insidious stuff out of my house. It was a losing battle.

A sound behind me, loud in the pervasive quiet, pulled my
head around. It was a taxi, and I excitedly flagged him down. He
wanted an astonishing amount for a ride to the train station at
Siracusa, a few hours away, and after I picked up my lower jaw
from the pavement, I sighed and got in. There wasn't much choice
at that point. He was genial enough—he could afford to be with
what I was paying him—and when I told him where I was ultimately
headed, offered to take me all the way to Palermo for the princely
sum of a few hundred dollars. What a jerk. These guys see a lone
woman struggling with a suitcase, the "Tourist!" light goes on in
their heads, they begin to salivate, and immediately calculate how
much they can squeeze out of her. Thanks for nothing.

I had several hours wait for the train to Palermo, and the ride
was a long one. We stopped at every little village along the way,

Siracusa

55

which would have been quite interesting had the circumstances been more relaxed. As it was, my mind was racing. What was I supposed to do once I got to Palermo? Sure, I knew some people there, but it had been some time, and this season marked the annual exodus to vacationland. Even if someone could put me up, what was I supposed to do after that—waltz right in to Massimo's apartment, pick up my son, and say, "Cheerio! Thanks for babysitting!" Did I really think they'd just shrug and let me walk out of there with Alex?

The train finally pulled into Palermo. As I stood on the platform alone—for the other passengers had once again melted into the ether—I was struck by the sudden inspiration to call an American friend in town. Sarah lived with her Sicilian husband, Stefano, and their young son Fabrizio, and perhaps they'd be able to help me somehow. It's amazing what the memory latches onto. Some numbers won't let you forget, and in this instance, I was glad for it. Sarah answered the phone and listened to my story. Her voice choked with emotion, and she ordered me to stay right where I was. She'd be there directly. Also, I was not to worry about having a place to live. Their home, she assured me, was mine also.

When Sarah arrived at the station, something in me quietly snapped. The sight of a familiar face, so far from home, broke into pieces my stoic veneer, and I fell into her arms, weeping. As we shared hugs and tears, she told me that she and her little family had only yesterday returned from a two-week vacation to Ireland.

What an amazing coincidence! Yet, as I was to learn while I limped slowly through this shadowed valley, there were no coincidences in God's economy, only pieces of a meticulously crafted plan.

4

Facing the Opposition

Guarda te stesso prima di parlare di me.
Look at yourself before talking about me.

A tremendous weight was off my shoulders, with now having a place to hang my oversized sunbonnet. It gave me, however temporarily, a base of operations. Sarah and her husband were perfect hosts—a family, really—and hovered over me with all kinds of suggestions and encouragements.

With American options effectively cancelled, I'd have to pursue legal alternatives through the Italian system, a prospect that filled me with dread. U.S. laws I knew, at least well enough to assert my rights in my own country. But it was beginning to dawn on me that I'd entered into a different arena: the fight rules were not exactly Marquess of Queensbury. The last thing I wanted was to end up in a legal free-for-all, getting pummeled by the opposition without knowing how to defend myself.

The first order of business, therefore, was to secure an attorney. Finding one in the off-season was another matter entirely. With the list I obtained from the American consulate in Palermo, I burned up the phone lines. For a solid week, I tried. Nobody, literally nobody, was available to even take my call. Like many other professionals in Palermo, they'd all hightailed to cooler climes or just snoozed under beach umbrellas somewhere for the next two weeks. I couldn't believe it. An entire Italian state devoid of personal legal aid! What did people do who were charged with capital crimes—petition the judge for dismissal?

I could see it already.

Prosecuting attorney: "Your honor, (or whatever they called them here) I find I must move for dismissal on the grounds that the lawyer of the accused is on vacation."

Judge considers a moment. "Sound wisdom, counselor. Next case!"

Then, sternly, the judge turns to the relieved defendant: "The next time you kill someone, be it vacation time or no, I'll send you to jail! Now, mind your manners."

Silly, yes, but honestly, what was I supposed to think?

To top all this frustration, I had sent up a trial balloon (no pun intended) that immediately became a collapsing Hindenburg.

It's impossible to underestimate the strain of constant worry on the human spirit. You hear some people ask in amazement—I know I've said the same things—"How could she have done that? Is she out of her mind? What was she thinking?" No answer suffices, really. Until you're there yourself, until you know the intimate terror of a tragedy that won't end, there's nothing to be said to make others understand. All I know is that since I was exhausted, suffering from those wretched anxiety attacks and gnawed at day and night by the fear that I'd never have my son again, well, I had to do something. I had to assume some modicum of control. At this point, it had been two months since I'd seen Alex.

So, I went to him.

The day after I arrived in Palermo, I tried calling Alex, pretending to be yet in the United States in order to forestall any suspicion on the part of Massimo's parents. I was told by the grandmother Lucia that he was at Massimo's house and with his grandpa, Giovanni. That was all the information I needed. The location was burned in my memory. It was the last place I lived with Massimo in Palermo before leaving him for good. Good friend that she was, Sarah not only was privy to this little sortie, but an accomplice. She prompted me to take her car instead of the bus, on the off chance I was able to get Alex away. After that, it was anyone's guess what either of us would do.

As Sarah and her family lived a few miles away in the coastal town of Sferracavallo, it took about fifteen minutes to actually get into Palermo proper. Now, driving among Italians is an experience in street survival. You get used to being yelled at, honked at, cut off, and generally made a moving target by everyone with a driver's license. Compared to this asphalt asylum in Palermo, California drivers are the most polite in world history. By the time I got to Massimo's house, I was almost nostalgic for some good old-fashioned, laid-back American road rage.

I pulled up near my former home and cautiously got out of the car. Not knowing what to expect, nor wanting to be prematurely recognized, I had my blonde hair tucked up into a wide-brimmed ladies hat like I'd done in Malta. I found I was slipping back into defense mode. In my previous years in Palermo, I'd learned that Italian men have a fascination for women with blonde hair, especially Americans. They'd make a real nuisance of themselves strutting, puffing out their chests, and expecting me to fall over in a dead faint at their exuberant masculinity. It got to the point where I couldn't so much as take a leisurely walk without pre-planning what karate stance I'd have to assume.

As I walked toward the house, I noticed an elderly man helping a child into a small blue Fiat. My heart stopped. It was Giovanni, and he was with Alex! I broke stride only a second while the pent-up emotion from a turbulent two months welled in me and threatened to explode in a volatile mix of love, joy, relief . . . and seething anger. The mother's rage at the whole situation became a palpable thing, and I suddenly felt that I was completely out of control, as if moved by the will of someone or something outside me. I walked purposefully to the car, opened the passenger door where Alex was sitting, and said as cheerily as I could, "It's Mom, honey, and I'm here to see you."

As I reached in to hug Alex and pull him out of the car, I felt a presence behind me and turned to face an absolutely livid old man. He raised his fists and swung at me. I parried his blows as best I could and tried to maintain my balance as he struck with one hand and pushed me with the other. A thought passed through my mind that if he had a heart attack right then and there (and his rage seemed enough to spur a coronary) then I'd be in serious trouble. I backed away from the car and cried out for help to a fruit seller some short distance away. He just stood there and watched as if this kind of thing went on all the time. I broke free and ran across the street to a Mormon church. Many Mormons lived in Palermo, peddling their religion. I related the attack to some people inside, but they also refused help, even forbidding me the use of their phone for a call to the police. What a great witness to their faith!

Because Giovanni had not followed me inside, after a few moments I wondered if he'd left. Exiting the building, I stood at the front entrance as Massimo himself strode toward me, screaming in anger, "What are you doing here!?"

"Are you crazy?" I shot back. "What do you think I'm doing here? I want to see my son!"

Massimo chopped the air with his hand in a sign of finality. "No! Absolutely not. He doesn't want to see you anyway, and you shouldn't be here. Go home!"

I stepped forward at that point, my anger and his, an even match. "If you think I'm going to leave after coming all this way, you think again. I'm not going anywhere without seeing Alex."

He shoved a forefinger in my face. "Katie, don't you make trouble! He belongs here, and he's with family."

I was astounded. "You want to talk about trouble, Massimo? Your father just assaulted me. How's that for trouble? Let's call the police and see what happens."

He dismissed it with a shrug and a sneer. "So what? You think they'll believe you?"

That unsettled me some, but I stood my ground, leveling a hard stare at him. "I'm not going anywhere till I see Alex. You won't stop me."

For a tense second or two we regarded each other over a two-foot gap, a distance that seemed more like an abyss. How could I ever have convinced myself that I might grow to love this man? He was a complete stranger to me. Finally, he threw up his hands in frustration. "Oh, all right, all right! But just for a minute. Then you go. Got it?"

I agreed because it was the only choice I had at the moment. Crossing the street under the collective gaze of the crowd who'd gathered to see the spectacle, I entered the house and gave Alex a long hug. He was terrified, looking at me in a strange kind of way, and I wondered what they'd been telling him about me. Massimo would have to spin quite a horrid tale to convince Alex he didn't belong with me in the States. That moment, I got a glimpse of what I was up against. Massimo didn't just dislike me—he hated me, wanted me completely destroyed, even in the mind of my child. He wouldn't even leave that sanctuary unsullied.

Those few minutes were way too short; my arms felt so empty when I stood to leave, at their insistence, of course. I turned to Massimo and stared him straight in the eye. "I'm coming back. You're not keeping us apart."

Massimo heaved an exasperated sigh. "You drive me crazy. Come back, then . . . tomorrow at four o'clock."

As I left the building and went to my car, the heaviness of all that had happened settled on me. My head swam, and my legs felt like lead. I kept thinking, *This can't be real. It's some kind of bad dream. How could they do this to me, to us?*

What kind of savage lust for revenge could have propelled Massimo into . . . this? I was incredulous. As I got into the car and sat down, I felt dazed, and confusion fogged my sight. What was I going to do? I didn't know, but one thing was a given—I wouldn't tuck tail and run. Enough was enough. I had to find a savvy, sympathetic lawyer and turn him loose on the lot of them. Maybe I could get some mileage out of Giovanni's punching me. I still ached from the blows. The only reason I hadn't pressed them on the assault right then was out of fear they'd somehow turn the whole thing around and make me look like the aggressor. I found out later that's exactly what they did.

61

That night was a sleepless one. Lying on the bed with my eyes open, breathing ragged as I fought panic attacks, I watched the day's incidents replay on the dark ceiling and combine with others of my previous life in Palermo. It was an agonizing photo patchwork of being a stranger in a foreign land; fighting to learn the language; raising Alex pretty much by myself and struggling to preserve a crumbling façade of marriage. The voices were

Some apartments by the sea in the Province of Palermo

there in that still night, too, of Massimo's accusations of my worthlessness, of him on the phone with other women, and my own voice pleading with the doctors in Santa Cruz, "Help me. Help me . . ." The fear clawed at me, and though I desperately sought the respite of sleep, the images and the voices kept prodding, making me remember.

I slept at some point because I woke exhausted and thinking of Alex. My mind immediately began freewheeling, throwing around fears, inane ideas, and tantalizingly blithe hopes. *Maybe I can just take Alex*, I thought. *By now, they must all recognize that since I'm here, I've won. They've got to let him go. The law is on my side, Alex is an American citizen and the case is clear-cut*, blah, blah, blah . . .

I had no way of knowing that this day would rule the next few years of my life.

I didn't bother Sarah for the use of her car, but took the afternoon bus into Palermo from Sferracavallo. At precisely four o'clock, I knocked on the door to Massimo's house, held my breath, and went in when Massimo opened up. He grimaced at me, and I likely returned the favor before proceeding across the living area. I'd spent years in this place and knew it like the back of my hand. As I strode purposefully to Alex's room, I noticed that as soon as he let me in Massimo moved to where his girlfriend, Anna, was standing and speaking softly to an officious-looking man I didn't recognize. I paid him little attention as I sat on Alex's bed—his door was open—and gave him a smothering hug.

As I released him, but before I could speak, I saw that the man from the living room stood over me. "Katherine Molnar?"

I nodded, my mouth suddenly dry. He handed me a sheaf of papers, and spoke in Italian.

"You are being served with a court order. You are permitted access to Alex only at his father's or his grandparents' homes between the hours of 4:00 p.m. and 7:00 p.m. daily. You are forbidden to take him anywhere unsupervised. Do you understand all this?"

"How can this be? I'm his mother!"

"During an emergency hearing this morning at court, the judge had the restraining order drawn up."

I was aghast. "Just like that? I wasn't informed of any hearing. Don't I get a chance to state my case?"

The man was emotionless. "That's all I know. You will abide by the court order under penalty of law."

This was all too much. For the most part the courts were closed at this time of year, and to get a case heard was nearly impossible, especially on such short notice. Did Massimo have legal connections? His best friend was a lawyer. Maybe it was his father's doing. Giovanni was a respected university professor, had many high-level contacts, and used his influence to pull a few strings. I later found out while in court that the distinguished, mild-appearing grandpa had told the judge that I'd brought with me two big men to help me strong-arm Alex away from him. How ridiculous was that? If I'd really brought two barrel-chested thugs with me, didn't the judge think they could handle one old man? I'd be halfway home with Alex by now if that had been the case.

I was heartbroken. The man who had handed me the court documents turned and left without another word to me. I looked from Alex to Massimo and Anna, then back to Alex. *I can't do this,* I thought. *How can I restrict myself to "visits" to my own son? I'm not a stranger; I am his mother!* And Massimo had broken a multitude of laws, not me. How could I fight against a family so organized, so virulent in their opposition to me?

I struggled through the rest of the visit with Alex, not wanting to relinquish any time with him, but trying hard to keep the tears from coming. At one point, Alex looked up and asked if I could spend the night. My "Ask your father" response was greeted by a firm "No!" from Massimo, who listened to every word that passed between us. Massimo was taking no chances. Court order or no, he didn't trust me, nor should he have. I would have done everything I could to spirit Alex away in the middle of night, while everyone else was sleeping. Provided Alex would have come. I saw in his eyes the confusion, the uncertainty about who I really was. The family here had told him untrue things about me, and I'm sure at that point, he didn't trust me either. It was encouraging, though, that he wanted me to stay overnight.

Despite this tremendous legal blow, I wasn't about to give up. In the short time he'd been here, my son's thinking of me had been twisted, but I'd make sure to be there every day to undo the damage. There was no way I'd allow them to turn Alex against me. With each visit, I was determined to help him see the real me. When the time came, and I had to keep believing it would, I'd need him to trust me implicitly.

The visit (how I grew to hate that word!) ended all too soon. I hugged Alex, told him I loved him, and brushed past Massimo without so much as a glance.

Out on the street, I stood for a long moment in the late summer heat and looked around at the half-empty sidewalks. People were still out having a good time, vacationing away. It didn't seem right that they should be oblivious to my pain. While they all enjoyed sunny beaches, dancing, cruises, whatever, my world was quietly falling apart.

I walked slowly to the bus stop, intermittently crying. When I got home and told Sarah, we cried together.

Several days of ceaseless phoning to law offices compounded discouragement to near despair. Out of the blue, I was called by an attorney in Milan. It seems my father, whose position of prominence allowed him many professional contacts, phoned the man, a personal friend, informing him of my trouble. This concerned gentleman gave me the name of one Marco Russo, a lawyer he felt certain would be available once he heard my story. Given a phone number to call, I found it was answered at his mother's summer home. Mr. Russo had followed the lead of his vacation-bound compatriots and skipped town, but his mother, on the other end of the line, assured me she'd give him my urgent message. A few days later Mr. Russo called and set up an appointment to meet with me the following week.

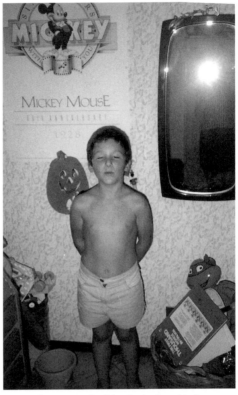

I took this on my first visit with Alex. The look on his face was confusion; he didn't know how to act and what to say with all going on.

Physically, Mr. Russo was unimpressive. He was about my age, of small stature, and although I half expected his youthful appearance to be matched by a gushing sympathy, he seemed at first too reserved, regarding me almost poker-faced despite hearing the desperate circumstances. I showed him all the paperwork I'd brought with me from the States and asked him if he had much experience in these kinds of cases. Although I wished for a better response, he basically seemed to dance around the question and the issue was left hanging. I didn't wish to press him further, for fear he'd back out of the case, but the nagging doubts about his previous experience in this kind of sticky situation left me with an uneasiness.

Despite its subdued beginnings, however, our relationship grew. He would prove to have a big heart and became much more than an attorney. In private consultation, his smooth professionalism gave way to only partially restrained outbursts of indignation. "The nerve of that man," he'd fume. "Who does he think he is?"

In the months following our initial meeting, Marco showed over and over that his heart wasn't composed of dusty legal tomes. As a husband and father of two, he was consistently outraged that Massimo was putting me through this. "Don't worry," he'd sometimes say with an almost paternalistic air. "We'll get Alex back for you."

For all that, we were really up against it. We couldn't get around the fact that the Italian court had indeed granted full custody of Alex to Massimo. He held all the legal aces. For several months, we went round and round. Marco filed one court document after another, attempting to get us a hearing that would lift the "order of protection." Unrestricted access for me was the first step. We'd worry about getting Alex out of the country after we cleared this hurdle. Compounding the situation was that, in the eyes of the Italian court system, I was still married to Massimo. A divorce in the United States didn't seem to sit very well with the Italian authorities and apparently wasn't recognized as a valid dissolution—or at least that's how it was treated. It may have been deliberate obfuscation on the court's part, or a delaying tactic, or maybe it was just the Italian machismo kicking into overdrive because they hated to concede any kind of victory to a woman, especially an "outsider." I was learning that whatever went through the courts here took a long time, and people got used to waiting. There would be no quick resolution to this mess, and I felt knocked down again and again.

All this time I continued to visit Alex daily. I was like an employee punching a time clock: in at 4:00, out by 7:00. In an ironic twist, Alex didn't even stay with his father but in a special room at his grandparents' home. This was the same house where Massimo and I had lived for a while after we were married. He'd been getting on his feet financially, and to save money (he was always a cheapskate anyway) he made the decision to move back with his parents "for a couple of months." That turned into two years. This was actually an accepted social practice. Adult Sicilians often still lived at home or moved back in with the folks for some reason or another. Nobody seemed to mind. Privacy was a main concern with me at the time, but it was offset by having Nonna* around to look after a very young Alex when I needed to go shopping or just take a walk. Also, her being there was a great "in-house" way to learn Italian. Since she spoke no English, I had no choice but to learn to speak the language.

But the brutal bottom line for me was that, after Massimo had gone through all this to get custody of Alex and deliver me an emotional coup de grace, he did not even live in the same home as his son most of the time. He had his separate home and life. Having torn him from my side, his vengeance complete, Massimo now charged Alex's upbringing to his grandparents!

Soon after I began the daily visits to Alex, another big change took place, designed to keep me in line. Being let into the house one day at the usual afternoon hour, I noticed a younger man sitting at the dining room table, off to the side. He watched me pass, and I in turn gave him the once-over. I didn't like the look of it, and got that sinking feeling again. Once in Alex's room, I sat on the bed, hugged him, and asked as nonchalantly as possible, "Honey, who's that man out there?"

"Oh, that's Tony."

"Why is he here?"

Alex shrugged. "I don't know. But Nonno* says he'll be here every day while you visit me."

My suspicions were confirmed later when I found out that "Tony" was an off-duty police officer in the pay of Massimo's family, posted as "guard" over me during visiting hours. All of them

---

*Nonna - Italian for "Grandma"
*Nonno - Italian for "Grandpa"

were afraid that without continuous supervision, I'd snatch Alex and hide out with him until I could leave the country. They knew I still had enough friends in Palermo who would provide us with a safe house, and maybe they figured that there was some kind of expat underground railroad that could assist the escape back to the States. Once in the U.S., the Italian authorities couldn't touch us.

So this was it. I couldn't afford to kid myself any longer. I was in this for the long haul, and I had better get used to the idea. With this realization, the germ of a plan was beginning to form in my mind, not so much a plan of rescue as an initial stepping stone to that ultimate course. It became obvious at that point that there was no way I could fight the family on their terms. For them, this was a home game, and they set the rules. They knew far too many people in power, and had the influence to get things done their own way. They made sure that my every legal avenue was closed, and they settled down to wait me out.

All right, then. I wouldn't disappoint them. Their strategy was to wear me down, make me give up and go back to the States. I'd meet them halfway. I'd show them that their way was working, that my nerves were shot, and I was too exhausted to fight anymore. I wouldn't leave, but I would, in their eyes, become a neutralized threat. If I could put on a convincing performance, maybe they'd let down their guard. And the first slipup on their part would be the opportunity I needed to get Alex away from them. I didn't know how I was going to do it, but I was absolutely determined to keep my eyes and ears open and my mouth shut. I'd play the part of the beaten foe, and hope they'd ease up on the surveillance.

Summer was nearly over. September was a few days away and with it was the beginning of the Italian school year. This signaled another heartbreak as I'd anticipated that this whole mess would have been cleaned up by now and Alex would have started school back in the States. It obviously wasn't going to happen. When his grandparents proudly outfitted him for entrance into the local Catholic school, I looked on in defeat, wanting them to see the hopelessness in my eyes. All the while I looked ahead, thinking, *Okay, maybe not this year, but next.*

At about the same time, another surprise unfolded. I still lived with Stefano and Sarah, and coming home one day Sarah took me aside and with a shy smile told me of a secret that she hadn't even revealed to her husband: she was pregnant. I was so happy for them both, and we hugged and laughed. But in the midst of the rejoicing, I knew what this news portended for me. I'd have to find another place to live. As generous as the two of them had been with me, I couldn't expect that to continue. Another family member was on the way, and it was time for me to find my own place to live.

5

The First Lonely Year

Dimmi con chi vai e ti dirò chi sei.
**Tell me who you are with,
and I'll tell you who you are.**

Hope for the best, and prepare for the worst. How trite that sounds from armchair quarterback mode, but live in a never-ending tragedy and the old saying really does take on a life of its own. The gist of it is that you live one day at a time, make it through the night, then in the morning take a deep breath and do it all over again. As it was, so early in the game, I still hoped for a good resolution to this travesty, while steadfastly refusing to face the possibility of a worst-case scenario. Perhaps that was the better way. Had I for a moment seriously considered the odds against my ever recovering Alex, I might have gone completely mad. And if not for clear-thinking friends propping me up when I was on the verge of collapse, pumping me with encouragement when I'd run dry, and sometimes funneling a few extra dollars my way to take the edge off my financial worries, I'd have been the poster child for defeat.

So far, I'd had a lot of financial help. Before I left for Malta, my lawyer in Santa Cruz handed me an envelope containing five hundred dollars to help "fund the cause," and some of my nursing colleagues had also passed the hat. While all this assistance moved me deeply, it wouldn't be enough for the challenges ahead. Though my job was being held for me by a sympathetic employer, I was being forced to put some bridges to the torch, so I made

the call and reluctantly resigned. I also phoned the girl to whom
I had subleased my Santa Cruz apartment and asked her to get
my things in storage. I wouldn't be going home anytime soon.

Thanks to Stefano and Sarah, it really wasn't too difficult to
find an apartment to rent in the fall. By then most of the tourists had already left, and villas, apartments, what-have-you stood
empty. Managers and owners were more than happy to have a
winter renter take up the slack, and with careful inquiry a person
could find a place specifically tailored to his or her financial state.
Stefano located a cute little place in the lovely seaside resort of
Mondello where an incredibly blue sea rolls against a white-sand
beach. Ringed by steep cliffs and mountains, it is postcard perfect.
It was also on the local bus loop, with the schedule conveniently
paralleling my own daily trips into Palermo.

The apartment was a first floor, typically Mediterranean-style
dwelling with red tile roofing and rounded brick archways. It was
small and simple, but furnished; this was a great blessing since my
dwindling stash of lire wouldn't allow for the luxury of even a bed
purchase. One window opened up right in front of a clothes line,
rather handily, I would discover, because the apartment's one big
lack was a washer/dryer. For the years ahead, I'd be scrubbing my
laundry by hand and weighing that clothesline down almost till it
was bowed and threadbare. In the coming years, going home to
visit Mom and Dad in Jersey would be highlighted by the delight
I found in doing laundry by machine. My first time home from
Mondello, I nearly squealed with delight when I lifted the washer
lid and stuffed that gaping maw with dirty clothes.

But the apartment was in such a nice setting that I found little
cause to complain. Off to one side was a small courtyard where I
could take in the sun when the weather cooperated. The now empty
beach was a block away, and the piazza, a village meeting place much
like our own American town square, offered the opportunity to
lounge in the sea air and drink espresso (at least as long as the little
shops remained open), meet with friends, or daydream under the
waning afternoon sun. The dozens of summertime street vendors

normally choking the streets were mostly gone, too. But after the hectic summer, the prospect of a more languid pace was appealing.

Stefano waited while I signed the landlord's lease, a six-month deal because the lower winter rates were all I could afford. Come May, I'd be given the boot in favor of a high-paying tourist. With my signature on the bottom line and the apartment key in my hand, all business was concluded, and we said our good-byes. Giving Stefano a hug, the thought crossed my mind that my two dear friends would be glad to get their home back. Much as they loved me, there was a lot of baby prepping that needed doing, and I'd just get in the way. As I was to learn later from the Old Testament in the Book of Proverbs, even good friends can wear out the welcome mat. Thinking back on that time, "Withdraw thy foot from thy neighbour's house; lest he be weary of thee" prompts a smile, but it is advice I still heed. Many relationships can be saved when a guest knows when to gracefully bow out.

Yet, as the sound of Stefano's car grew faint, then evaporated altogether, I felt like crying. Standing in the middle of the floor with the small suitcase by my side, I was suddenly, dramatically, completely alone.

What a mess. Everything in my life was up in the air. I had to get organized—and fast—if I wanted to make it. That meant finding work. Actually, after only a little word-of-mouth advertising, I picked up my old job giving English lessons, and worked out a four-days-a-week schedule. My initial trickle of students quickly became a steady stream, and I earned enough to keep the wolf away from the front door, plus I had a little left over. One thing I'd absolutely forbid was interference with the precious few hours I had with Alex daily. Any other work hours were fine with me, or if it came to it, I'd go hungry before I'd surrender even a portion of my allotted time with him.

Not that I ate a lot anyway. My appetite had never fully recovered from my previous years with Massimo, and this new crisis exacerbated an already bad situation. I lost more weight and felt exhausted all the time. Coffee became my liquid fuel, and though often jittery with a caffeine buzz, I could make it through the day so long as I had a full tank.

I also reconnected with a loosely formed group of mostly American ladies, many of whom were married to native Sicilians. We normally met one night a week for dinner, alternating homes, in which we'd discuss everything from relationships to local news to politics to fond memories of our home countries. What a wonderful bunch they were! With them, I could laugh, cry, vent, get hugs, and all kinds of encouragement, and find the strength to keep going. "Never give up!" they'd repeat, mantra-like, along with the angry, stone hard, "Don't let him win!" It was hard enough, they knew, to be an American in Sicily, without having the problems that plagued my life. But we all had issues, and in some respects that meant we were all combatants in the same trench. Their breezy conversation helped blow away the dark cloud that seemed to perpetually hang over my head, and their efforts to distract me was a life ring thrown to my floundering sanity.

As a group, or just in twos and threes, we took lots of trips on the weekends, to the lovely little towns along the coast and inland. Sicily really is a fantastic vacation spot and a great place to live under the right circumstances. But, as alluring as it otherwise could have been, the island became a prison without bars. I could travel the length and breadth of it but couldn't free myself from its iron grip. As long as Alex was a prisoner, I was too. This attitude began to fester, coloring my interactions with Sicilians and how I perceived the culture and the country itself. It was here that I'd first met Massimo, here I married him, here my spirit first descended into a dark crevasse of emotional abuse, panic attacks, and serious depression. And now it was here that my mother's arms were forcibly restrained from gathering up my child and sweeping him away to a place of safety. I grew to resent it all—the people, the language, the laws, the rules imposed by an alien society. Unpredictable panic attacks threatened to engulf me, and the insomnia was a living thing, a shadowy parasite feasting on my nightly unrest. Sometimes, as I paced the floor at three in the morning or hugged my knees as I sat alone on the cliffs overlooking

Mondello Bay

Mondello Harbor

A moment of refuge for me on the beach

Mondello, I craved an empty spot made just for me—an isolated place in the mountains where, whenever I took the notion, I could turn loose all the frustration and scream until there was nothing left.

The shoreline by my apartment became my refuge. The long, empty beaches were an open invite for reflection, and though the weather turned cooler and drizzly, I'd spend hours leaving a lonely set of footprints in foam-washed sand, remembering, wishing, and planning escape. I'd sit back from the surf, stare out at a fall-burnished sea, and envision a real life over the horizon or watch solitary mewling seagulls forking their wings into a stiff Mediterranean wind and wish I was one of them. Their freedom was heartbreaking. Why couldn't that be just me and Alex, spreading strong wings and facing into the east, toward our California home?

Maintaining my daily visits with Alex at his grandparents' house proved a continual sharpening of my sense of futility. Certainly this was by design. Carefully watched, guarded like violent felon, hung over with a fabricated criminality, it was all I could do to weather the daily insult without complaint. I didn't dare show what I really felt. The ex-cop in the other room was no doubt filing a sheaf of mental notes, and any outburst, no matter how justified, would be presented to Massimo as a lever to use against me during the next court hearing. But they couldn't control my thoughts. *How dare you!* routinely echoed through my head. *Just you wait. One day . . .*

The flip side of the anger was outrage that Alex even lived there instead of with his father. I had thought this would be a rather awkward position for Massimo before the courts, considering his officially declared fondness for Alex, but despite my bringing up this lunacy before a judge a half-dozen different times, it never was addressed. Nothing, in fact, seemed to make any impression on any judge at any time. Everything I said seemed to fall on deaf ears. I was stuck in a revolving door of legal paperwork, while my lawyer continued to plead with the court for joint custody or, at the very least, unsupervised visits at my own apartment. Always there were the hearings, then the interminable wait for a decision.

One tremendous blessing for me came in the form of Sarah's translating expertise. In her official capacity as court translator, she handled all the paperwork that came for me from California and never charged me. It would have cost a small fortune to hire someone both skilled and court-approved to do that sort of work. Over the years, Sarah was always available and gave my documents top priority. I don't know what I would have done without leaning on her shoulder.

Out front, there wasn't much I could do. Behind the scenes, however, I barraged the U.S. State Department with pleas for help. Over the phone, those beleaguered employees listened as I wept, berated, cajoled, and did just about anything else that entered my head to get them off their diplomatic duffs to do something. Boy, did I get tired of hearing that old refrain, "I'm sorry, Ms. Molnar. Our hands are tied . . ." How I wanted to scream into the phone, "Don't any of you have children?! What if it was one of yours, with your own reputation smeared?" Honestly, how many times could they expect me to politely listen to them tell me that I was on my own?

I became such a regular caller that when I mentioned my son's full name (Alessandro), they immediately responded, "Oh, yes, you're Katherine Molnar . . ." Heavy sigh. *Just call me Katie*, I'd think ruefully. *We might as well be on a first name basis, since you're not getting rid of me.*

It had been a year—a year!—and I was no closer to getting my son back than when I'd first come to Malta. Frankly, I didn't know how I'd hold out much longer. I was living as two people—the fake one who stood before the courts as a quiet, self-assured American, and the other, real one who emotionally resided in her own private asylum. The whole sordid affair went on and on, without respite. It was like being on a treadmill pre-set to the same sluggish pace that everyone in the whole of Sicily seemed used to. I wished fervently for something to change, for my lawyer and me to go in a new direction, and go in a hurry.

Be careful what you wish for . . .

One afternoon I was called to my lawyer's office, and he handed me some documents with a flourish. His anger came out as an accusation. "What do you know about this? Is that your signature?"

Studying the papers a brief moment I nodded, then realized these were the same papers presented by Massimo to the judge in Santa Cruz, months before, during the custody hearing. Marco was furious. "Do you know what you've done? You signed these papers but didn't show up for the hearing!"

"But . . . I thought . . . I don't understand . . ." I stammered, re-reading some of the documents; I felt my knees nearly buckle. Horror swept over me at the words, ". . . California has declared to have its own exclusive jurisdiction . . ." Nobody in that California courtroom had read carefully enough. Along with everyone else who'd read it, I had thought the documents Massimo presented said that the Italian court recognizes California's authority to grant me full custody. But a careful reading showed only that California "declared to have its own exclusive jurisdiction" in this custody case, not that such jurisdiction was officially recognized and officially honored. In other words, my parental custody of Alex was only recognized as long as I remained in California. I had been under the assumption that the hearing in Palermo—called for by Massimo—had been cancelled or at least overridden by the California custody judgement, that my custody of Alex had been a done deal. The reverse was true. Since I never showed up for the hearing, the Italian court had deemed me an "uninterested mother" and awarded full custody to Massimo who, of course, had planned this whole thing from the start.

I broke down, sobbing uncontrollably, and begging Marco to keep me as a client, to help me. His demeanor softened, and he beckoned me to a chair while I poured out my heart to him long into the night. He listened patiently, more like a father or older brother, breaking in every now and then with a word of reassurance. And he never charged me a dime for all those hours. When I left his office after 9:00 that evening, I was drained. I crawled into bed that night swathed in hopelessness, thinking, *What more can they do to me?*

I was about to find out.

Out of the blue, I was served with an order to appear before a court-approved psychologist. I couldn't believe it. Being summoned to a mental health evaluation was a new low, even for Massimo. Being declared "uninterested" was not enough, it seemed; his family appeared determined to prove I was a rubber-room candidate. That wouldn't be hard if my life continued being emotionally pummeled. During consultation with Marco, however, it was determined it could possibly work out in our favor. If I could demonstrate both my desire and capacity to care for Alex, it could sway the judge. So, prior to meeting with the court shrink, Marco set up several meetings with our own psychologist, Marcello Lombardo, a middle-aged, rather jocular fellow whose inherent good nature was a tonic to my nerves. I answered a battery of questions and thought the meetings had gone well.

Later, I met with the court psychologist on a gray, rainy winter day, my nerves jangling as I entered the office area. The breath caught in my throat as I saw both Alex and Giovanni sitting to one side of the room in preparation for Alex's own interview by Marco's psychologist. It just so happened that both psychologists were in the same office building. Alex smiled, and Giovanni's stony gaze rested on me only a moment before he resumed looking straight ahead. I don't know what feelings I had anticipated, but the humiliation of my son watching his mother being professionally grilled galled me. I was immediately relieved to see a woman behind the desk. Perhaps she was a mother herself and would surely understand what a miscarriage of justice this was! After a cursory greeting, she waved me to a chair and peppered me with questions: What do you think of the present situation? Would you be willing to live in Palermo indefinitely if you were granted shared custody? What is your current income? Etc., etc. Some questions came packaged with insinuation, or at least that's how they struck me. I bristled silently and answered as pleasantly as I could, very much aware that she noted every miniscule impression.

Intense as it was, it could have been a lot worse. If she'd given me one of those "word association" tests, the whole interview would have gone south in a hurry. I can see it now:

She: "Massimo"	Me: "Hate"
She: "Law"	Me: "Stupid"
She: "Court"	Me: "Kangaroo"

Oh, my! That would never do. But in retrospect it's still fun to think about.

The really hysterical thing concerning the whole interview is that they had no clue how perpetually close I actually was to a breakdown. I never got the professional help I'd been seeking in the aftermath of my "marriage," and I was just beginning to mend when Massimo took Alex. The strain of the past year had only magnified pre-existing problems, and to a large extent, I still relieved the pressure through alcohol and, when I could legally get them, tranquilizers. I hated doing it, but I simply couldn't function any other way. Yet I felt no guilt in refusing to explain all this. It was marriage to you-know-who that had catapulted me into this mental state in the first place, and his stealing of Alex merely compounded it. If anyone had anything to apologize for, it was Massimo and the purveyors of this whole convoluted "justice" system.

My problems aside, there had never been any question of my caring for Alex. Utterly devoted to him, shielding him at times perhaps too much, I poured out affection on him like I'd done with no one else. He was the bright spot in my life, the actual reason for going on when everything in me screamed for a halt. Robbing us of each other and poisoning his mind against me was, from my perspective, a death sentence against my heart. The sheer hatefulness of such a maneuver had infused me with a strength that forbade me to surrender.

About halfway through the interview, Marcello Lombardo entered the room. He smiled a greeting, then seeing Alex, placed

Alex—Taken on one of my visits

a hand on his little shoulder. "And what about us, young man? We too have work ahead of us, eh? Shall we get to it?"

As he began running Alex through his own psychological regimen, an interesting thing happened. Marcello had been poking fun of his increasing girth, patting his pot belly with one hand. He liked food too much, he laughed, and immediately Alex brightened. His excited voice sounded loud in the quiet room. "Hey, I know who you should call," he said, and rattled off the name of a well-known weight-loss center in California, one he'd often seen advertised on TV. Marcello chuckled and quipped that he'd give them a call next time he was in the States. Funny as it was, for me it also offered a measure of hope. His accent was changing, his cultural perception adjusting to Sicilian life, but Alex still had what he considered fond memories of life in the U.S. I wondered what else hid in the corners of his mind and how we could leverage that to our advantage sometime down the road. I noticed too, with subdued alarm, that the woman querying me didn't bat an eye.

I felt both our interviews went well, and I left the building confident that at the next hearing the judge in this case would consent to a change in the status quo.

After a two-week wait—doesn't anyone in this country do anything without a yawn?!—I got the call to meet Marco at his office. I hurried there and walked through the door, scarcely daring to breathe. His secretary waved me in. Marcello stood conversing with Marco, and when they turned to me, I could instantly see the news was not good. I closed the door softly. Marco sighed and shook his head.

"No good. They rejected our request for shared custody."

"What?!" The anger welled, and I felt like hitting someone. "That's crazy. What reason did they give?"

Marco made a face, half sympathy, half disgust. "Your mental health evaluation."

His sad eyes rested on me, and he suddenly looked like a man who'd been beaten up. He spoke slowly. "The court-appointed psychologist recommended, on the basis of your 'cold personality' (the words hung in the air) that Alex stay with his father. You see, you are a 'passive' person, uninvolved with your son's emotional needs."

This was absolute nonsense. Everyone who met him knew Alex to be a happy child, full of energy and throwing himself with gusto into the world around him. Kids don't get that way through parental neglect. We'd always been so much more than just parent and child—we were friends, and to refuse to see that was to be willfully blind. I began to wonder then and there if the "interview" had been a mere formality, if the "evaluation" was predetermined and would be used against me no matter how I had responded.

The room's silence was suffocating. Both men regarded me as with the pitying affection one gives to the helpless. There was nothing more to say. I thanked them and left.

Throughout the winter, I continued to support myself through English lessons and actually reached the point in student enrollments that financial worry was a thing of the past. Sometime, during another hearing I was not privy to, the judge ordered Massimo to pay the rent on my apartment. I reveled in this blow to my ex's ego, a small victory but one that stung him where it hurt.

The heavy gray skies of winter were beginning to yield to the approaching tourist season when I tallied my prospects for a new place to live. The lease on this place would be up soon, and the landlord would be here, too, with his hand out for double the cash I'd agreed to six months earlier. I had put the word out among friends and didn't wait long before I got a nibble.

A heart surgeon friend from southern Italy, Gaetano Moretti, gave me a ring and over the phone began describing a place right in Mondello that he felt was tailor made. Thrilled because I loved living by the sea, I met both him and a representative of the rental agency a few days later at the piazza. Together we drove a couple blocks away, to a very narrow side road I'd never noticed. We stopped outside a gate, which the agency rep opened with a key, and drove in the last few feet. Rolling to a stop, we got out and

stood in front of a small, two-story complex of three connected apartments and two by themselves to one side of the courtyard. Another smaller apartment off to the side, beyond another gate, seemed to beckon. Once inside, I fell in love.

The place itself was small, but fully furnished and immaculate, having an entrance floor laid out in a beautiful mosaic tile. The front room held a table and four chairs, and a daybed that could fold up into a couch. To the left was a spacious, high-ceilinged bedroom with a floor adorned with more of that lovely mosaic, but of a different pattern. The little kitchen was situated down the short hallway, a small area containing a stove and fridge, but oddly, no sink. When I mentioned this to the agency rep, he smiled and opened two wooden double doors, and we followed him out onto the patio. There was the sink, with cupboards attached to the outside wall. A bit unusual, a challenge in winter, maybe, but I couldn't resist. I bonded with the place immediately.

The apartment became a kind of sanctuary, a shelter from a world of hurt. I could curl up here, listen to music, and retreat behind a gate barricade at the end of each crazy day. For some reason, I also didn't feel quite as alone as I did at the other place. It's as if this apartment had been expecting me, somehow keeping itself empty until I walked through the front door. A covey of good neighbors welcomed me, looked out for me, and made me one of their numbers. Behind the gates of this little paradise, many little trees hung heavy with fruit during the summer. The whole time I lived there, I bought neither lemons nor bananas.

As a homecoming gift, Gaetano paid the deposit. He just smiled, shook his head, and waved off my protestations. Looking gently into my eyes, he said, "One day, when you and Alex get to the United States, you can pay me back . . . or not. But for now, consider this a present."

I never knew when we'd cross paths again, as he lived in a different part of Italy, but his gift and his words were an acclamation of faith. He knew we would succeed—Alex and I—and return where we belonged.

I only wished I could be as certain.

6

A Visit from Grandpa

L' acqua lo bagna e il vento l'asciuga.
The water gets you wet, the wind dries you off.

Just before moving into my second apartment in the spring of 1993, I received word from my lawyer that another hearing had been scheduled, prompting him to adopt a new strategy. Marco insisted that someone from my immediate family fly to Palermo to be with me during the proceedings, that a physical representation of Alex's "other" family might help to flesh out the distant relatives who also loved and missed him. It was a great idea, and I thought, if handled correctly, might produce rulings that would permit me freer access to Alex and would dispense with the guards who accompanied him everywhere.

That part of the restraining order particularly galled me. I was never alone with Alex. We were constantly watched, eavesdropped on, hovered over; I had mastered the over-the-shoulder look, for even in our most intimate moments together I never knew just how close that ear was to the door or who would be checking up. How I longed to whisper all my heart to my son, to encourage him in his remembrance of his native land, to promise outright that we would one day return together and live a normal life. I recall one day arriving for my usual afternoon visit, and as I was crossing the street, a car pulled up in front of Giovanni's apartment. I stood there and quietly seethed while Massimo's girlfriend, Anna, got out with Alex, and led him by the hand to the front door. There I was, his own mother, forbidden by law any kind of unchaperoned outing with my own son. But this woman, not even a family member, could drive the length and breadth of Sicily with him unhindered. I found this injustice infuriating and heartbreaking.

I volunteered my dad to stand with me at the hearing. If Massimo's family could play the prestige game, so could I. Dad's character was unimpeachable—a world traveler, renowned representative for the language and culture of his own heritage, distinguished professor at Rutgers University in New Jersey, and founder and president of the American-Hungarian Foundation and Museum. He had dined with at least one American president and rubbed elbows with the social elite. He was articulate and carried himself with authority. That Alex had such a grandparent, and one willing to go to bat for him, should, I reasoned, speak volumes to the presiding judge.

Massimo had often argued before the court that the disinterest of my parents was evident in that they neither bothered to visit their grandson nor to maintain close contact with their own daughter. Utilizing this lie, he could shore up the "uninterested mother" accusation and press for more restrictions.

Dear, precious Mom, though desperate to come as well, couldn't leave New Jersey. With the development of another brain tumor, she was warned by her surgeon to stay close to home. Although not yet cancerous, the tumor required continuous monitoring, and another bout with the scalpel was a very real possibility. She poured out her heart in a letter, though, to be presented to the judge. Hers were the pleadings of a broken heart. Across the miles, she begged for one more chance to embrace her grandson in her own home.

I picked up Dad at the Palermo airport in a loaner vehicle. We hugged and shared a few quick words before locating his luggage and getting back to the car. Once into traffic, we made for a Mondello pensione, a small hotel where he was booked for the week. My place, only a block away, was obviously too small for both of us, while the *pensione*, a quaint, charming place situated on a cliff above a busy tourist avenue, would offer a needed place of respite for Dad. I knew once he'd been through the legal wringer here, he'd need some quiet time.

After checking in and getting his luggage squared away, I took Dad back to my little place or the "summer residence" as the locals called it. There I cooked his favorite food, an old-style vegetable soup. As we sat and ate, we traded half-baked ideas of the hearing ahead and what we hoped would be the outcome.

I had little appetite myself, but I was glad to watch him eat.

Mom and Dad

Lifting the spoon to his mouth, he'd pause and inhale, smile faintly and meet my gaze across the table. Oh, Dad! How glad I was to see him, to have a blood relation stand with me; but as I watched him a pity stirred. He looked tired, haggard even, and despite the brave veneer, I knew he was a bit unnerved. Dad had always been a head-to-head kind of guy, unafraid of confrontation, especially when he knew himself to be in the right, but after more than a year of separation from both his daughter and grandson, after repeated court maneuvers to thwart Alex's return, he had little idea what to expect. Though we spoke vaguely of hope and justice, neither of us let the talk go too far. Emotions were just below the surface, and a hard honesty would prick the careful bubble we'd momentarily spun about ourselves.

Watching him enjoying his soup and pretending that all would be cordially sorted out, my heart reached across the years. *How little we had in common in those early days*, I thought. My Apuka was the sterner part of my upbringing whose impressive self-discipline had unfortunately stifled the outward flow of emotion. He was Professor Molnar or President Molnar, a pillar of the community and universally loved by his students and peers, but at home a gushing sentimentality was almost a breach of decorum for him—not that he didn't love. On the contrary, his commitment to family was unshakable. Blood ties were inviolable, and he'd fight like a wolverine to protect one of his own. But he was old school Hungarian, and unbridled emotion was best left to other cultures like the hair-trigger Irish or the flamboyant Italians. He worked hard, provided well for his family, and earned the respect of his peers—proof enough of his love, he reasoned.

For my part, my innate rebelliousness had always gloried in bucking the status quo. A proper child when very young, in my early teens I grew to loathe propriety, flaunting my disdain by deliberately choosing the wrong friends and the wrong path. In front of Mom, I always pretended to be pure as the new-fallen snow, and she bought it so easily, perhaps because she preferred the security of the "perfect family" illusion. Dad was not nearly so naïve, I knew, but his control over me had by that time spun wildly out of his grasp, and in frustration, he surrendered both my discipline and instruction to Mom.

So many wrongs and so long ago. I looked across that little table at my Apuka and loved him, inwardly overjoyed to finally have him as an ally. Ironically, it was the outcome of my rebellion that finally began bonding us all. Alex proved such a blessing, a family addition whose infectious good nature and infatuation with life was a healing balm. *We'll get him back, Dad. You and I.*

We discussed his seeing Alex that very afternoon. Dad was not only curious, but planning strategy. "You going to let them know ahead of time?"

I shook my head. "No. I'm not sure how they'd react. They might try to keep you away by saying it wasn't part of the deal. Besides, every time I've been upfront with them, they used it against me. Not this time."

Dad eyed me cautiously. "You think there'll be trouble?"

I was past the point of caring. "I don't know what's going to happen, but you've come all this way. They're not keeping you from Alex, and that's all there is to that."

We had a few hours to kill. When I noticed that Dad's chronic asthma beginning to manifest, I suggested he retire to his room and partake of the mid-day siesta, also a local custom. The pre-summer heat was bearing down, and the streets were emptying of both vendors and locals. He could rest in the quiet of Mondello from 2:00 p.m. to 4:00 p.m., and then we'd board the bus to Palermo an hour later in the piazza.

With satisfaction, I thought it a subtle viciousness that we would arrive at Giovanni's house unannounced. I savored the image I had of the shock of them seeing my father, and although I hoped for no confrontation, I prepared for it. I didn't really give it an awful lot of thought, just stiffened my spine and plowed ahead.

About 5:30 p.m., we got off at the bus stop near Giovanni's. Arriving, we were greeted by the doorman and were immediately transported into a scene like an old Bob Hope movie. Flustered and completely stunned at the company I'd brought, the doorman was slapstick personified, first stammering a reply then lunging to the intercom to announce our arrival. A man was coming upstairs with me! You'd think Dad was CIA or something, the way the word caught in his throat. I half expected the Keystone Kops to come tearing around the corner to arrest us. If the situation hadn't been dead serious, I'd have laughed out loud.

Entering the building, we took the elevator to the third floor, knocked on the apartment door, and when Alex's Nonna answered, went on in. Giovanni, Lucia, and Massimo's brother, Alberto, stood in various parts of the room with mouths halfway open, as if wanting to speak but unable. I announced my father, formally introduced him in Italian, and forced a smile as the polite handshaking and mumbled embarrassed greetings began all around. With none of them having met before, it seemed the common civilities should be observed, but the scene's absurdity appeared lost to everyone but me. If it wasn't for Alex's being forcibly kept in Italy and by necessity me as well, the meeting would never have taken place.

Giving them all only a moment, I marched on, followed closely by Dad, and entered Alex's room. The look on his face was very nearly cherubic. "Grandpa!"

He jumped off his bed, where the scattered papers of his homework laid and wrapped his little arms tightly around Dad's waist. "You're here! I didn't know you were coming! What are you doing here?"

"What else?" Dad replied with a wide smile. "I'm here for a visit! I can't let your Mom have all of them, now can I?" Dad scooped him up, holding him close. "My Alex," he murmured. He was fighting back tears.

A tremendous bond had always existed between the two of them, and so I took a backseat in deference to that. Their joy was infectious. Alex spent the entire visit in his grandpa's lap, chattering away in the stream-of-consciousness talk that comes with his age. I interjected a few things here and there, but mostly I just watched, smiling but with breaking heart. The thoughts rolled around in my brain, and I thought sardonically of visiting day at the state penitentiary: loved ones hug, smile, exchange rehearsed pleasantries ("Oh, it's not so bad on the inside. Food's okay, I got my own cell. Hey, how's everyone at home? Tell them I miss them and that I'll be out soon . . ."), then it's over. The iron doors clang shut, and the walls wrap around again like a tomb.

I looked around the bedroom. No bars, but a cell nonetheless.

As if to punctuate the irony, Lucia entered the room with a large tray of tea and biscuits. Having spent two years here with Massimo, I noticed the tea cups and saucers were from her best china collection. She smiled, poured, and assumed the mien of a gracious hostess, treating us as honored guests. Such contrasts abounded. I believe that in her own way, she was genuinely concerned that we all feel welcome and could enjoy this short time together.

Neither Giovanni nor Alberto made an appearance, and I couldn't help thinking that they'd been on the phone with Massimo. Oh, the look on his face would have been priceless. Massimo wasn't often knocked off balance, but this one surely upset his equilibrium. I couldn't suppress a smile. Take that.

It was 7:00 p.m. How I grew to hate that hour! Every day the clock tolled the end of all my joy and a return to an empty apartment, and this day it slid all too quickly between us. I looked at Dad and choked out, "It's time."

He nodded, and after one lingering hug and a hoarse, "I have to go, little man," eased Alex from his lap and stood. The look

A visit neither will forget

on Alex's face killed me. "Why, Grandpa?" he asked, genuinely puzzled. He twined his fingers with Dad's, keeping his gaze fixed on him. "Can't you stay overnight?"

Dad put on a brave smile. "No, son. But I'll be back. I'm not going home just yet."

To this day I don't know how I did it, that day, and every day for years on end. But we turned away from Alex, strode across the room, and left the apartment with barely a word of goodbye to our "hosts." Not a violent man by nature, I'm sure Dad wanted right then to punch somebody's lights out. I know I sure did.

The next morning, Dad and I walked up the steps of a gray, dismal building, one I would grow to know so well in my seemingly endless sojourn in Sicily. Built during the Mussolini years, it was an architectural depression, squared and forbidding. We passed through a brace of military guards with submachine guns slung over their shoulders, and upon entering the building passed through the obligatory metal detectors. Guards were everywhere in the hallways. In Sicily, armed, uniformed men are just part of the everyday scene. Like anything else, you get used to them after awhile, and often they just become part of the street background. Sometimes, however, they are more obvious. I recall one time standing on a street corner at a busy intersection, waiting to cross when a motorcade swept down the avenue. A black, tinted glass limo, shielded front and behind with a heavily-armed police escort, cruised toward me. I stared, transfixed. Uniformed men scanned the streets from partially opened windows, the barrels of their automatic weapons in plain view. As they rolled past, I was swept by those same black muzzles and felt my throat go suddenly dry. I later learned it was an escort for a "Mafia Judge," one of the few magistrates fearless enough to take on the Mob.

In a tiny, upper-level room we waited with other onlookers and plaintiffs/defendants for the arrival of the judge. This was just one of many places in this very building I'd had my case heard. The rooms all bore the same ho-hum appearance, kind of a makeshift office with a table, a few chairs, and a couple of windows looking out onto the street below. Marco Russ was there and waved us over. Massimo stood with his lawyer. Glancing up, he took note of my father and then busied himself with paperwork. The judge, wearing a simple suit and tie, entered with the clerk, a rather harried-looking individual overburdened with files. The court was called to order.

Massimo and his lawyer (a one-time friend, I thought) took the initiative to speak with the judge. We, in our turn, offered my mom's letter, along with several letters of recommendation from family and friends back home, attesting to my good character. I was personally asked to speak, and I requested free access to Alex, without the ever-present chaperones. Marco had previously filed for joint custody, which we both realized was very nearly laughable in light of our well-heeled opposition. So the unsupervised visitation was a more circumspect approach. The judge did note my father's presence with approval, no doubt to the chagrin of Massimo, who banked on the image he'd cultivated of my parent's disinterest in either their daughter or grandson. With Dad at my side, that exposed the lie for what it was.

Sarah was also there. Called forward, she testified concerning my character. Good old Sarah laid it on the line—Katie was a wonderful, devoted mother, steadfast friend, hard worker. Alex loved his mom dearly, and the attestations to her good character were always evident in the happy child. Massimo's character did not fare nearly as well. Sarah was blunt in her recollections of his distaste for me as his wife and of his tearing me down behind my back.

The judge would consider all sides, he said, and render a decision at a later date. More delays, but we expected as much. I was ordered to turn over my passport to the court clerk as a show of good faith. I took this as a hopeful sign because it seemed to point to a relenting of the judge's previous position. They didn't want me to flee the country if Alex was in my custody, and that could only happen with unsupervised visits. Smiling, I handed it over, making a show of complete cooperation.

No one in that room had any way of knowing that a few

months prior, in January 1993, when I had returned to the States for a week in order to sell my California possessions, I contacted the Philadelphia passport agency and reported my passport lost. It wasn't, of course, but I needed a second one for a then undefined escape plan. I was processed and received a new one almost immediately; this I squirreled away for future use. So, though it looked like one more capitulation on my part, the courtroom surrender of my "only" passport was nothing but show. In fact, I was quickly learning to mask all feelings of resistance. More and more I was impressed with the fact that the only way I was going to win anything in this epic struggle was to fake it, let Massimo and Company think they had the upper hand and mentally file away anything that might be of some use to me at a later date.

It is fascinating now, so many years after all that emotional trauma, that I can relive those fantasies of escape. They were many during those years—constant, in fact. The POW mentality had me always planning, strategizing, imagining. Not digging tunnels underneath enemy barracks or cutting through barbed wire barricades, perhaps, but breaching an all-encompassing security apparatus just the same. When with Alex, I was always under guard, regarded with suspicion. My plans took many different routes, often spur-of-the-moment thoughts prompted by a particular scene I witnessed. Watching the fishing boats weigh anchor and sail out of sight, I'd consider hiring someone of that humble profession to take on a couple of passengers and get us to Malta. No one would think twice about a fisherman plying his trade far out to sea. I thought about renting a car, kidnapping Alex, driving for the first hundred miles then changing vehicles. Once, when staying overnight at his apartment, I considered slipping some sleeping pills into Massimo's drink before bedtime. Drugged senseless, Alex and I would be long gone before he roused enough to phone the police. But with nowhere to hide, no contact waiting to shelter us, I nixed the plan in short order—just another thought flitting through an adrenaline-charged mind.

The very first time I tinkered with the idea of re-taking Alex by subterfuge, I was standing by the sea. Still living with Stefano and Sarah at the time, with my California apartment, job, and belongings all hanging in limbo, I'd gone to the Mondello beach along with Massimo and his girlfriend. Amazingly, it was at Massimo's suggestion. "We're taking Alex swimming," he said, with a decided lack of cordiality, "and you can come along if you want."

Once there, ignored by the two adults and only intermittently engaging with a happily playing Alex, I stood and watched a group of young guys roughhousing on the beach some distance away. Rowdy and thuggish-looking, they appeared grossly out of place, as if they were more at home in dark alleyways and cramped tenements. My mind wandered, and watching their physical prowess, I considered what it would be like to enlist their immediate aid. They could easily beat up the out-of-shape Massimo and spirit Alex and myself away to their dark corner of the city and arrange with their black market friends a clandestine passage for us to some faraway European safe house. From there, it would be an easy skip across the Atlantic to home.

My gaze must have been intent, alarming even, because Massimo's demanding voice broke into my reverie. "Who are you looking at? You know those people don't you? You'd better not be planning anything! There are other people around here watching you right now. You won't get away with it!"

A look of surprise must have crossed my face to find he'd been reading my thoughts. From there, his tirade degenerated into character assassination. "Why did I have to get stuck with you?" He regarded me with disgust. "I can't believe my bad luck. Of all the planes that go down everywhere, crash into the sea, why couldn't you be on one of them? You are such a burden to me!"

I was stunned and looked to Anna for womanly support. But her gaze slid away in apparent disinterest. I'd thought I plumbed the depths of his hatred for me, but I hadn't even come close until that moment. How could I have shared any of my life with this man?

I was to find this moment of suspicion was for him anything but an anomaly. My unexpected arrival in Sicily and stubborn refusal to leave when commanded birthed in him a large, unreasoning fear. He gave me far more credit for escape planning than either my funds or contacts would ever allow. Nor were his threats of unseen watchmen idle ones. Apparently, at least in the beginning of my stay, he really did have something of a network going, his own (probably unpaid) spy ring. As I was preparing to leave after one particular visit with Alex, he approached me out of earshot of our son. "You're planning something, aren't you?"

When I honestly denied it, he pointed his finger at me. "Don't lie! I know you are. One of your relatives flew into Palermo today, and you're meeting her, huh? Well, you better not try anything. I have you watched!"

Come to find out that Massimo had someone checking the airport arrival lists, and a passenger named Molnar (my maiden name) disembarked in Palermo. Although I knew it to be a mistake, it did clue me into some of his operating procedures . . . and his growing paranoia.

Such paranoia was not baseless, however. I took every opportunity—indeed, made my own when I could—to subvert his system of secrets and spies. When playing "Cops and Robbers" with Alex at Giovanni's apartment, I'd hide out in Giovanni's office, quietly closing the door in pretense. Anyone coming suddenly into the room, though angry with me for being there, would likely assume it was part of the game. While Alex looked for me throughout the apartment, I'd quickly root around in Giovanni's files, looking for anything having to do with Alex and myself. I wanted to know well in advance of every court hearing just what I could expect from Massimo's family and any "evidence" against me. Using this ploy, I frequently discovered useful information and was never caught.

That day on the Mondello beach, a light went on in my head, and I knew there could be no more flirting with openness or any incautious revealing of thoughts. For any hope to survive, I had to outwardly play by their rules and make them think I was only a stupid American woman completely at a loss in this land of foreign laws and customs.

While awaiting the judge's decision, we continued visiting Alex as a family. Dad wanted to cram in as much as he could and realistically assess the chances of Alex's returning home. He would fill his heart and mind with the sights, sounds, hugs, and interests of his grandson, then when he got back to New Jersey would transfer them as best he could to an impatiently waiting Mom. My mind was often occupied by scenes of her slowly pacing the floor in that big, empty house and of her hopes for the phone to ring with any kind of good news. Unfortunately, she would have to wait like the rest of us.

The day before Dad left, our visit with Alex took place in the sunny day room that had been decked out specifically for him. Alex's toys, books, even a computer game hooked up to the television provided him with a little place of his own and a world of entertainment. This day, however, he mostly sat on the couch on Dad's lap again and scarcely took his eyes from him. The scene was heart-wrenching, as Alex repeatedly asked, "Why do you have to go?," while touching his American grandfather's face as if to remember it by feel. I had trouble keeping back the sobs as I sat and watched. When the visitation ended and we stood on the street waiting for the bus, my sadness hardened into anger. "This is outrageous," I said to no one in particular, but Dad didn't respond. He was too busy wiping away tears.

Dad left early the next morning, and the man who seemed so distant when I was a teenager had again bonded with my heart. I felt like a little girl again, alone in my apartment. I needed my Apuka.

After my months-long bombardment of telephone calls to Marco's office for any information, we were thrown a court-approved bone. No joint custody—surprise!—and no unsupervised visits, but . . . Alex could spend a couple of chaperoned hours with me over Christmas. What a letdown. That meant Massimo and whoever else he decided to bring along, plus the possibility of one of his unseen sentries on one end of the street or the other. I

Dad and Alex

simply couldn't believe it. Now the guards would be invading the sanctuary of my own apartment as well! I felt cheated and abused.

After the initial shock passed, I found myself looking forward to the visit. Hope is such an incredible thing—resilient, unquenchable, always grasping for just one more reason to exist. *Maybe this is a start*, I thought, *maybe instead of the mile we asked for they gave an inch, but at least they gave. Maybe . . .*

It was a never-ending cycle of hope, despair, and hope again. The "maybes" often crowded around me like a horde of excited schoolchildren, laughing, shouting to get my attention whenever I was close to hitting bottom. I was desperate for something concrete, but all I really had was a vaporous hope that shifted with each new breeze of defeat. But at least it was there. And ultimately, what each subsequent legal beating accomplished was a stiffening of my resolve, which was to keep playing the game, but plan for "The Time."

One of the most depressing aspects of the whole obscene farce was that literally no one in the local market, bakery, café— all part of my daily rounds—knew that I was a mother. Always alone, my purchases minimal, I appeared the embodiment of the transplanted American, a wannabe Sicilian who preferred the single life to the tie-downs of a family. At the same time, I didn't want them to know the embarrassing truth and fall under their suspicion as well. How I ached, as I saw other moms on the street with their children, laughing, scolding, or simply holding little hands as they went about their business. That should be me . . . that *was* me, once. The pain knifed deep, and I nurtured a burgeoning dislike of everything Sicilian. These people had no right to this intimacy with their own children. If I couldn't have it, neither should they. Inwardly I raged daily, deeply resentful of every one of them for what was happening to me. Somehow, they were at fault too; it was their country that chained me, took my son, my dreams, and my freedom. To see those people smiling, laughing in conversation, strolling absentmindedly with their children made the gall rise in my throat.

The months eased by, and with the approach of Christmas my enthusiasm took off. Chaperoned or not, my son was coming to my home. My home! In the two weeks prior to the visit, I shopped, cooked, and cleaned for all I was worth. Christmas Day arrived and with it Alex and a very bored-looking Massimo. Almost immediately Massimo gravitated to the phone and sat conversing with someone for the next half hour or so. I was riding so high, I basically ignored him and swept Alex into our own little, meticulously prepared world. There were gifts for him to open right away, but as per our special little custom, we got right down to the "Treasure Hunt," with clues written in English and hidden all over the apartment. It was a hectic, raucous event punctuated with lots of laughing, and by the time it ended the floor was wonderfully strewn with ribbons, clues, and wrapping paper. Oh, it was good to have the presence of a child again in my own apartment.

Leaving Alex to his booty, I set the small table with every American trimming I could think of. When it was set up, I called them both to the table. Alex bolted upright and flew across the room, but Massimo grimaced, putting on a show of disdain for his court-ordered guard duty. "I'm not hungry," he fairly groaned.

I smiled. *Good,* I thought. *I didn't want to share it with you, anyway.*

Do you know how hard it is to find a good Christmas turkey in Sicily? There were moments, during a frustration-laced shopping day that I nearly considered floating a few bucks to the mob—they'd be able to procure me a decent bird! What I ended up with was a not-quite-melt-in-your-mouth specimen, but with all the fixins, lunch was a blast. Afterward, a flurry of friends came round to play board games, and one of Alex's special buddies engaged him in a one-on-one computer battle.

When they all left, and I was alone with the quiet and the mess, I felt strangely whole. Tomorrow would come with the inevitable waking alone, but for the moment, it was all okay. We'd had an absolutely wonderful time, and though the whole affair

A visit at my apartment in Mondello

lasted a scant two hours, for me it was a moment out of eternity. I was to find later that, retreating after a particularly hard day, I could relive that visit over and over and retrace every step Alex took through my front door and into my personal living space. It would become a kind of shelter for me in the following year, a secret retreat far away from a hard and dangerous world of courts and suspicious relatives, of cold-eyed lawyers, and shadowy observers who watched my every move.

The same world that still held my son.

7

Stranger in a Strange Land

Megghiu si 'nsigna cu lu fari chi cu lu diri.
Experience is the best teacher.

"*That's* not possible," was the response on the other end of the phone. Crisp and unyielding, it took me by surprise and shut me down so that I had to momentarily reorganize. I guess I simply wasn't used to being dismissed without, at least, a proper hearing. I sighed. Here we go again.

"Um, well . . . I'm looking at it now."

"It" was a sinister black stain that had oozed over the entire ceiling over the last couple of weeks and begun to creep languidly down my bedroom walls. It started as a single black spot, like spilled ink that hung over my bed waiting to pool and drip. It quickly became an eye, a blurred, malevolent orb that stared down at me, unblinking when I awoke in the morning. Eventually, it became a mouth; its gulp widening to the four corners of the room. Daily, I watched it grow in both size and temerity till I'd loathe going to bed at night, envisioning while sleeping being wrapped up in its thin black tendrils. It was the last thing a gal with a panic-attack problem needed. I could smell its subtle aroma of mold, much what you'd expect to encounter in a centuries-old crypt. It left a taste in the mouth that flavored my food, so that cooking became a contest of scents to see which would overpower the other. "It" always won.

Unfortunately, the absentee landlady was adamant in her refusal to believe me. Have you ever looked up the word "adamant"? While it does mean "stubborn," it also refers to an impossibly hard stone or mineral. That's what I was up against. As I stood there telling her "day," she was just as stubbornly responding "night."

She bounced the dialog ball back into my court. "No, it can't be. There's nothing wrong with my apartment."

At this point, my patience was playing hide-and-seek, and I was losing. "Look. I'm staring right at it. My eyes are open, okay? I'm not making this up. There's a huge black whatever all over my ceiling and it's spreading. I would like something to be done about it."

"No, it cannot be. Why do you bother me?"

"Because my ceiling is being eaten alive!" I paced the floor as much as the phone cord would allow, and in best Sicilian style flung my hands as if swatting flies. "You need to come here, okay? Just take a look, and see for yourself."

Her response put me over the edge. "No, I'm too busy. I can't come, and that's all."

I felt, rather than heard, my voice elevating to a harpy-like crescendo. Later, I was grateful there had been no crystal in the room.

My landlady never did come.

One thing I was to learn the hard way was that, for Sicilians, there was no decibel level comfort zone. In fact, the louder the better. Watching people on the street, you'd think every verbal volley would escalate into blows, but really, as a people they seemed to love it. Want to make a point? Shout! Disagree with your friend? Then get in his face and let it all out. It may not change his mind, but you'll feel better about yourself. Then both of you can laugh and go have an espresso.

What a strange world where I'd been imprisoned! I'd have thought my prior years as Massimo's wife would have prepared me for this enforced cultural immersion, but I was to find there was still so much to learn. Often I felt a twinge of Grade B sci-fi run up my back, a chill, as it were, letting me know that I was trapped in some alternate universe where the rules of life as I knew them just didn't apply. By appearance, it was a stunningly beautiful place, where a romantic blue sea meets a spotless stretch of white sand, where green cliffs hug the bays like ancient citadels, and unmatched architecture takes the breath away. But the people—good-looking, robust, energetic—proved themselves a wonderful, chaotic breed that could be counted on for nothing so much as their cavalier disregard for convention and utter disdain for emotional restraint. I tried—oh, I tried!—to fit in and to go with the proverbial flow. But every time I got in the stream I found myself paddling in the wrong direction.

Sicilians are a world apart and proud of it. Irrepressibly enthusiastic about life, they grab it by the throat, put it to work for them, and plant their feet at any opposition but ready with a laugh or a song because they know "it will all work out." To a transplanted American, like myself, this approach is bold, confusing, and often troubling. Their impulsiveness is a carelessly thrown monkey wrench in the gears of an American's carefully planned day. Sanity in Sicily is maintained only by understanding where the culture comes from and accepting that it's just the way things are.

Considering themselves Sicilian first and Italian second, their innate pride in their own culture and homeland is all over everything they do. Though Italian is the common spoken language, you can still get the flavor of Sicilian by hanging out in the areas and kinds of businesses characteristically reserved for the "lower classes": street vendors, open-air market sellers, fishermen. Sprinkled with Italian, Arabic, even ancient Norman words—holdovers from previous empires—the language is at once fluid and musical. To hear the merchants call out in the Palermo marketplace or in the weekly Mondello mercatinos is to be transported back in time. For all my developing resentment toward the land because of my horrible circumstances, I nonetheless loved to stand and listen to the ancient lyrical callouts of "Fresh fish!," "Ripe tomatoes!," "Sweet fresh fruit!" It was so beautiful, it took my breath away.

Cut off from the mainland for so many years, conquered over the centuries by various marauding armies, used to having their land pillaged by occupation forces and neglected by the Italian government, Sicilians have quite naturally developed a pugilistic nature. In other words, they like to fight, if not as often with fists, then with words. A duel with the tongue is considered just part of the everyday experience, and believe me, like the old-time swordfighters, they have their own set of warm-up exercises, parries, and killing thrusts. In all the cultures I've experienced worldwide, Sicilian is, hands down, the most vocal, stentorian, and verbally exuberant. During conversation, they get in your face and stay there. They haven't the slightest concept of personal space, and wouldn't give a hoot if you explained it to them. Hand gestures proliferate, from the enigmatic "question circle" (putting the fingers together with the thumb in a circular pattern and placing it directly in the other person's face) during an agitated question-and-answer session, to the rigorous flapping of the arms when in disagreement or disgust, to the more varied and standard crude gestures. Their body language complements their intense and clamorous speech.

Every day in Sicily was a lesson in surviving culture shock. A trip to the store, bank, or whatever resulted in a kind of mayhem-turned-teachable moment. The concept of waiting patiently in line till your turn comes along is as foreign to them as spoken Mandarin. Instead, counters are literally mobbed. And while living in Sicily, unless I wanted to be ignored by the clerk, I had to learn to use elbows and shoulders to keep from being mashed out of the place altogether. Routinely, those behind rubbed up against me, pushing me forward or to the side. A stranger's breath on my neck was just part of the game, where no amount of withering stares or caustic comments ("Do you mind?!") would give them pause. It was something a person got used to or planned her business during the daily siesta, when most everyone else was napping.

Their driving was along the same lines. On the road, they were positive lunatics—cutting me off, nearly sideswiping me during a pass, yelling threats out the window. And they had an absolute love affair with the horn. I wouldn't be sitting at a stop light for a half second after it changed, and the guy behind me, and the one behind him, would give their horns a body slam. I had to learn to drive like the rest of them when I was behind the wheel of a loaner, jockeying for position like I was an Indy 500 contender, double-parking whenever I could; no one parked correctly anyway, and the police didn't bother with such trivialities. And like them, I also pretended my speedometer was merely a dashboard decoration. I had to if I wanted to get anywhere by car.

Perhaps if I'd looked more like I belonged, the transition would have been easier. But my paler complexion and blonde hair made me a stand out in any crowd. Fair hair is strikingly conspicuous in a country of dark-haired, swarthy people, and it acted as a magnet to men. While that could work both ways, most of the time this was unfortunate, for it repeatedly garnered unwanted attention. While walking down the street, minding my own business, as they say in those cheesy news stories, invariably some guy would imagine that my pointedly looking the other way was the perfect subtle come-on. He'd actually follow me—"stalking," as they call it in the States—for blocks, cooing out, "Bellllllaaaa," which means "Beeeoootifullll," coupled with the ever popular "Dove` vai?" or, "Where are you going?" Or he'd get right in my face, walking backward while trying to impress me with his smooth conversational technique.

"You're not from around here," he'd ooze, "I can tell."

Really? How astute, I'd think, punctuating it with a bored rolling of the eyes.

On and on he'd go, prompting me with a "Where are you from?" But he didn't want me to actually *talk*, unless it was to remark admiringly on his bulging biceps or Casanova-style appeal. And persistent? You couldn't shoo this kind away with a double-barreled shotgun. When it came to their favorite pursuit—women—they were deaf, dumb, and blind to blunt rebuff and the most degrading insults.

Normally, I'd begin with a curt, "Leave me alone!" and in short order escalate to ridicule.

"You're stupid!" I'd wind up shouting or "You're ugly!"—anything to humiliate them to the point of breaking contact. It never worked because they had no sense of shame. You just couldn't embarrass them. They were totally on a mission, and a pretty obvious one, by the way they leered at me. The only way I could lose them was to walk fast, weave in and out of crowded areas, or duck one way into stores and leave by a discreet exit.

Certainly not all Sicilian men were like that. But by and large, the whole society was governed by an irrepressible machismo, which men flaunted and to which women were expected to yield.

The bright, shining exception to that standard was Fabio.

I'd met him while sharing Stefano and Sarah's apartment. Coming home one night about the time for the late evening meal, I was introduced to a very young, handsome, and amiable cousin of Stefano. A former member of the carabinieri, the elite national police force that worked both the military and public sectors, Fabio was a refreshing change from the overbearing bravado I was getting accustomed to. His courtesy and gentlemanly manners seemed at odds with my concept of an armed-to-the-teeth guard of "Mafia judges." At dinner, conversation naturally swirled around my Alex dilemma, and I immediately gained another sympathetic ear.

"That's horrible!" Fabio said with deep feeling. "There must be something that can be done. This is not right!"

While I appreciated his newfound support, I really didn't think much about him after he left for the evening. He was nice enough, disarmingly polite, and very easy to look at (!), but my mind was perpetually on other things. I'd only recently gotten out of a devastating relationship with a husband-turned-kidnapper. I had no intention of becoming entangled with another Sicilian man of an as yet unknown caliber.

After moving into Ashur, the complex that contained my first tiny apartment, I began to notice a young man who seemed vaguely familiar. It clicked that this was the same Fabio I'd met a couple of months earlier. It turned out he lived in the same apartment complex. When I called out to him the first time, he turned and smiled as if he'd won an American lottery. We became good friends, and when I left a few months later for my second place at Via Mondello, he . . . well . . . followed me there. Not like the other men, but rather in a hello-again-Katie-just-thought-I'd-stop-by-for-the-hundredth-time kind of way. He was always showing up, and we'd go out for dinner, take long walks on the beach, or just sit and talk. No doubt after the first few months our neighbors were beginning to think of us as an item, and the very last thing on my mind, again, was a serious relationship. On top of that, he was nine years my junior, which at the time seemed an unbridgeable gulf. So, every once in a while I'd sit him down and he'd patiently endure "The Speech."

"Now, I'm not here for a boyfriend, Fabio," I'd unvaryingly begin. "I'm here to get my son back. That's all. I like you, but you know we can't get serious. There's just too much going on."

Nodding emphatically and with a look of persuasive innocence, he'd agree, every single time. "Of course! Yes, yes! I completely understand."

That settled, we'd go right back into the same comfortable routine—him showing up, us laughing and talking, going out to dinner, walking along the beach.

Whatever his hidden intentions, Fabio was the dearest of friends. He well knew my terrible situation, and his genuine sympathy was moving. More than that, he respected me. That really threw me to the point that I'd begun to ask myself, "Is this guy even Sicilian?" He was the antithesis of all I'd come to expect in the local manhood. His kindness, generosity, and good nature became a rock I could cling to in my storms of emotion. When suffering from panic attacks, I'd lie on the couch at Via Mondello while he read aloud from what became my favorite book—a history, written in Italian, of an 1800s English explorer of ancient Egypt. I'm not sure that the content had much calming effect (although I've always been fascinated by world history), but I do know I enjoyed the sound of his voice, warm and soothing. I felt like a kid, lying there, listening. I didn't realize it then, but my heart was being nudged, ever so gently, in a direction counter to my loner survival instincts.

His knightly conduct extended even to my defense against adversarial weather. While enjoying lunch one Sunday afternoon at his mother's apartment, a winter rainstorm began beating against the windows. As certain areas of Mondello were prone to flooding due to poor gutter runoff, I watched with increasing anxiety as the weather intensified. I knew if we didn't leave quickly I'd have to temporarily find another place to live. Even if I did make it into my apartment before full flood, I'd be stuck inside for a few days, till the waters on the main drag receded.

Fabio—at his mother's apartment

Unable to relax, I told Fabio and his mother I'd have to go. It was only a five-minute fast walk to my apartment, but we had no time to spare. Once on the street, we had to skirt channels of fast-moving water and deep pools where low spots in the streets had been filled. We stopped off at a local market for a couple bags of groceries (knowing that I'd be housebound for a day or two), and then without explanation Fabio insisted we drop into one of the piazza's espresso bars where we were regular patrons. "Fabio!" I said with urgency. "What are you doing? We don't have much time . . ."

Going directly to the counter, he spoke quickly with the help. They smiled, handed him something, and when he turned, I saw that he held two very large black plastic garbage bags. "You don't think I'm going through that out there without some protection?"

We hurried out the door and proceeded up the street. An impromptu lake had formed on the main road, and before we started for the gate leading to my apartment, he put on his make-shift wetsuit. Stepping into the trash bags, one leg in each, he tied them around the tops of his thighs and gave me a look that said, "Well, what are you waiting for?" He looked ridiculous, and I laughed. "Up," he said with a smile, jerking his thumb at his back. I hopped up, piggy-back, with a sack of groceries in each hand, and he slogged through the rushing water. We passed a lone woman driver, who wasn't actually driving since her car was flooded. She sat in her car with the windows rolled up while the waters flowed by at about steering-wheel level. Her eyes followed us with the evident suspicion that we were two sanitarium escapees, and on our part we were amazed she sat there, waiting either for deliverance or the flood to recede. We made it to the apartment, and Fabio settled in to dry before braving the flood on his own. We never did find out what happened to the woman. When I went past several days later, both she and the car were gone.

Fabio was always looking out for my interests . . . and in thinking about it years later, for his own, too, when the situation warranted it.

In the spring of 1994, when my group of English students was thinning out, in order to make ends meet, I took a job at a posh

Palermo tennis club. The hours left something to be desired, as I'd rack up twelve-hour days, six days a week, and get off work after midnight. Plus, all the standing left me with temporary nerve damage resulting in a persistent numbness in my left foot, which lasted for about a month after the job ended. But in general, I liked the job. I discovered that in the proper atmosphere of relaxation, many of Sicily's upper strata were surprisingly "unstarched" and would exchange good-natured banter with me, as they soaked up the sun by the pool. The doctors, lawyers, and judges congregating there threw lire around like confetti, so the tips flowed like the proverbial wine. As a bonus, I was treated almost as royalty by the management due to—ta-dah!—my hair color. About time it worked in my favor. "Ha!" the boss would say in derision of the other exclusive clubs. "Let them get their own blonde!"

It was a big business draw for the management, and they utilized it to maximum advantage. I could almost see them sending their own infiltrators over to the competition, pretending to be busboys and bartenders, all the while telling the other guys' patrons, "Hey, have you been over to the competition lately? They have a *blonde* working there!"

Throughout that several month stint, Fabio was self-appointed chauffeur. Often he'd drive to the club and wait till my shift ended to give me a lift home. Sometimes I kept him waiting over an hour, but he didn't complain. I know my late night situation prompted his concern, but there were a couple of different aspects to that.

"You shouldn't let just anyone drive you home after work," he'd chide. "You don't know what could happen." Well, yes, but I suspect what he really meant, at least in part, was, "I am jealous and don't want anyone but me driving you home."

For all Fabio's intimations of danger for a lone woman, I hadn't really felt threatened in Sicily. Crime was generally low at the time, and for all the blatant machismo, attacks on women were rare. Still, I carried in my purse a small container of pepper spray that I'd brought with me from the States, and which I was ready to use at the slightest genuine provocation. My apartment in Mondello could be reached from the road only by way of a gate that opened up into a narrow, high-walled driveway—more like an alley. When coming home late, this heavily shadowed path could be very intimidating. With my eyes constantly darting from one dark corner to another, I always kept one finger on the button of my upholstered weapon, ready to blast an intruder with 100% unadulterated cayenne. Hit the button till the canister ran dry, bash him over the head with the empty can, and run like crazy was the only plan I ever had.

The "weapon" went with me pretty much everywhere, except when I went to the courthouse for hearings, since they ran everyone through security. I actually forgot about it once when Sarah and I were at the consulate in Naples. She needed to renew her passport, and after entering security, we both placed our purses on the conveyor belt to have them run through x-ray. I realized with horror that the pepper spray, considered a prohibited item in Italy, would show up clearly on the screen. Images of sudden arrest flooded my mind, and I held my breath. On the other side, though, they handed us our purses and bid us a polite "Good day." I think I exhaled in relief so explosively that the building's windows bowed outward.

The item may have been prohibited, but that was only on paper, and I, as well as everyone else in Sicily, knew it. If it had ever gotten lost or malfunctioned, I could easily have gotten a replacement or even upgraded my armory if I'd been willing to go to the quarters of Palermo that routinely arranged such things. I passed the entrance to such places all the time on my way from the courthouse: narrow streets slithering deep into the city, coiling around dark, ancient buildings, and interconnecting in a maze safely navigated by only a few. In Palermo, there was always a way to get what you wanted, if you knew the right person and handed over the right amount of money. There were rumors that deep in the guts of the massive, open-air market known as

Capo, other less visible sellers plied their trades and sold wares not mentioned in polite company. More than once I stood looking down those constricted corridors and tinkered with the idea of hiring some mercenaries for a caper of my own. But with no contacts or guarantee of safe conduct and not nearly enough money, I shelved the scheme each time. I didn't want to end up on the police "disappeared" list.

Women tourists often make the mistake of going unescorted into these same dark, winding streets. Enthralled by the medieval atmosphere, gawking at the fifteenth-century buildings leaning in close from either side, they never see the helmeted speedster zooming past with outstretched arm, snatching a loosely held purse as he and his motor scooter quickly vanish. I learned to

Capo—The open food market

keep my purse close, and only one time had any trouble. Standing on a crowded bus on my way to visit Alex, I felt an unusual nudge against my shoulder, the one that supported my purse strap. Looking quickly down, I caught a thief with his hand actually in my purse. Lambasting him good, loudly telling everyone on the bus, "This man is a thief!," I forced him away from me, with him just as loudly denying every accusation. Throwing his hands up in feigned innocence, he made for the door and exited at the next stop. No one said anything; they just went back to reading, looking out the window, or talking with the person beside them as if nothing happened.

This "don't get involved" trait seemed so ingrained in Sicilians that they'd give the impression they could witness a murder, and in good conscience, forget it ever happened. For them, it was actually a matter of survival. On the street, one never knew who was attacking, robbing, or harassing whom or for what reason. In the birthplace of the Mafia, it was considered wise to simply mind your own business. Lots of people had "connections" or family ties that could stretch a long way. No one wanted to run the risk of getting a visit in the middle of the night or being waylaid by a mysterious stranger months down the road because of some well-intentioned interference in a private fight. This would help explain the total lack of response or sympathy from passersby when I was being manhandled by Giovanni on my first day in Palermo. Any onlooker knew his actions would be backed up by then unseen *famiglia*. For all they knew, keeping their distance would equate to keeping their skins.

Ah, but Sicilians have no such detachment when it comes to their food. Eating for them is one of the main reasons for being alive. They regard their food with an absolute passion, and I quickly grew to share that sentiment. Sicily has the freshest, most delicious food anywhere! Shopping at the open-air mercatinos (especially the Capo) after another frustrating court hearing in Palermo, was a balm to my nerves. Not that it was soothing! On the contrary, it was as if I'd entered into the belly of a huge, benevolent, and thousand-year-old beast that writhed with a happy, perpetual movement. The sing-song calls of the merchants, the whirlwind of scents, and the rainbow of bright fresh fruits and vegetables . . . it was a carnival atmosphere; once in, I found myself not wanting to go home to that lonely little apartment. Here I was alive, with the world for a moment completely shut out.

In all honesty, not quite everything was to my liking. I couldn't develop a taste for the foul-smelling cow spleen sandwiches (okay, I didn't try!), and no matter how a market cook or master chef flavored a bundle of intestines or garnished up the plate, it still looked like, well . . . animal entrails.

If Sicilians are passionate about their food, they are unrestrained fanatics in their coffee habits. Whether you order espresso (a regular coffee, chokingly strong by American standards), ristretto (even stronger), or my favorite, cappuccino (espresso with steamed milk), the place is a coffee lover's health spa. It is normally drunk standing up at a coffee bar, in actual porcelain cups (They hate Styrofoam!) and is never sipped, but finished off in two or three gulps. I discovered it was in bad taste to order a cappuccino or anything with liquid milk in it after the morning hours. Drinking milk in the afternoon, even to flavor coffee, was for some strange reason looked upon with disgust. They'll give it to you, but regard your craving as unveiled barbarism. As was the idea of traditional American coffee. Sicilians coming to the States balk at drinking the stuff they have derisively dubbed acqua di polipo or "broth of the octopus." To them, its only purpose is medicinal, to be slugged down quickly with two acetaminophen in case of migraine.

Three times a day for most Sicilians, literally everything comes to a screeching halt when the "coffee mood" strikes. Numerous times I've stood on the street corner in Palermo and watched public busses stop dead in the middle of traffic, and the driver unconcernedly exiting the bus to spend a few moments downing coffee and visiting friends at his favorite bar. He'd be in there till the riders had enough and let him know it by leaning on the horn and shouting their outrage. After a while, he'd saunter outside, wiping his mouth with the back of one hand, while with the other casually waving them to take their seats, and placating them with an unhurried, "Okay, okay, I'm here. We're going."

You'd think this attitude would infuriate paying customers and they would flood the bus headquarters with complaints. But Sicilians are forgiving in this respect because everybody does it and not only for coffee breaks. The Western concept of "time," that things have to be done within a certain period, somehow missed landing on Sicily's shores when it was annexed by Italy a hundred and fifty years ago. You know, when a Sicilian looks at his watch, it's not necessarily to check the time but to admire the timepiece. *Hey, it looks good on that wrist! Maybe I can dazzle the girls with it.*

While I was there, it took forever to get anything attended. The snail's pace of the court system left a bitter taste in my mouth; accordingly, any problems with the bank, government offices, or even with a landlady would take a long time to resolve. For instance, in the summer at my apartment in Mondello I learned to correlate my shower times with my upstairs neighbor. If either one of us forgot, the grossest of plumbing problems quickly surfaced—literally. In response to the increased water usage, prompted by the sudden influx of tenants, the pipes would back up. Sewage coming up the drain itself prompted a near-frantic phone call to Fabio. Well, the problem was out of his league so we tried to get a hold of my invisible landlady. Unable to contact her, we tried a twenty-four-hour emergency plumbing service. A woman answered and Fabio hurriedly explained the problem. She had him wait a moment, while her muffled voice relayed the situation to an associate. We both listened in astonishment as the phone line jumped with uproarious laughter. They never did come to the apartment.

Such was the case with the killer mold. At times like this I was so very grateful for Fabio. What a gift that man was! He brightened up my life with more than kind words and gentlemanly conduct. When my disinterested landlady refused to come to the rescue, he could be counted on to take over, often without my asking. Discovering the mold problem on my ceiling and walls, he quietly planned strategy and waited till I'd gone on my Naples trip with Sarah. Upon returning to Mondello, I walked into a spotlessly white, clean-smelling apartment. Fabio had redone the whole interior with mold-killing paint, and the transformation was astounding. In on the happy deceit from the beginning, Sarah stood in the doorway, smiling, while I squealed in pleasure and threw my arms around my paint-spattered hero. Little did I know at the time the major role this knight in shining armor would play later in my life.

Fabio

8

A Plague of Doubts

Manciari amaru e sputari duci.
Keep up a good front though things are tough.
Lit. Eat bitter and spit sweet.

What is it like to live every day with a growing sense of fear?
It is an exile into the shadow lands of uncertainty, of always
waiting for the dread "thing" to come around the corner or loom
suddenly before you in an alley at twilight. It is the perpetual
knot in the stomach that rebels against the imposition of food;
at the same time, it is the craving for an elusive peace, a hunger
that cannot be sated. It is the feeling of utter helplessness in a
nightmare from which you are unable to waken . . . only it's not
a dream, and your eyes don't flutter in sleep. That's part of the
problem—you don't sleep at all—and the gaunt face that stares
back, unblinking, from the morning mirror seems a painting
of someone you once knew from long ago. The vibrancy, the
laughter is gone; all that remains is the marred reflection and
captured in aged oils of a life sheared away and interred in some
unmarked grave.

I woke with a start, muscles contracting, kicking, or running,
maybe. A moment ago, it had been so real. Alex and I had succeeded; we were getting away. The plan had worked, things had
fallen beautifully into place, and we were exiting this mess that
passed for a badly acted play. But on opening my eyes, the room
was still there, I was still there, and the quiet, oh, the terrible

quiet of early morning, where the only sound was the breathing I tried hard to ratchet back from my adrenaline-pumped "escape." Thinking of Alex (when did I not?), I wondered if he had these kinds of dreams, too. I lay on the bed, feeling the thump of my heart in my temples, and wept.

In the Fall, I started doing English lessons again, and it proved profitable enough to net me a decent income; but the routine of paid conversation with native Sicilians was wearing on me. It was necessary to invite these people into the sanctuary of my apartment, and though most of them were quite nice, I found myself host to another simmering resentment. Since as teacher and student we quickly exhausted all routine conversation, more and more I was being used as a sounding board, a therapist, almost. As I listened to their personal problems, their complaints about family members or coworkers, I was drawn into their private lives. I hadn't bargained for this. In contrast to my own colossal situation, their petty murmurings were no more than minor inconveniences.

Despite the friendship extended by some of my students (one young couple had even taken me shopping and to dinner), a coldness seeped into my feelings. I continued to view all Sicilians with a smoldering anger, and any relationships with them that developed along the way became like sandpaper on a raw wound. It didn't matter who they were: the old woman on the street, the teenager on his motor scooter, the young mother with her children . . . yes, especially them. It was shameful, but I held them collectively responsible for Alex's being here and for my own subsequent confinement to an island whose culture and people were the opposite of everything in my own makeup. It was like being stuck in a photographic negative. All that I expected to see black, was white, and vice versa. Even as I began to understand their ways, I hated them for making me do it. Like it or not, I was becoming assimilated, conforming to their standards and beginning to act like them. Even the language took on a life of its own. It was alarming that in get-togethers or conversation with friends, often with the cadre of expats that formed my unofficial support group, portions of common English would suddenly evaporate from my vocabulary. I'd go blank, fishing for a particular American word or phrase, thinking, *Now, I know that word. Come on. This is so stupid!*

Alex was turning the corner, too. Every day I watched him becoming more Italian, squeezed into it by his schooling, his friends, and of course, Massimo's family. He spoke the language like he'd been born there, flawlessly reciting classic poetry from his schoolwork, and though he was still fluent in English, his voice was taking on an Italian accent. His memories of American life were slipping away, his connection to his birth culture rapidly fading until I was the only reminder. If things kept on in this perpetual stalemate, I'd lose him to this place.

I wasn't about to let that happen without a fight. I would not let him forget those things that tied him to America. My mom, a schoolteacher, devised with me a sort of clandestine counter-cultural attack. She sent me English grammar and composition books, which I slipped into Giovanni's apartment during my visits. In secretive moments, Alex and I would crack open the textbooks, and I'd grill him on the lessons, constantly throwing glances over my shoulder or listening with one ear to the hallway for approaching footsteps.

"This is our secret," I'd whisper periodically, and with a complicit grin, we'd huddle and work. When my visitation time ended, I'd leave with all the evidence. It was crucial that I kept up the "defeated" façade. Any inkling that I still planned to get Alex back to his home country would sound a death knell to my visitation privileges.

Alex himself was once the catalyst for a dramatic surge of hope. During one of my low points, I arrived at Giovanni's apartment and headed for the day room, which is where we had most of our visits. Alex's face lit up as I entered the room. Running to me, he tightly grabbed my hand, "Mom, I have to tell you about a dream I had last night."

Visiting Alex at his grandparents' home during Christmas

His infectious enthusiasm sent my depression spinning out the door, while he chattered away in English (which I insisted he'd do during our visits). In his dream, Alex and I had held hands, jumped forward, and landed in my parents' house. After telling the dream, he looked up at me and said, "Let's do it again." We took a step forward and jumped, pretending to land in that distant, New Brunswick living room. Repeatedly we "jumped" over time and space, laughing and hugging each other afterward. So, I wasn't the only one thinking about home. Or perhaps God had visited him in the night. Whatever the source, that day my battered soul touched the stars. It was the boost I needed to keep going.

Another point of encouragement came in the unexpected form of a day trip to Ustica. Alex and Massimo, along with Massimo's girlfriend, Anna, had made plans for a week-long vacation on the island, and amazingly the judge handling the case ordered a few hours' chaperoned visit with me. Although predictably miffed, Massimo was forced to comply, and I made the two-hour ferry trip on a hot, sunny, beautifully standard Mediterranean day. I went with a lot of mixed feelings. The island people had been wonderful to me when Massimo and I had been there together years earlier, but even then they'd warned, albeit subtly, about my hookup with this man I barely knew. It was here I became pregnant with Alex. And it was here I made many dear friends who looked at me sad-eyed and wondered about my future.

When the ship tied up, it was a lonely walk from the Ustica marina to the town square. No one awaited my arrival at the dock, and there loomed the promise of Massimo's frowns and unsavory quips throughout the day. At the piazza, I saw the three of them. Alex ran to meet me, and though Massimo exhibited his usual displeasure at having to play chauffeur, he motioned to the parked car, and we bundled in for the drive to the beach. Alex and I talked nonstop for the short drive, then burst from the vehicle as soon as the car rolled to a stop.

Those warm sea waters were made for a day of play. I'd brought along a small inflatable raft I'd purchased for Alex, and he had a blast with it. Once, when resting on the hot sand and watching him, I thought of us both climbing onto that pitiful excuse for a lifeboat and using our hands to paddle away from there. We'd go all the way to the horizon, then sink below it, forever out of sight of this prison land. If Massimo suspected my thoughts, he kept his own smug counsel. Quite at ease, he was well aware that a "snatch" was out of the question. The only way to or from the island was by boat. When my allotted half day ended, he personally escorted me to the ferry dock and actually waited there till the ferry's lines were drawn in, and the little ship eased away from the dock. His was the last familiar face that day in Ustica. I wasn't even permitted to see Alex wave goodbye.

Hope is a funny thing. Its willful disregard of overwhelming circumstances keeps the breath circulating in a body otherwise dead. His ship splintered by a barrage of cannon shot from the English ship Serapis, Revolutionary War commander John Paul Jones defiantly shouted across the drifting gun smoke, "I have not yet begun to fight!" Savaged by a grizzly bear in 1827, mountain man Hugh Glass, his body a mass of open wounds, refused to give up the ghost as he crawled and limped nearly two hundred miles through the wilderness to safety. Silly, I know, but I was every inch one of their number. In the face of every scrap of evidence to the contrary, I still believed I would get Alex home with me. Even with the image of Massimo standing dockside with arms folded and face impassive, I had an unreasoning faith we'd make it out of there together.

In my varied readings about Jewish survivors of the Holocaust, never-dying hope was a recurrent theme. Despite the gleeful brutality of Nazi guards, the starvation and diseases that scythed them down by the multiplied thousands, despite the pall of black smoke from chimneys and the human ashes that settled in the compounds like soot, many still fought for each new day of life—if not for themselves, then for a loved one. With each morning came the chance of liberation or that somehow, for some unfathomable reason, they would make it out alive. Maybe this was what propelled me to seek help from another direction altogether.

Though raised in a "religious" home, I'd long since given up any pretense at prayer. But this legal and moral war had exacted a fearful toll on my heart, and I realized that I was getting nowhere without the help of God. I knew about Jesus, certainly. I'd been "witnessed to" enough by the wonderful missionary lady who had lived next door to Massimo and me during the fitful years of our marriage. I always listened politely, but the message never "took." But I did relearn that Jesus is God, that He is the Savior, and that He answers prayer. I was willing to try anything, however sporadically, if it would get us out of this impossible situation. You know, no atheists in foxholes and all that sort of thing.

Catholic presence is everywhere in Sicily—feast days celebrating the lives of saints, big and little church buildings all over the place, multiple shrines to venerated "somebodies" or other . . . and on it goes. Palermo itself boasted a statue of its patron, Santa Rosalia, and from Mondello, you could see the mountain where she stood. So I figured dipping my toe into Catholicism was a good place to start spiritually as anywhere. In Palermo, sometimes after yet another discouraging hearing, I'd step into one of the massive Catholic churches to pray. The architecture was truly astounding—marble floors and pillars, vaulted ceilings, huge murals of Christ or the lives of saints taking up vast portions of ceiling or walls. Usually empty when I visited, the buildings' semi-darkness shot through with rows of votive candles on wrought-iron stands, I felt the atmosphere was surreal, as if I'd stepped from a modern Palermo street into another century. The sound of my footsteps on the cold stone floor was haunting; I was the only person in the world. Kneeling in the pew or sometimes lighting a candle (although I think I broke "the rules" since I was not Catholic), I'd petition God for my son. I never bothered with form prayers or reading from a missal. I just gave it to God straight, from a mother's bleeding heart, "Please, give me back my son."

Even in my apartment, the urge would take me, and I'd lift my eyes to where I felt heaven should be, and make impossible promises that I had every intention of keeping. How many times

I had vowed, "God, I'll turn my life over to You if you help me get Alex back," I'll never know.

The silence from heaven was deafening. So I'd slip the drug and alcohol crutch back under my arm and hobble off into another grueling day.

It's ironic how God answers when no one is looking.

Though my expat friends carefully monitored my feelings and continually offered both encouragement and diversion, I periodically "escaped" Sicily on my own. I hated leaving Alex even for a short time since I never knew in my absence what mischief would be planned by Massimo. But a visit to my parents' home in New Jersey would be a strong tonic to nurse me back into a fighting stance. Their lovely New Brunswick house, which had seemed so confining in my rebellious youth, would now appear palatial in its warmth and companionship. All of us—me, Mom and Dad, and my brother, even though living elsewhere, were in this together. It's strange, how tragedy can either make or break a family. Alex's kidnapping had brought us together in a way we'd never have been otherwise. It had changed us all. For them, the old tough, uncontrollable Katie was gone, replaced by a gentler, very needy person who soaked in all the love she'd rejected as a young thug. Dad, shed of his characteristic reserve, consistently paid my round trip tickets from Sicily and was quick to ferret out a need where he could help.

Summer slid into fall and with the onset of damp weather, the loneliness again settled in hard. American holidays were the hardest to deal with, away from both family in the States and Alex in Sicily, unless granted special dispensation by the courts. I had to get away, take a break from the stress and reorganize both my thoughts and feelings. The past one-and-a-half years had taken its heavy toll. I needed distance between me and this convoluted country, a breather before I got back up from the mat and started swinging again. I called Dad, and he booked me a flight home.

Though I missed Alex terribly, the respite was wonderful. It was during this 1993 "furlough" that Mom broached a new angle, something I hadn't really given much thought. At the elementary school that day, she'd been approached by a woman whose two small children were in Mom's charge. The woman's husband, an editor for a New York-based magazine, was interested in my story. Maybe he could help. Mom, with affectionate Hungarian, ended the conversation with a firm, "You should see him, Kati."

You bet I did. I phoned his office, and Tom Swenson got right down to business. Delighted to hear from me, he immediately threw the ball into my court. He had heard snippets, but he wanted the whole thing. "Tell me all about it, Katie," he said, and listened while I peeled off one emotional layer at a time. I rattled off names, dates, what-have-you, and told him I could send the newspaper clipping from that short piece in the Santa Cruz newspaper from nearly two years earlier—all the specifics he'd doubtless verify before officially pursuing the story. When I finished nearly in tears (that was a given), he thought a moment, then excitedly ran through some angles we might be able to pursue.

"Okay, here's what I think. Sometimes it's a good idea to light some fires, really go public. So far your exposure has been local. A good story on you and your situation could change all that. What if we sent some of our people to Sicily with you, a writer and photographer? We could shoot your visits, tell your side of the story, let people see up front what you have to deal with on a daily basis."

The thought of that sent chills through me. "Oh, no. That would look so bad to the courts. It would probably hurt my case over there."

Pausing only a moment, he pitched again, "We could give you a video camera. Could you do some filming yourself? Kind of a video journal. We could work with that. Plus, we could still send a man along with you, who would do the actual writing, transcribing . . ."

I considered it, but the uncertainty surrounding the venture prompted caution. How in the world would I get that thing unseen into Giovanni's apartment? "Well, maybe," I said, "But I'll have to think about it some more."

Tom didn't push. I had the strong sense that it wasn't the story he was concerned about so much as getting Alex and me home where we belonged. I really liked the guy and wished I could offer some avenue to accommodate him.

Feeling bad because I wasn't giving him much leeway, I gushed apologies. "I'm sorry, Tom, but I have to be very careful. Believe me, the family will use anything they can to discredit me. I wish we could do something more dramatic, but I really don't know what."

His tone softened, no longer that of a professional news-hound but as a father of two children. "Katie, I understand if you don't want this kind of coverage. That part's really not all that important to me. Getting your child back is." He paused as if considering something, and I wished I could see his face, read his expression. It seemed like a long interval but was only a second or two. "You know," he said, "we covered a story a few years back, about an agency that sends out 'teams' to recover children stolen by noncustodial parents. They go all over the world. They're professionals. They might be able to help."

Stunned, I could hardly speak. "You're kidding. There are people who actually do that sort of thing?"

He smiled. "Oh, yeah. They've been pretty successful. The group is called CTU, Corporate Training Unlimited. You might want to give them a try."

He gave me the phone number, wished me the best, and hung up. With my hand still on the phone, I went over his words again and again: "They send out teams to recover children stolen by noncustodial parents." Thoughts started zinging through my head. *What are these guys—mercenaries? Do they carry guns? How much do they charge for their services?*

I did a little research on my own and afterward just sat and let it all sink in. Headquartered in Fayetteville, North Carolina, and founded and run by Don and Judy Feeney, CTU was comprised of ex-military commando types who act as personal security and security consultants for a variety of organizations, including multimillion-dollar businesses and the U.S. government. The group also arranged paramilitary sorties—minus the hardware—into other countries for the purpose of retaking children kidnapped by the noncustodial parent, just like Tom said. CEO Don Feeney was a former member of the elite Delta Force, the U.S. military's counter-terrorism/counter-insurgency response team. Along with his wife, Judy, they coordinated rescue operations for civilians—like me and Alex.

There were possibilities there, but dangers, too. This was a pretty radical diversion from the court system, and although I had for the past nearly two years toyed with this very possibility, I ultimately decided against it. Too risky, and for some inane reason I still felt the Italian courts might eventually see it my way and at least grant joint custody. I kept the phone number tucked away in my purse. When things got really rough emotionally, the idea resurfaced and sat unmoving in the back of my head, not insistent, just waiting, like a cat ready to pounce.

On my way back to Palermo, I stopped for a day in Rome. Peter McAuliffe, one of my father's business contacts and a friend, had heard of my plight and was eager to help. When I met with him a day before leaving for Sicily, he told me, "Look, I'm good friends with Monsignor Trigona at the Vatican. I talked to him yesterday about you, and he's interested. You know how it is in Italy. You have to know somebody to get anything done. Connections mean everything there. I'm sure he can help you."

The possibility of speaking directly to a man of such impressive religious stature sent my heart soaring. He was a priest, a higher-up, and the whole of Italy is influenced by the Catholic Church! If I could adequately present my case to him, I just knew he'd intervene in some way. Even the courts would have to take his involvement seriously. Mr. McAuliffe handed me a phone number. Before I left the next day, I called the Vatican, probably passed through a secretary (I don't recall), then spoke with the man himself. I was thrilled. "Yes," he said encouragingly, "Peter called earlier. He told me you had something important you wished to discuss, and I told him a meeting would be arranged."

I could not believe my good fortune. Without knowing my story, he agreed to see me. His kindness was evident by this alone, and my enthusiasm blossomed. I made an appointment, and he told me to call again when I reached Rome.

When I arrived in Rome in late afternoon, I purposely chose a hotel close to the Vatican, within short walking distance. The next morning I showered, had a quick cup of coffee, then rang the monsignor's number. "Yes, of course," he said, rather tiredly, "I may not be able to speak with you for a long interview, since I'm not feeling well and need to rest, but certainly, come over anyway, and you can explain the situation."

He told me the particular entrance to go to for a pass into the Vatican, and I was on my way. I walked through St. Peter's Square under a low gray sky that threatened rain. A chilly wind skittered a handful of dead leaves across the pavement, and the locals, huddled within upturned jacket collars, walked hurriedly and with heads down. St. Peter's Basilica and the Obelisk, normally so warm and inviting in the brilliant summer sunlight, now stood hard against pasty clouds that were remote and untouchable. My heart was thumping. Not as a tourist this time (I'd been here often on organized tours), I approached, with a combined hope and dread, the Vatican entrance where I'd been directed. I had officially left Italy and was then on foreign soil.

Situated in the sprawling metropolitan complex of Rome itself, Vatican city is nonetheless a sovereign city/state, with its own laws. Though sitting on a very small plot of land, the Vatican is center stage for the world's billion or so Catholics, most of whom would consider the pontiff's word the final one. For more than a thousand years, the popes had reigned as Vicarius Christi, the Vicar of Christ, before whom even European kings bowed. This time I felt, perhaps, like a medieval supplicant, an awe-struck commoner ushered into this religious fortress to beseech—grovel, if necessary—the help of a personage of enormous power. I didn't know exactly what a monsignor was, except that the title carried a hefty rank in the Catholic hierarchy.

At the entrance, where I had been directed, I was met by very polite but businesslike security personnel who inquired of my name and purpose for being there. They put a call through, presumably to verify my story, and issued me a temporary pass. Escorted from there by more security, I was taken to a spacious hallway where some of the elite Swiss Guards were posted. From there, it seemed they were all over the place: doorways, entrances, and exits.

Though known mostly for their flamboyant dress, the Swiss guards are not merely decorative. All men, and all Catholic by religion, they are a highly skilled group who are entrusted with the protection of the pope and of others within the Vatican's walls. Visitors will see them standing guard at various entrances and exits to the Vatican, and their imposing presence—made complete by a gold-handled sword—harkens back to the Medieval age of knighthood and fealty to the ruling prince or king. They are a force to be reckoned with.

Under this impressive escort, I was taken to another section where the public is forbidden access. The walk there was incredible; I felt awed, excited, and kind of important—all at the same time. The interior was enormous, a honeycomb of grand hallways, priceless works of art, and a bewildering array of rooms. It was the most lavish, opulent place I'd ever seen in my life. I was led to a closed door and told to wait with another contingent of the Swiss Guard.

The monsignor hadn't yet arrived, and although the dead time offered an opportunity to rehearse my plea for help, I was too nervous to remember any of the words. While I gawked at the palatial surroundings, I shot a furtive glance at the guard standing within an uncomfortable few feet. He stood impassive and erect in his red, yellow and blue traditional uniform; I didn't even see him blink! Amazingly, despite the solemnity of the moment, a mischievous idea suddenly sparked. A smile teased the corners of my mouth, and I flicked another glance at my stone-faced guardian. Images of the London sentries at Buckingham Palace did a slideshow in my head, along with stills of all the antics that these poor beleaguered soldiers had to put up with from both Londoners and tourists alike: dancing, making faces, standing on their heads, all to get a reaction from the impassive sentinels. I wondered how my own personal manikin would react if I, you know, just stuck my tongue out at him real quick, plugged my ears with my thumbs and wiggled my fingers, or something equally absurd. But I just didn't have the nerve. Sigh. All these years later, there's a sense of loss at blowing the chance of a lifetime . . .

About ten minutes later the monsignor arrived, seemingly a very kindly looking man who introduced himself in almost perfect English. He was glad, he added, to meet someone sent by his friend in the States. We entered the very large, richly paneled room where stood tons of books in wall bookcases. In the center of the room was a large table, and around it on all sides were chairs. It appeared to be a business office of some kind, a meeting room where lots of people met to discuss Vatican issues. Monsignor Trigona motioned me to a chair and sat directly across from me. After a moment of small talk, he asked why I had come to see him.

The story spilled out of me in all its sordid detail—the emotional abuse, the divorce, the kidnapping, the travesty of the court system. By the end of it I was crying again (How can one person have so many tears?!), and he waited, watching me for a moment, until I regained my composure. "I don't have anywhere else to turn, Father," I concluded. "I was hoping you'd be able to help in some way."

"Are you Catholic?" he asked suddenly.

Taken aback, I stammered, "No, actually, I'm not."

It was as if something passed between us, an unseen wall or barricade, and his demeanor immediately changed. He abruptly said, "I'm sorry, there is nothing I can do," and as he stood added, "I'm not feeling very well today and need to retire."

I tried to speak but the words came out chopped and not making any sense. It seemed as if he was literally pushing me out the door, maybe not physically, but by his harsh dismissal. As we left the room, he turned and walked away down the immense hallway, leaving me to the guard who had waited outside the doorway. Immediately I was escorted to the nearest exit and that quick, I was outside again.

I stood in the chill air for a long moment, unable to fully comprehend what had just happened. Shock settled on me and a volley of thoughts echoed through my mind. *A priest does this? A priest! How could he just turn me out like that? He didn't even offer to pray for me . . .*

I left the "state" of Vatican City and began the short walk to my hotel. By the time I got there, my steps had quickened and shock had given way to outrage. The thoughts kept coming. *Hypocrite! Is this the Vatican way—you're either "in" or "out," and "Heaven had better help you if you're out, because we won't?"*

Once in my room, I made a beeline for the phone and dialed long distance, "Mom, you're not gonna believe what just happened . . . !"

I spat it all out and sure enough Mom was aghast. One of my parting shots was, "And you can tell Dad's friend . . . !"

Poor Mom. I didn't really mean to give her an earful but she was a convenient dumping ground for my jumbled emotions. And she was really quite gracious about it, offering what meager encouragement she could from six thousand miles away. How I wished for one of her hugs right then!

The slow, agonized drag of months continued. After an interminable series of do-nothing hearings, I decided to change lawyers. I really liked Marco Russo personally, but he was proving ineffectual. A neurosurgeon friend of my parents' recommended a Rome attorney who, upon hearing of my situation, offered to take my case for free. I met him only once, a very nice man and willing to help. But upon reflection, I decided there really wasn't much he could do, so geographically removed from my situation. In March of 1994, I applied to still another Palermo lawyer, a woman by the name of Antonella Bellino who possessed a good command of English, had an undergraduate degree from a prestigious American university, and studied law in Italy. Maybe with a two-pronged legal assault, we'd get somewhere.

In the meantime, the visits continued without change. Well, almost no change. I was actually becoming bolder in my dealings with Giovanni. Remarkably, his original intimidating attitude toward me had somewhat softened. This was likely due to the passage of time and my appearance of helplessness, but he hadn't counted on the anger building within me. During one visit, as I entered Alex's room I noticed several candy wrappers in the small corner wastebasket. I fished them out and counted them. Five candy bars. It tripped a breaker in me somewhere, and I blew a fuse, marched out to where Giovanni was reading a newspaper in his favorite chair, and shoved the handful of crushed paper almost under his nose. "Look at this! Don't you put limits on how much of this stuff he's allowed to eat?"

Giovanni lowered his newspaper and smiled. "What is this? Why are you so upset? He's a boy, and boys love chocolate. Nothing wrong with that."

I sighed heavily in exasperation, "Nonno, Alex is gaining weight. Have you seen how pudgy he's getting lately? It's not good for him to eat too much candy. Do you want to be responsible for him becoming unhealthy?"

Giovanni relented and became almost paternal. "Okay, okay. No more gorging for him. I'll put the candy out of his reach."

"Thank you."

I tossed the wrappers in the kitchen trash and returned to Alex's room. We sat down on his bed and had a long talk about the importance of self-discipline and good diet. It was the first of many such talks, and as I was to discover later, my concern was to play a crucial role in our being reunited.

Giovanni surprised me in other ways. In the spring, he invited me to come watch Alex perform with his classmates at the Catholic elementary school the family had enrolled him in since his abduction. Surprised, I thanked Giovanni and accepted the invitation, walking alone to the school to meet them there. The two of them waited outside the compound; Alex waved happily and ran to hug me. While I had passed this imposing building many times, I'd never been inside. Walking around the perimeter of the stone wall surrounding the elementary school compound, we came to a massive, wrought iron gate, and stopped there while Giovanni pressed the button on an intercom attached to one wall. The gate unlocked, and we entered a courtyard where everything was set up for the play.

It was a beautiful, sunny spring day, comfortably warm, and the courtyard soon flooded with parents. I noticed immediately that I was regarded with nearly hostile suspicion by the nuns, and none of the other parents bothered to speak with me. Massimo was there with Anna, and they both ignored me. I sat with Giovanni in the seats set up outside and felt the stares. It was humiliating. I knew what they'd been told or had otherwise learned through one medium or another. Although Palermo is a city, it's still considered small-townish in atmosphere, at least in this area. Everybody seems to know everybody else's business. No doubt I carried the brand of the "uninterested" American mom who made life difficult and refused to go away like any decent sort.

But Alex made it all right. During the play, in which the kids had all dressed up as various animals, Alex continued to turn and look full at me, favoring me with a big smile every single time. The nuns and all the rest of them could say or think what they wanted—my son loved me, he believed in me, and that was enough.

My group of English students began dropping off as summer kicked in, and so I switched gears to waitress at the tennis club. The hours were exhausting, and I never seemed to get enough sleep. Often during my visits with Alex, we'd be happily exchanging news when suddenly my words would hang suspended, and I'd nod off for a second or two, with my mouth open! How embarrassing. Asleep in the middle of a sentence, I sometimes couldn't remember exactly where my words had left off, and I'd wind up either repeating myself or moving on to another subject in the hope I'd stay awake. I'm glad nobody ever took a picture of me during those moments. I never missed a visit, though. Tired or not, I put my time with Alex first.

That fall, an upcoming hearing had me in a hopeful mood. The judge was a woman who had two children. Finally, someone in authority who would understand! Surely a mother of two could grasp the importance of being with her children. *Antonella Bellino presented my case well*, I'd thought, *and the judge appeared to consider everything carefully*. Watching her closely, I felt sure that in this realm of misbegotten machismo, a mother's voice of reason would be heard and agreed with by another woman in power.

It was not to be. Her ruling made it clear that the status quo would be maintained, that my daily straightjacket visits were appropriate and the restrictions placed upon me just. The response from my lawyer, "Wait. There will come another ruling, and maybe then . . ."

For days afterward, I walked around in a fog of despair. Thanksgiving was only a week away, and holidays were the hardest to get through with my sanity intact. Those days I could share intimately with neither my son nor my family back home. The pressure was building again, and I couldn't stand being in close places. Panic attacks swept down on me like a dark bird, settling heavily on my chest and beating frantic wings against my face. I couldn't think straight. The numbing effects of alcohol and drugs could only go so far, and I refused to up the dosage of either because I didn't want to collapse into addiction. I was dropping weight again because I couldn't force myself to eat regularly. My legs were extremely thin and half the time didn't want to support my body.

It was time to get away again. I wanted to scream, curse, and pull my hair because "they" were making me leave yet one more time without my son. The horror of being so routinely helpless metamorphosed again into rage. It threatened to consume me, and I grew increasingly fearful that, one time, in front of them all, I'd lose it, come unglued, and start breaking things or hitting people. For both my good and Alex's, I needed a respite.

Covering Alex with kisses and holding him tightly one last time, I left Palermo on a flight to the States. Thanksgiving was always a good family time in New Brunswick, and my parents would be all over me with consolation. It would be a month-long emotional massage.

At Mom and Dad's, there was a lot of time to think. Not brood, actually, but turn over in my mind incidents and relationships, and try to make some sense of them. I kept coming back to one inescapable conclusion: this whole thing just wasn't working. The treadmill of time continued to run at the same unhurried pace, and the oppression of waiting smothered my soul. "Wait," my lawyer had said. What a joke. Wait for what? More of the scripted farce called "custody hearings" or for Massimo to conjure up more indictment against my motherhood? I wanted to scream. There was no longer a purpose to any of this. All the struggle I'd put into defending myself, the heartache endured and tears wept were irrelevant, at least in relation to measurable success. After two-and-a-half agonizing years, I was no closer to regaining a mother's right (right!) to be with her only son.

Mentally, I replayed my own efforts. So far, I had been extremely careful, done it all by the book—their playbook, that is—jumped through every hoop, bent into every contortionist legal position, backed away and kowtowed to all restraints imposed upon my relationship with Alex. I had taken absolutely no chances with anything. I had stupidly hoped that justice would be served, that I would be handed my son and told to depart in peace. Now, I saw clearly, and I was sick of the whole mess. I had no idea how things would work out, but one thing I knew: I was through being pushed. Only Massimo had profited by my overarching caution. I gave it a good, swift kick and sent it flying out of my life.

Mom, Dad, and I had a family conference. With the outcome of the last hearing, they knew what was coming and surprisingly I didn't have to talk them into anything. They'd already decided what needed to be done. I think they were surprised it took me so long to come to the same conclusion.

139

For the moment, the fear was gone. I was mad clean through. Searching through my purse, I located my little address book and turned the pages till I found "the number." Staring at it a moment, I felt I was about to cross over into something. No . . . I already had.

I picked up the phone and dialed. A moment passed while it rang on the other end. A pleasant woman's voice answered.

"Hello," I said firmly, "Is this Judy Feeney?"

Alex's first birthday party in Palermo after Massimo took him.
I was invited. It was humiliating!

On another birthday, I was allowed to give Alex a court-appointed birthday party at my place. I made a paper-mache lemon piñata filled with candy. The other children had never seen one before.

Above: Second visit to my
apartment at Mondello

A surprise visit by Alex
and Giovanni to the tennis
club where I worked

Making cookies at my place during one of his court-appointed visits

9

A Line In The Sand

Chi non rischia ninente ottiene nulla.
Who risks nothing, gets nothing.

There is a story, probably apocryphal, that on the evening before the massed attack by Mexican general/dictator Santa Anna, the one hundred fifty men at the Alamo gathered in the courtyard of the former mission to hear a short speech by the American lieutenant-colonel William Barrett Travis. The Mexican army was readying for an all-out assault on the former Catholic mission. Five hundred yards from the Alamo, the troops covered the land like locusts. Inside the fort, the men, one with a wife and child, could expect no quarter. Santa Anna's command was final: surrender or be killed. Outnumbered more than ten-to-one, a massacre was inevitable. The hope of reinforcements from the outside world waned with each passing moment. Travis stood before them, eyeing them silently. Then, drawing his sword, he shoved the point into the sandy ground and walked backward. When he stopped, a line of carved earth separated him from the volunteers.

Sweeping his gaze over the men, he said solemnly, "Whoever is willing to stand and fight let him come over to this side of the line." There was little hesitation. Crowds of men hefted their long rifles and strode silently and grim-faced across the line to Travis. The legendary Jim Bowie, sick with fever and unable to rise from the cot they'd brought him out on, said

A happy moment playing together

weakly, "Boys, will some of you carry me across?" Two men standing beside the cot lifted it, and with Bowie, crossed over. In less than a minute, every man stood with Travis, save one. He was dismissed, and disappeared into the night, hoping to make it past Santa Anna's guard posts. The others looked to their weapons, took their positions in the "fort" and waited for morning. They would sell their lives dearly.

The light of a rosy dawn bled slowly into the eastern sky. Santa Anna's bugler sounded the Deguello, eerie in the early morning quiet. The plains shook with sudden cannon fire, and the battle cries of a thousand charging infantry rose in a blood-chilling swell. Travis, in plain sight on the wall, shouted, "Let 'em have it, boys!" and the Alamo's tiny garrison responded with characteristic Texas enthusiasm for a good fight . . .

※

Judy Feeney and I had spoken over the phone for a good half hour. She was very sympathetic, a good listener, and tactful in her responses. At her suggestion, I afterward wrote a detailed letter about the whole mess: my disaster of a marriage, the emotional abuse, the divorce, the simultaneous custody hearings in California and Italy, and finally the kidnapping and the endless Italian legal proceedings. I also sent copies of the California court ruling in my favor and the arrest warrant issued against Massimo for kidnapping. They needed to make sure I was on the level, and this was just part of their own security.

When I had first spoken with her, I'd been angry. But as I thought through every word I put down, the anxiety was beginning to creep back in, peppering me with questions for which I had no immediate answers: Would they take the "case"? What kind of expenses do these "missions" entail? Would my parents help me out financially? What would be my part in all this?

Judy's reply, coming in the beginning of December, was a healing balm, "We will be praying for a favorable outcome in court this March for you and your son. Do not hesitate to give us a call if there is anything that we can do for you."

For the first time in nearly two weeks, I felt I could breathe easily. They would do it. As per our conversation, we both agreed to wait until March, after the next custody hearing in Palermo, before pursuing more drastic measures. Enclosed in Judy's reply package was a book she had promised to send. "This will tell you about our group," she said, and indeed it did. *Rescue My Child* details four CTU commando missions into foreign countries to retrieve children kidnapped by non-custodial parents. Judy wanted me to read the book and let it all soak in. She added a chilling reminder, "When you're done, get rid of it. It's important that it is not to be found on you or among your possessions."

As an added precaution, I tore off the cover before I left for Sicily. The bold print was easy to see from a distance, and even transferring it from hand to purse could be a giveaway. After reading it upon arrival in Mondello, I walked to a dumpster that I knew to be by the piazza, some distance from my apartment. Giving a quick look around to make sure I wasn't being watched, I tossed the book in and unhurriedly walked away. My initiation into this shadow world of covert operations left me with a sense of anxiety, unexpectedly overlaid with excitement. This was like a scene right out of a James Bond film, and I had suddenly become one of the characters.

Still, the book raised scary questions. Overall, it was a great read, mostly because it encouraged me that these kinds of things actually happened, and people like me weren't necessarily doomed to a life away from their children. The downside was that sometimes, things didn't go as planned. Don and Judy had once gone to Iceland to retrieve two children at the behest of a frantic father. Separating to avoid being conspicuous once, they had retaken the children; they were both stopped by the authorities at different locations. Miraculously, Judy, detained at the airport, was eventually permitted to board with her half of the family. Don, however, never made it out of the country. Outmaneuvered by the authorities, he was arrested and spent a year in an Iceland jail. Although he would later tell me that it was a generally good experience—Judy sent him tons of gospel tracts to hand out to the other prisoners—the separation had been very hard on their family. With children of their own, they well knew the personal risks involved.

Returning to Sicily on Christmas Eve, since I refused to be away from Alex over the holiday, I settled in to wait out the next few months. The days crawled by. Nurturing no real hope of justice in the courts, I consequently couldn't keep the phone call out of my mind or the possibilities it raised. Mental images flitted about constantly, portraying one extreme scenario after another. I went from seeing myself with my arms around Alex in our California home to viewing the world from behind a latticework of prison bars. It really could go either way.

In the meantime, I honed sharp the only weapon I had at my disposal—acting. I completely took on the role of the defeated American. For the previous years, I had done this to some extent but allowed room in my character for occasional righteous outbursts, like the candy confrontation with the grandfather. No more. Now, I threw myself into despair mode, appearing downcast when they opened the apartment door for me during visiting hours, and afterward dragging my feet dejectedly on the way out. Backtalk and bristling at insult was a thing of the past. I had to make the family see what I wanted them to see.

And, you know, it worked. Little by little, I could feel the death grasp on Alex and me loosening. Even Massimo seemed to be coming round to the idea that I was beaten, no longer a viable threat, and though the humiliating routine of visits continued, the old watchfulness and narrow-eyed suspicion that had hallmarked the family was on the wane. Inside, I warmed with satisfaction. It was energizing to know that I wasn't so helpless after all, nor was the family so all-knowing that they could see through my ruse. I had found the chink in their armor.

The March court date eventually swung around, and I went through the motions. The same day of that courtroom farce (it's pointless to even state the outcome), I phoned my parents. In New Brunswick, Mom answered. "Tell Judy let's go ahead," I grimly told her, "Enough is enough."

For three years, I had lived at my own Alamo, assuming the fetal position behind crumbling emotional walls and weathering the ceaseless potshots of the opposing "army"—the useless court system, the assassins of my character, and of course, my ex-husband as commander-in-chief—and I hated them all. I had meekly taken all I was going to.

Something happens deep inside when a person is pushed too far. He, or in my case, she takes abuse after abuse, hoping it will stop on its own, that right will win out, and she'll be vindicated and left in peace. But the provocation continues, like the steady drip of water or the finger poked repeatedly in the chest; until one day, when nobody notices, something inside snaps. If she has any reserve of courage, she finds herself looking down at her own line in the sand and defiantly steps across into a new way of life. I was once told that a man with nothing to lose is the most dangerous man in the world. Double that for moms deprived of their babies. My days of being pushed were over.

My parents arranged a meeting with the Feeneys and without telling me, picked up the tab. The couple drove from their home/headquarters in Fayetteville, North Carolina and booked a room at a hotel near my parents' home. The first meeting held in the motel restaurant was like a reunion of old friends. An immediate bond formed. For hours they discussed my situation. Don was especially taken with my dad's rock solid determination to get over there and get the job done. Dad was as gung-ho in his attitude as any commando. "Get my grandson back," he said with finality, "no matter what it takes."

They all met again the next day at my parents' home to discuss options and probably for Dad to make the initial payment. One thing I was to learn was that "operations" of this nature are of necessity very spendy undertakings. Extensive planning aside, there were hand-picked operatives to be called in, flights needed to be booked, contacts notified, extra "help" hired on, etc. Meals, hotels, car and boat rentals—everything costs money, lots of it. On top of that, there was the time element. A group just didn't go in the first day, make the snatch, then take the next convenient flight home. The operation could last months, with the crew engaged in constant surveillance of the target and maintaining a high level of readiness. Plus, there was always the danger. As *Rescue My Child* made plain, any number of things could go wrong.

Long before any of the crew arrived in Mondello, Judy and I arranged to keep in touch by phone. I never used my home phone, fearing it might be bugged. Massimo was just paranoid enough to have implemented that without my knowledge. He was well-connected in Sicily and could easily find the right man for the job. So I usually called Judy from a pay phone near the Mondello piazza after my visits with Alex, using a phone card that would bill it to my parents' home. By that hour of the evening, the crowds would be thinned considerably, but I was always careful to survey my surroundings and take note of anything unusual. If any suspicion were aroused, I knew when to terminate the conversation and immediately leave the area. Our long-distance exchanges involved regular updates about Alex and me, encouragement from her, and sometimes glimpses into the everyday workings of their commando society. A bit nervous about our upcoming meeting in Mondello, I asked Judy how I'd recognize her.

"Don't worry about it," she said, almost casually. "We'll know you. And sometimes, before we meet face-to-face, we'll put a tail on you."

This sent little shivers up my spine, "What?"

"Sometimes we have to," she explained, "to make sure you're not being followed by one of your ex-husband's buddies or whoever. The last thing we want is for them to associate us with you. Besides, you'd never know we were there. You could be sitting on a bus, and we could be right next to you. We'd follow you first to see if anyone else was tailing you."

Incredible. With every answer, I was more certain I was doing the right thing. But in my quieter moments, especially at home at the end of the evening, I was engaged in my own private battle. There was "the voice," that distant, nagging little panderer of doubt that whispered the inevitable questions: *What am I getting into? What if I get caught? What happens when . . . ?* It took a determined effort on my part to shove those apprehensions as far back in my mind as I could and refuse to allow myself the luxury of dwelling on the flip side of this deal. The very real possibility loomed that if we all failed, I might never see Alex again. At the very least, I could be deported and banned from the country.

Without my presence, Alex would fall prey to Massimo's disin-formation campaign, and this time, he'd have the legal papers to prove it. With a prison record, however short, it would be a simple matter for grown-ups to persuade a nine-year-old that his mother really is the person they portrayed these past years. *Shut up*, I'd think forcefully. *I'm not going there.*

Most of the time it worked, and I devoted myself to the immediate. The rather unexpected result was that a confidence overtook my apprehensions and trampled them good. I began to believe it would work. No matter what happened, I was sure Alex and I would be on our way home in no time.

My mother and I kept in touch, and she informed me of her decision to have the brain tumor removed before we got Alex back to the States. She wanted to be well on the road to recuperation when her grandson walked in the door. She always spoke as if the rescue was already a done deal, and her attitude buoyed my morale even more. I'd need all I could get in the coming month.

A big problem that would certainly arise if I didn't initiate countermeasures was the issue of my ongoing relationships in Mondello and Palermo, specifically my expat friends I routinely hung out with, and, of course, Fabio. It turned out he was the easier of the two to deal with. Inviting him over for a private conversation, I sat him down and told him as much as I dared. I really had no choice. By then we had grown quite fond of each other, although not progressing to the use of the "L" word. He naturally wanted to spend lots of time with me, and while the operation was in progress, that would be impossible. As an ex-cop, one of the elite Carabinieri, his crime antennae would be up in a heartbeat if I distanced myself from him without explanation.

Our conversation was short and to the point. Sitting him down on the couch, I took a breath and said, "Fabio, I have to ask you not to come over for a while. I've got some friends who've come from the States, and I'm going to be spending a lot of time with them. It's not about you. It's that . . . well . . . I have something planned . . . and you just can't be around . . ."

Fabio put up his hand, "Don't tell me anything. I don't want to know."

I really didn't know what else to say, except a weak, "Thank you."

Getting up to leave, he smiled. "Be careful," he said, kissing me on the cheek. "And if you need me for anything, get in touch with my mother."

After he left, I stood staring at the closed door, thinking, *He knows.*

I didn't have time to dwell on it. Anyway, Fabio wouldn't have offered any assistance if he'd intended to stop the process; he didn't even warn me about, well, breaking the law he'd sworn to uphold. Though maybe not an accomplice, actually, he was proving himself an ally.

With Fabio agreeing to stay away, I implemented "phase two" of my dropping off-grid strategy. With my group of expat friends, I brought to bear the acting skills I had gradually perfected over the last three years and especially over the last couple of weeks with Massimo's family. What they saw in me was a disturbing slide in the direction of a full surrender to the powers that be. "I'm really tired of all the fighting," I whimpered. "I don't think I can keep going. Maybe I'll never get Alex back . . ."

Whoa. This proclamation knocked them for a loop. This sounded so unlike the spitfire they'd grown to know these past few years endued with all manner of motherly concern. They buzzed about me with hugs and encouragement.

"Oh, Katie! Don't give up now. You've put so much into this fight."

"Don't hand a victory to Massimo! This is just what he's been waiting for."

"Oooooo, I'd like to punch him!"

"Three years, Katie—three years! Think of it. You don't want to throw it all away . . ."

I waved them all off, told them I needed some space, and that they wouldn't be seeing much of me in the coming weeks. I hated to deceive them, but if I didn't cut the ties, I knew that sooner or later one of them, no doubt with good intentions, would get in the way at the wrong moment. There was also the issue of their safety. If any had been privy to my plans, they would be viewed by the law as accessories, which in Italy could mean a long prison sentence. I even played it up big in my lawyer's office and made sure she communicated my "depression" to Massimo and family.

On the other hand, the whole thing was a balancing act and called for delicate maneuvering. If I'd overdone it, I could have been perceived by my friends as possibly suicidal, and they were just dedicated enough to post a guard at my door or even have someone live with me to prevent me from "harming myself." The idea was to drop off contact one quick step at a time, instead of all at once. Later, when I met any of them on the street, I'd offer one excuse after another why I couldn't meet for dinner or other outings like, "Oh, I have some new students right now" or "It's been a long day and I'm kind of tired. Can we make it some other time?" These were not satisfactory, of course, but they did the trick.

Only once did I come close to having my cover blown. About to step out for a clandestine meeting after "the crew" from the States arrived, I heard a car pull up and then the quick approach of footsteps on the stone patio outside. Taking my hand off the doorknob I silently fled to the bedroom area. An insistent knock on the door prompted me to cower behind the heavy wooden shutters. A voice called to my upstairs neighbor.

"Is Katie around?"

It was Sarah, and I could hear the worry. "No," my neighbor replied, "I haven't seen her for some time now."

The interior of every Italian villa or apartment has shutters made out of wood or other heavy material. These keep out the heat during the summer, keep it in during the winter, and shut out the sun so when you close them the room is cave dark. It also keeps out intruders and locks from the inside. Anymore, all my windows were routinely shuttered as part of the plan, so there was no real danger Sarah would spot me, but I still tried to make myself as small as possible against the wall. After what seemed like an eternity of chatting, Sarah said goodbye, and I listened to her footsteps trailing off. A car door shut, the engine revved, and she was gone. I waited long enough for my neighbor to go back inside before I opened the door and slipped through the courtyard and into the street. Even then, I had to scan the area to make certain Sarah was gone and I wasn't noticed.

Even before the Feeneys arrived, I was getting a feel for this cloak-and-dagger stuff. It was strangely exhilarating in that for the first time in years, I was taking the lead in something. I was exercising control—however limited in scope—over my formerly impossible situation, and (ha!) Massimo didn't have a thing to say about it. Not only that, but he didn't even know. The all-powerful, all-seeing Massimo, with his manifold connections and cabal of spy buddies, was completely in the dark.

My last long-distance phone conversation with Judy set my heart to pounding. "It's all lined up," she said, "and we'll be there in a couple of days. Where would you like to meet?"

I gave her directions to a nice seafood restaurant overlooking the water, and she cheerfully said, "We'll see you there!"

As I walked back to my apartment, my mind was in a whirl. This was it.

Fabio dressed up as Santa one Christmas and daringly showed up at the grandparents' apartment.

Notice USA map in my apartment. I just had to take a photo of Alex under this.

10

The Infiltration Begins

Giudicari e 'nniminari, Diu sulu lu pò fari.
Only God can judge and foretell.

I don't know what I expected. I suppose in my mind they were a group of burly men in military fatigues, steely-eyed and speaking in clipped sentences, their clothes bulging with hidden weapons. When addressing me, they'd say "ma'am" a lot, like "Just leave this in our hands, ma'am" or "Try not to get in our way, ma'am." Without exception, they'd sport buzz cuts under their boonie hats, and every clean-shaven jaw would be square as a block of chiseled granite. Altogether, they'd be fascinating . . . in a scary kind of way.

For weeks, I had anticipated this day. It's difficult to explain, but the upcoming "operation" took on the characteristics of the surreal, and at times, I questioned whether it was all a dream. *Who are these people anyway? I don't even know them. Are they soldiers of fortune or what? How do they go about something like this?*

I'd heard stories of commando raids and seen the old WWII movies where elite strike forces were sent behind enemy lines to rescue American officers from the Nazi command. The films always had happy endings, with the last scene showing the merry band (minus the inevitable few lost to enemy fire) geared up and heading into their next mission. But this was no movie set, and nobody bothered to write the final scene.

I had spoken with Judy over the phone about a half hour earlier. Although in the past she had traveled to Palermo, Mondello was an unfamiliar territory. At her suggestion, I waited near the phone booth from which we'd had so many conversations over the last two weeks. The team would zero in on the beacon of my blonde hair, and we'd go into the restaurant together.

At nine o'clock in the evening, the street traffic had eased considerably. Few people walked by, mostly strollers out for the evening air. Although no one paid me any attention, I felt guilty standing out in the open and fervently hoped no police would come by and give me the once-over. In that event, I'd have to start walking and that would translate into another night of waiting. We were so close now; an anticlimax to the evening would stretch my nerves to the breaking point.

At last, a pair of headlights burned in the distance and a car slowly approached, pulling up alongside me. The woman driver beamed a relaxed smile and said through the open window, "Katie?"

"Judy?"

In response, a pretty, petite blonde stepped out of the car, enclosed me in a mother hug and began dissolving the tension with the easy sort of chatter characteristic of old friends. "How are you?" she asked. "We have so looked forward to meeting you. Your parents send their love."

A big guy in the passenger's seat leaned out of the shadows so I could see the warm smile on his face.

I was instantly won over. Finally, finally they had come, these mysterious, wonderful strangers who were going to cradle Alex's life and mine in their capable hands. I slid into the back seat, and we drove the short distance to the restaurant meeting place.

Judy was anything but what I'd expected. I thought maybe she'd look like a bouncer, big-boned and brawly, with a hard, raspy voice and sardonic wit. What I got instead was everybody's mom, all smiles and feminine softness. As I was to shortly discover though, this beguiling appearance was only the half of it.

Underneath, she was as tough as any of her "colleagues." Theirs was a dangerous business, and although spurred to these rescues by caring hearts, the prep work necessitated rigorous physical and emotional training. She was skilled in hand-to-hand combat, surveillance, evasive driving, and all kinds of counter-espionage techniques. Plus, she was no stranger to on-the-job injury. During one rappelling session, she fell a considerable distance to the ground and broke her back. Even that didn't keep her out of the game too long.

Judy introduced me to Temi, a native New Yorker of Spanish ancestry who made his home in North Carolina. Swarthy, moustached, and topped with a thicket of jet-black hair, he would blend in nicely with the Sicilian population. As for qualifications, he looked the part. Broad-shouldered and barrel-chested, this ex-U.S. Special Forces sergeant would make a nice addition to any mercenary group. I was just glad he was on our side!

The three of us were escorted to a corner table where we were able to talk quietly but freely. We ordered our food, and as we ate, we made sure to smile a lot and assume a casual air. There had to be no appearance of conspiracy or furtiveness; although, those descriptions accurately characterized a good many people in the "darker" quarters of Sicilian society. This section of Italy was renowned for its backroom deals and insidious "business arrangements" sealed with an under-the-table handshake. We couldn't afford to be viewed that way.

Don Feeney and the rest of the crew would not be arriving for another two weeks. I was to learn that Judy was generally the "point man," sent in ahead to scope out the terrain and basically establish a presence. As a woman, it was easier for her to get into a country and move around without attracting attention, and in her "dumb American tourist" role, she easily won friends and assistance from the locals. Her job consisted of micromanaging a multitude of tasks: spending time getting to know the area, familiarizing herself with a variety of car and pedestrian routes, investigating possible exit strategies, and daily pumping me for

Temi

information which, when gone over in minute detail, would help formulate a plan of escape. By the time her husband Don came into the picture, she'd have a lot accomplished. With a plan worked up, the group would spend time in the fine-tuning process. First and foremost, she was there early to initiate female-to-female bonding and build up the trust so necessary for an operation of this nature. She also functioned as a kind of mental health assessor, evaluating my emotional state and ensuring that I would be able to function under massive stress.

She knew immediately that I was at the breaking point. The three-year strain of separation from Alex had done its dark work. Dangerously thin from not eating, my stomach routinely churned with nausea, and my eyes often burned from lost sleep. I was rushing toward my endurance limit at breakneck speed. I really, really couldn't take a lot more of this. One more good push from the courts or Massimo and my next address might well be the psych ward at the Palermo hospital. This mental state was a double-edged sword. If I was not able to manage the additional stress of a difficult rescue, the situation would unravel and place everyone involved in danger of imprisonment or physical injury. The other side, though, was that with nowhere else to go for help, I felt I was ready to do anything to get Alex back. I discovered that one of the essential ingredients to a successful rescue was the willingness—indeed, the fervent desire—of the wounded parent to place herself (and sometimes himself) completely into the hands of Feeney and Co.

Judy had to be absolutely certain that I would follow their instructions to the letter. There could be no hesitation or the entire mission would be in jeopardy. I suppose I was easy because by the time Judy and Temi arrived, the groundwork of relationships had already been laid. My parents, CTU, and I had formed into one inseparable unit. When I sat with Judy and Temi for the first time, it was as if I said, "Okay, here I am. Here's my problem—fix me!" That was exactly what Judy had been hoping for.

Ironically, my alcohol/tranquilizer "diet" worked in our favor. For a rescue to be effective, the mother, who was by then an emotional train wreck, had to be controlled, and Judy was the compassionate controller. It was critical that I hang on their every word and move with them in unison. In this respect, the drugs kept my fear factor in check without impairing my ability to function normally.

Pleasant as she was, Judy got right down to business. "Okay, we need to map out several things: Alex's daily routine, how far he lives from your place, and who is usually at the apartment. We also need to discuss the options for transporting you and him out of the country. We can rent either a small plane or boat. There are plusses and minuses to each method . . ."

And on it went. The toughest aspect of the mission would be getting access to Alex. He was literally guarded 24/7, and any snatch that occurred might happen on the spur of the moment, as opportunity presented itself. My part in the charade would take many forms. I was to continue to downplay my by-now heightened sense of hope and portray the defeated mother. Because I would not have any spare time, my English students would be informed of a sudden termination of my services. This didn't prove too difficult since with the onset of warm weather, many would be vacation bound anyway. Plus, I was to act as navigator, driving around with them in their rental car and familiarizing them with both the area and Sicilian customs so they could become appropriately assimilated.

Temi listened attentively while Judy did most of the talking. As the lady boss, it was her job to set things up properly and communicate those plans to me. And it was his job to follow orders and if necessary, wing it in the event of separation. Big, strong, and quiet, he was the kind that won my trust just by being there.

This initial meeting would be the last time we'd be seen together in public, at least in any town where I'd be recognized. Also, from then on, when with them I was to don my "Malta disguise" of large hat, sunglasses, and with my hair tied back or tucked underneath the brim. Judy would also dye her blonde hair a nice shade of brown. When out with the crew, I was a "tourist" traveling with other "tourists." If seen by anyone who knew me personally, I was to say that Judy and Temi were friends of my mom's from the States who I just happened to run into.

The discussion was a bit overwhelming and sent my adrenaline level into the red zone. My heart thumped, both from excitement and fear. I was overjoyed to be sure, but the whole idea of this "operation" still took some getting used to. Judy did her best to put me at ease and for the most part succeeded. Yet, I kept thinking to myself, *I can't believe these people risk their lives to do this*; I determined afresh to be an asset when the time came.

From the restaurant, we all went to the nearby hotel where Judy and Temi had booked separate rooms. Judy asked if I needed money to purchase the things Alex needed for the trip home.

As much of my time had been taken up with the pre-meeting arrangements and keeping my own outward emotions in neutral, I hadn't been working steadily. Opening her purse, she pulled out a sheaf of about five hundred dollars and handed it to me. It was a pittance compared to the oversized wad of bills it had come from. The bankroll literally filled her purse. I found out later that mom and dad had nearly cleaned out their savings and borrowed on their home in order to finance the undertaking.

Before we parted for the evening, Judy encouraged me. "Tomorrow," she said with a smile, "we kick it into gear. Alex, here we come!"

We met some distance from my apartment at a prearranged time. Showing up in a rental car, Judy and Temi pulled up alongside and scarcely stopped long enough for me to jump into the back seat. "Remember," Judy warned, "keep low."

They pulled out into the lane, and we were on our way to Palermo. Within fifteen minutes, we were in the Palermo traffic stream.

I can heartily recommend for any aspiring mercenaries the Palermo traffic as a quick means to sharpen survival skills and as a sounding board for their strength of character. Not only is the average Sicilian driver an expert with vehicular weaponry, he is also a master interrogator, proficient in striking terror into the fainthearted. Forget the hot lights in the face and the beatings with a rubber hose—the methods Sicilians use to break their enemies are the steering wheel, the horn, and the blood-curdling screams out the driver's side window. A soldier of fortune wannabe should be put mercilessly through this wringer as part of the application process. If he makes it through one day of it without taking on the glassy-eyed stare of the severely traumatized, he could, with confidence, be sent to the front lines of any war on the planet. As a veteran, Judy scored amazingly high on this stress test. While I can't say that I actually heard her, I can well imagine her muttering some carefully chosen words. "Maniac!" or "Jerk!" comes to mind, and perhaps punctuated by her deliberate, sharp swerve at the opposition. I could have once heard her rasp quietly, "Take that," but it might have been just wishful thinking on my part. Still, she was skilled enough to come within inches of an aggressive Sicilian driver and put a little, long-overdue fear into him.

From my backseat supine position, I directed her to various strategic places in Palermo: Alex's home with his grandparents and the Catholic school he attended, to name just two. Then, and in the weeks following, we talked over and over about Alex's routine at home, school, church, and whatever . . . all I knew. Like everyone, a pattern marked his life, and the whole crew would have to learn this particular one by heart to be ready for an opportunity to take him back. Judy and Temi also asked about Alex's likes, dislikes, favorite haunts with friends, what kinds of foods he preferred, and all the seemingly inconsequential things that make up a person's way of life. As nearly as possible, they had to know him as I did and picked my brain for details. They asked highly specific questions about Giovanni's apartment as well: How many entrances/exits to the building? Does it have a doorman? What about a lobby? On which floor does Alex live? Can it be reached by stairs, elevator, or both? Are they located to the left or right as you enter the building? Do the doors, both to the building itself and Giovanni's apartment in particular, open in or out? What is the layout of the apartment? How many rooms are there and where are they located? Overall, the information provided a detailed analysis, and by putting it all together, they might find that proverbial chink in the armor, the one thing overlooked by those who comprised Alex's "security cordon."

I also learned a lot that day: what it's like to lie face down on the back seat, how to position the spine to minimize the pain of extended contortion, and that (surprise!) the thirty-something body doesn't have nearly the flex it did ten years prior. Although I sometimes managed to sit upright without attracting undue attention, I generally maintained a fairly close relationship with the lower half of the vehicle. Periodically, I'd raise my head till it got eye level with the passenger window's bottom edge, just enough so I could see to direct them and just as often I'd duck when I thought I might be endangering the mission. Sometimes, particularly in congested areas where the possibility of being spotted was greater, I hid out on the floor of the vehicle. My knees or elbows would find small stones or other irritating memorabilia left by the previous occupants. All told, some of the glamour was already beginning to wear off this undercover stuff. By the end of the day, I was exhausted. It could have been worse, I guess. They could have put me in the trunk.

The second night after Judy and Temi's arrival, we met and drove to a rather isolated restaurant some distance from Mondello. After discussing the next day's plans, the pair dropped me off a couple of blocks from my street and disappeared into the night. There was a lot to think about on the short walk home, with my footsteps the only company. As always, I had my finger on the button of my trusty can of pepper spray; but my mind was running rampant, and I spaced out all possible danger within the shadows. When I got to my apartment, I went inside, closed the door, sat on the sofa, and had a complete meltdown.

It was bound to happen. The human spirit can only take so much pressure before it breaks. In my case, the stress—both inside and out—suddenly made shambles of my planned rescue. My mind was whirling with questions and fears; and if I didn't get immediate answers, it would all be over right then and there. Snatching up the phone, I broke the rules and called Judy at her hotel room. When she picked up on the other end, my dread poured out in a flood.

"Judy," I sobbed, "I just don't know about this. What happens if something goes wrong? Suppose Alex rejects me. What if he doesn't want to go back to the States . . . ?"

Judy's voice was firm but encouraging. "Okay, now. Take it easy. I'll be right there. Hang on."

I boomeranged back outside and in fifteen minutes, Judy pulled up at our predetermined spot. She took charge, and I let her. "Let's go somewhere we can talk," she said.

We ended up at a restaurant a little outside the city. It was eight o'clock, the Sicilian dinner hour, so the place was pretty lively. So much the better, to cover both our conversation and the upset that was all over me. Despite my lack of appetite, Judy prodded me to order, and as we sat there picking at our meal, I opened up.

"Look," I said desperately, "I'm not sure I can go through with this. I have so many questions, and to be real honest, I'm scared."

She nodded in sympathy. "Katie, this isn't unusual. Everybody gets last minute jitters. Even me. And the mothers, oh boy, you should see them. You're not the only one this has ever happened to. You wouldn't be normal if it didn't."

I regarded her through my tears. "What do you think our chances are? Really, I mean. You told me yourself that sometimes things go wrong . . ."

Her eyes never wavered, and her voice was gentle, yet confident. "That's true. There are no guarantees. We've had our share of failures. But . . ." she leaned closer and the mother in her reached over to touch my hand, "we've gotten a lot of kids back, too. Katie, we still keep in touch with some of them—the mothers and the children we helped rescue; and I'll tell you, they're happy. You can't measure that kind of success."

"But that's them. There's always a chance that it won't work out for me . . ."

Judy's smile was a beam of sunlight. "Look, we have a great chance of getting you and Alex out of here. From everything you've told me, he loves you very much. And yeah, it might be rough for a while, but I believe it will work out. Katie, we can do this. You have to believe that."

Actually, I did. It was one of those intense situations in which hope needs to be vocalized, maybe several times, in order to allay the creeping fears that threaten to paralyze you. That night was my first and last breakdown. I had to be one hundred percent; a divided focus would spell the end of a three-year-long dream of being free of Massimo, Sicily, and laws that strangled my relationship with my own son.

Judy and Temi changed hotels often for security purposes. The three of us continued to meet on a daily basis, never at the same place twice, and often somewhere out of town or along the coast road. Our lives consisted of coffee, meals, discussion, planning, and a lot of driving around. And the questions, oh, I'd never been under such interrogation in my life! There were always just a few more. The little things about Alex's life and mine took on new meaning. When I thought I'd answered it all, even more surfaced. I found myself remembering and relaying all sorts of minutiae, things I'd never noted before. Nothing was unimportant. All my interactions with Alex, our conversations, the movements of Massimo and his family—it all worked together to form a panoramic of my life there. In military terms, I was involved in "intelligence." I had become the team's eyes and ears, a human portal into a very private arena. What a kick. In yet another ironic turnabout, this time it was Massimo who was under surveillance. He (indeed, his entire family) was being closely monitored, and he hadn't the slightest clue. From time to time, a satisfying feeling of justice swept over me, and the thoughts would come of their own accord—*How's it feel, Massimo? What goes around comes around.* Of course at that time, he didn't know what I was up to, but soon enough he would. He would.

About the middle of April, Judy's other half arrived in Malta with another two men, to secure a thirty-five foot sailboat from a local rental. Judy hopped a plane to Malta, the plan being to sail with the men from there to Palermo where the boat could be moored at a busy dock right next to a hotel where rooms had already been reserved for them. She and Temi had already made their "tourist" presence known on the Malta docks prior to meeting me, and she felt that since the locals already knew her, no questions would be raised when she pushed off with Don and a couple of friends—the captain and navigator who had been on several of these sorties with CTU for a stint of "fishing and sightseeing." The first glitch came with the weather. Rough seas kept the team moored at the Malta docks, and Judy, anxious to keep close to me, caught a plane back to Palermo to wait for them there. The three men managed a crossing of the Mediterranean but got only as far as Licata on the south side of the island. Several times they tried to sail north to Palermo but were repeatedly thrown back by violent storms. The boat was tossed like a cork in a bathtub, with the men in actual peril of their lives. After a heated argument in which Don and the boat's pilot, Randy McCall, nearly came to blows (Don wanting to try again with Randy considering the move suicide), they moored at Licata to wait further instructions. Don was ready to join us; Judy would meet him and the others in Licata, discuss rescue plans, and reorganize (since the boat was nowhere near its preplanned mooring at Palermo). Then Don and Judy would rent a car and drive back to Mondello.

Though Temi would stay behind and keep close tabs on the situation, the mother-to-mother relationship that had quickly built between Judy and me made me reluctant to see her go. She was the rock that I desperately clung to, and I'd sorely miss the female empathy and understanding she brought to the operation. For the anonymity it afforded, Judy chose to take the bus to Licata. Located in a far section of Palermo that I seldom visited and in which I knew no one, we were comfortable being seen together for a few minutes. That date, April 20, 1995, is seared in my memory. While showing her the stop where she could board, we passed a newsstand and the headlines of an English-language newspaper screamed out at us.

"Judy, look!"

I snatched the paper from its shelf and held it out for her to see. Across the front page, the startling image of a shattered office tower, spewing a column of ugly black smoke, rooted us to the spot. Streets clogged with crowds of onlookers, police cars and fire engines made a churn of our stomachs. Judy murmured, "I can't believe it," and for a moment we read about the previous day's bombing of the Alfred P. Murrah federal building in downtown Oklahoma City, USA.

Judy's bus pulled up, huffing exhaust, and she needed to board. I handed her the paper. "You can read it on the way. I'll buy another one for me."

Judy forced a smile. "See you in a couple of days," she said, then with the paper under her arm stepped into the vehicle and was gone. I stood there for a long moment feeling very lonely, fearing for Judy, myself, and now, my country.

The week Judy was gone passed quickly enough. My "body-guard" Temi, was left with nothing particular to do but look after me, keep his eyes and ears open, and wait till the rest of the group returned. So, we did what anyone in our situation would have done—we went tourist.

With Temi driving, we hit all the major tourist destinations in and around that part of Sicily. We had a great time and got to know each other more on a personal basis. One of the most popular tourist destinations is the site of the ancient city of Segesta. Built by some of the original inhabitants of Sicily several hundred years before the birth of Christ, the ruins still hold fascinating examples of Greek architecture, including an immense temple and amphitheater. It was a long hike from the parking lot, but the views from the top were stunning. Shimmering with the late afternoon heat, the hills marched off into the distance, eventually lost in the afternoon haze. A patchwork of farmland filled the valleys, and overall the very air seemed charged with antiquity, as if the distant past was really only a breath away. Temi and I spent most of a wonderful day there, talking about everything under the sun—our lives, personal likes, and the places we'd traveled. On the whole, it was good to just get away from all the planning and secrecy for even this little while and just be ourselves.

Well, almost.

When other tourists would happen by—this wasn't often as we were there on a weekday and the season was early yet—they'd stop and snap a photo or two. A few times, Temi just happened to be in the background, and in those instances, I noticed immediately that just before the shutter clicked, he'd turn his head completely away, as if looking behind him at something that just captured his attention. The end result was that the only part of him ever caught on film was his back.

A few times of this was all I could stand before querying him about it. After one group of tourists left, leaving us to the quiet of the wind moving through the crumbling columns of the Greek temple, I asked him point blank.

A wry smile creased his handsome face. "You kidding?" he asked. "I'm not leaving any photographic record of my presence here."

It was a neat day, but it left me with a lot to ponder. *Wow,* I thought, *these guys never let their guard down.* In the end, they were always planning, calculating, considering options, and . . . surviving. It struck me that, in the three years I'd lived here, I'd already become so very much like them.

Judy returned on time, accompanied by a thin, lithe, dark-haired guy with a small mustache and an animated disposition. I met Don at one of our many meeting places, a favorite tourist restaurant where the group of us could sit unnoticed amid the cacophony of international voices. Fortunately, Don would blend right in with the locals. The Italian part of his ancestry would work in our favor, we all joked, as long as he kept his mouth shut and prevented his Brooklyn accent from making its Sicilian debut. His conversational Italian skill was somewhere around zero on the proficiency scale.

He, too, was not what I'd anticipated, especially as the other CEO of this commando business. Gentle, friendly, and warm, he was the kind you'd tell your problems to and fully expect him to have the solution. He liked to joke when it was appropriate, but could turn on a dime and be all business if the moment demanded it. From our initial meeting, I realized that if you were a man, he'd be the guy you'd be glad to have as your best friend and would fear to have as your enemy. He also earned immediate points with me because he spoke with great respect of my father. The two had hit it off, and Dad's confidence in him not only humbled Don but prompted in him a strong determination to hasten this particular mission into a quick and favorable conclusion.

Don's cover was perfect. He wore his façade of CEO of the Shepherd Travel Agency like a well-tailored suit and came armed with a batch of business cards bearing the title, insignia, and phone number of the "U.S. branch." Anyone calling the number would be connected to a recorded message that said:

"You have reached the Shepherd Travel Agency. I'm sorry I'm out of the office right now, but if you leave your name and number, I'll be sure to get back to you as soon as I can. Thank you."

The "office" was simply a separate phone line, set up at the Feeney's CTU headquarters in Fayetteville, North Carolina.

Shortly after his arrival in Mondello, Don was actually called to prove his cover. One evening at about dinner time we wound up in a small coastal town about an hour's drive from Mondello. We'd spent the day reconnoitering, planning, checking out escape routes, what-have-you, and we were coming down from the adrenaline high we'd been riding all day long. Pulling into the parking lot of a seaside restaurant, we piled out of the vehicle and stretched the kinks out of bodies that had been strapped into a little European car way too long. The air was rich with the scent of cooking food. For a moment we savored the breeze, cool now with the sun's dying, then strolled unhurriedly to the entrance and went inside.

Being a weekday, we found the place only half-full, so we located an open table, sat down, and ordered. By then, I was picking up some of the crew's survival savvy and doing some things almost without thinking. When dining, for instance, we chose a table far enough out of the way to avoid being conspicuous, yet with a clear view to every entrance and exit—including the doors leading from the dining area into the kitchen. The team, myself included, made certain we knew who was coming and going at all times. This place, so far from my own stomping grounds of

171

Palermo/Mondello, was probably safe; but with this operation already underway, we weren't into taking unnecessary chances.

While waiting for our food, we passed the time in unimportant conversation, just chit-chat, when I noticed a man approaching. Zeroing in on our table, he stood there, smiling. An older gentleman in casual attire, he appeared very unthreatening. "You are American?"

Don looked up at him cheerily. "Yes, we are. How did you know?"

The man beamed and kicked into Sicilian overdrive. As he spoke, his hands flailed the air. "Ah, I knew it! Forgive me, but I overheard. I am Pino Vitale. I own this place. I'm sorry—I just had to talk to you. Do you mind?"

He extended his hand to Don, who stood to take it in his own. "And I love America," Pino added with enthusiasm.

Don beamed all friendliness. I watched in amazement as a transformation took place. This ex-Delta, war-hardened commando took on the demeanor of a young entrepreneur skilled in mixing business with pleasure. "Don Michaels," he said, with practiced efficiency, "Shepherd Travel Agency."

He waved his hand toward the rest of us. "We're touring Sicily, getting some ideas for travel promotions, that kind of thing."

Pino was elated. "Oh, ask me! I can tell you the best places. Please, please sit down."

The two exchanged rapid-fire conversation for several more minutes. Pino was a native Sicilian but had spent some years in the States, where he had run an Italian food restaurant. Homesickness eventually overcame him, and he returned to be close to family and the friends of his childhood. Some second-generation family members remained in the U.S., however, and there was lately talk among them of visiting Sicily, some of them for the first time. Don offered him a "business card" which Pino took with relish, uttering a vague promise to utilize Don's services when the time came. When our first course came to the table, he excused himself, and we settled down to eat.

As Pino made for the kitchen doors, I found myself nervously wondering if he would remember us if the cops ever came around . . . afterward. No one else at the table seemed too concerned. They were all busy eating and joking. I dug in, too, but this was yet another incident to ponder. All of the team seemed to have an almost supernatural feeling of who to trust and who to be wary of. It was uncanny. Long exposed to the kind of danger most see only in movies, these people had their senses honed to a razor edge and were always—often without being aware of it—filtering information and cataloguing it regarding people, surroundings, conversations, etc. This interworking of the senses produced the legendary "gut instinct" of soldiers, long-time cops, and CIA operatives. They couldn't tell you why, exactly, but when the silent alarms rang, they listened, and acted accordingly with fight or flight. I quickly made it a habit to fasten my eyes on them, do what they did, and relax when they deemed it appropriate.

Don and Judy in a more relaxed setting in the U.S.

173

Truthfully, I was doing good to take it one day at a time, make it through, and congratulate myself that I didn't go to pieces even in the planning stages because even some of the scenarios we routinely discussed made the hairs on the back of my neck stand straight up. One time it was suggested that if all else failed, the team might consider just going into Giovanni's apartment directly. Hey, they were military, right? They reasoned that if nothing else worked they'd just storm the Bastille. The thought of this terrified me. So many things could go wrong, and I didn't want to consider it. They could discuss all this with a nonchalant air, but I wasn't as courageous as the rest of them. Sure, I wanted Alex out, but I hoped for it to be a squeaky-clean operation. The whole time we were in Sicily together, I kept thinking, *How brave are these people? They've got nerves of steel! How can they do this time and time again?*

Sometimes, I nearly hyperventilated just listening to them. If they noticed, they were kind enough to keep it to themselves.

We spent a few days going over more plans and hoping for a crack at Alex soon. Don and Judy both were pretty sure if they could get access to him, they'd be able to spirit both of us out of the country. The first opportunity came quite unexpectedly.

While sitting in our rental car across the street and up a ways from Giovanni's apartment, we watched as Massimo's vehicle drove into view and screeched to a halt at the curb near the entrance. Massimo disappeared into the building and emerged a few minutes later with Alex in tow. They got into the car and as it pulled away, we followed from a discreet distance till Massimo parked outside a Catholic church about five blocks down the street. Alex exited the vehicle, waved to his dad and went inside for his regular catechism class.

While driving, Judy described the route and destination to me. My head was down low the whole time, my body scrunched on the floor and forcing poor Temi as far over on the seat as his big frame would allow. "Pull up over there," Don said suddenly. "I want to check it out."

My heart skipped a beat as he opened the door and casually exited the vehicle. I knew this church; the building was circular, with not many exits. If spotted and questioned by the priest or attendants, he might not be able to leave quickly enough to keep his anonymity intact. Don entered the building, and, as he later told us, hugged one of the marble pillars in the back, nearest the entrance. We didn't see him for some time, and the tension increased with each slowly passing minute. Judy spotted Massimo's father strolling up the street, and he reached the church entrance just as the classes ended and the children were dismissed en masse. Alex filed out with the rest, greeted his Nonno, and the two turned for the short walk home together. Don had by then slipped out of the church and came sprinting back to the car. Being on the floor, I could only hear the quick approach of his feet and then looked up to see him standing by the driver's side, clearly adrenaline-pumped. With his face intense, he said through the open window, "I know the route they're taking. If I have an opportunity, I'm gonna grab Alex. Stay close."

Judy's terse, "Okay. We're ready" threw a switch in my head. The air in the small auto was suddenly charged.

I listened as Don moved, ran back to the sidewalk, and fell into step behind Alex and Giovanni. I stared at the floor, scarcely breathing, mouth suddenly dry. Thoughts whipped around my mind. *Is this the day? How can it be? We didn't plan for this. I thought we were just supposed to watch!*

Actually, all systems were "go" if the snatch worked out. Impromptu, yes, but with Judy behind the wheel we'd be out of there before Giovanni got his bearings, and the boat, although moored a good distance away in Licata, would be reachable. No one would know which way we headed anyway, or whether we'd scoot immediately or hole up awhile at some prearranged hideout. The crew had been in tighter spots than this. So I reigned in my sudden fear and chided the frantic thoughts going through my head. *Trust them. They know what they're doing.*

Judy gave me a blow-by-blow as our car crept along the street, keeping pace with Don. He was rapidly closing the distance between himself and the pair until he was just a few strides away, close enough to snatch Alex, make a dash to the car, and hand him to me before jumping into the empty front passenger's seat. Giovanni notwithstanding, the snatch could have been easily made. A grandfather walking in his own neighborhood is the last person in the world to suspect approaching trouble. The tension in the car broke every now and then because of a short, stifled laugh, and Judy later told me that Don looked like a detective in a slapstick film, where the "tail" is trying hard to appear nonchalant while actually pursuing his prey.

Just—and I mean just—as he was about to lay hold of Alex, a middle-aged woman, coming from the opposite direction, recognized Alex and Giovanni and engaged them in animated conversation. They all began walking together as a pack. Don broke contact. We pulled the car innocuously to the side of the street, and after a moment, he opened the door and slid inside.

"Almost," he said disgustedly, and heaved a sigh. "So close. I almost had him."

Without turning around he added, "Sorry, Katie. Maybe next time . . ."

"Next time" was to be sooner than we'd thought.

11

The Pachino Sortie

Pentola guardata spesso, non bolle mai.
A watched pot never boils.

"Mom, you won't be able to visit me for a few days. I'm going away for the weekend."

I had just walked into Alex's playroom, given him a hug, and plopped down onto a large bean-bag chair. We usually snuggled a minute or two—fortunately, he didn't consider himself too grown up for that kind of thing—then settled down to talk over the routine of the day. With his announcement, he looked up into my face with his childlike concern, hoping to prepare me. He expected the usual reaction.

Normally, this kind of news, especially so sudden, would throw me into "angry mom" mode. Being forced to surrender even more of what precious little time I was allotted with Alex could turn the atmosphere directly overhead into stationary thunderclouds, and I'd rain and hurl lightning at anyone coming within that emotional weather pattern. But this time I had my antennae up. Anything out of the ordinary could possibly be considered an opportunity to retake Alex.

Behind a façade of sorrow, I listened as he told me—first hesitantly, then with building excitement—that Massimo had planned a weekend trip to Pachino to visit an old friend; his girlfriend and Alex would accompany him. Massimo and his friend often left for hunting trips from there, but since this wasn't the season, he'd been invited for a cookout.

I must have looked upset because Alex stroked my arm and said, "I'll be back soon. I'll miss you . . ."

But his voice faded into some hollow background, like an echo losing itself in a deep cave. My mind buzzed with adrenaline-charged thoughts. *This could be it.* I had a passing familiarity with that country, having spent a few days there some years back. Its relative isolation could definitely work in our favor.

After leaving Alex that evening, I met Don and company at our prearranged rendezvous. As I slid into the back seat and pulled the door shut, I rattled off everything that Alex had told me and watched as the mood in that little sedan turned electric.

It was a perfect setup for a snatch. Situated at the southern corner of Sicily, Pachino had about twenty thousand inhabitants and had lots of very old buildings and narrow, winding streets that would make it easy for us to lose a pursuer. Life moved a lot slower there, too, and this would give us more escape time before a major police response could be marshaled or roads blocked. Surrounded by arid, almost desolate countryside, it was of interest to nobody except those who called it home. It would be the last place Massimo would expect trouble. Best of all was that we could finally make use of the sailboat waiting at Licata. Pachino was a short sail from Licata, and the escape boat could moor at an isolated cement dock some distance from town. The boat's pilot and navigator would just sit tight there till we showed up afterward with Alex.

That Friday evening as I said goodbye to Alex I buried him in a hug. "You have fun, kiddo. Your mom's gonna miss you. You better miss me, too, or I'll be mad."

"Okay. I'll think about you while I'm eating and playing football," he kidded then turned serious. It was amazing how he could man up even at that age. "Really, Mom, you'll be all right. It's only a few days. I'll see you soon."

"Yes," I said with feeling. "You will."

The next morning, brilliant sunshine washed over the streets of Palermo. It was early yet, about nine o'clock, and with the city offices closed, traffic was relatively slack. Don and Judy had parked their rental car within sight of Giovanni's apartment. In a second rental car, Temi and I waited it out a couple of blocks away, he at the wheel and I (heavy sigh!) relegated to my spot on the floor. I lay there listening to the faint hiss of static from the black walkie-talkie in the front seat. The set suddenly crackled. It was Judy, sounding cool and focused. "They're leaving."

"We're on our way," Temi responded, and the floor underneath me moved as the car pulled into the traffic.

Although we never caught sight of them, Temi's transceiver buzzed with curt, periodic updates. A few miles out of Palermo, the traffic thinned, and I was able to sit up and placed both hands on the seat in front of me while leaning forward and glued my eyes to the road ahead. It snaked around mountains, flat-lined in spots but constantly hid from view the two cars we were pursuing. Aside from the occasional vehicle going in the opposite direction, we had the place to ourselves. It was a lonely feeling, being separated from our "partners," and I wished for a reassuring glance that they were indeed out there, heading in the same direction as we were.

It was an absolutely gorgeous spring day. The road hugged the coastline, and the Mediterranean Sea, glittering with the early morning sun, stretched out to the horizon. A scattering of fishing boats bobbed lazily on the cobalt waters while distant gulls, stark white against the blue sky, pirouetted effortlessly in the mild offshore breezes. It was the kind of vista that annually drew millions from all over the world, but it was an everyday scene to me. *How sad*, I thought, *that I couldn't ever relax and enjoy it.*

We hadn't gone another ten minutes when the radio went dead. It wasn't that Judy's voice got progressively fainter; suddenly she just wasn't there. I looked sharply at Temi. "What happened? Where are they?"

Panic edged my voice, and wild imaginings played out in my mind: an accident on a sharp curve; their being confronted by a previously alerted Massimo; a run-in with the police . . .

Without skipping a beat, Temi took charge. "Relax, Katie. It's no big deal. We'll find them."

Turning into a pullout, he left the engine running while studying the map he'd brought along. The quiet of the empty road intensified my anxiety. After a moment, Temi said, "Okay," and offered a reassuring smile. "I think we've got it."

"But how will we find them?" I asked, my voice an octave higher than normal. "We don't have any idea where they are."

Temi shrugged. "The town's not that big. There're only so many places they can be. Besides, we know where the boat will be waiting. Sooner or later, they have to rendezvous there with us. Don't worry."

Buzzing Don and Judy once more without response, he pulled back onto the roadway and in best Palermo style gunned it, leaving the radio turned on just in case.

Temi's attitude had a calming effect, and I settled back into my seat. I threw the occasional sideways glance at this ex-Special Forces guy who partook of a kidnapping with the same practiced nonchalance he no doubt exhibited when ordering a cheeseburger at a fast-food joint. What were these people made of? Danger of every kind was to them part of the routine. I wondered if they could function without it. For me, once was enough for a lifetime. If I stopped moving long enough to dwell on my participation in this caper, my nerves would be shot. *Never again,* I thought. *Not if I can help it.*

It took most of the day to get to Pachino, and as we approached it, the land took on a somber, rather depressing atmosphere. Although it was supposed to be an agricultural area, with some vineyards scattered throughout, it instead seemed forlorn in a dusty plot of weeds, low brush, and parched earth. Old West cowboys would have called it "hardscrabble." The term fit. Not a single cow, sheep, chicken, or any barnyard-type animal made an appearance, either on the road or in the "pastures" behind the endless latticework of wire fencing. The road was still mostly empty, and nothing, no one moved in the fields.

As the miles rolled by and conversation with Temi faded, my mind eased into other things. Only the night before, I'd spoken over the phone with Mom, discussing the surgery that was then only a few days away.

"Nervous?" I asked. I sure was, but didn't want to add to her concerns.

"Well, a little," she admitted, tagging on some optimism, "but at least we'll be over this hurdle. The last one, I'm sure."

A silence strained the distance between us. There was so much we both wanted to say. She was doing this now to be ready for Alex. Her hope never wavering for his rescue; she'd plotted the timing for this brain surgery as part of the overall plan—only she couldn't say so over the phone. She knew the possibility existed of Massimo having my phone bugged. It turned out he never did that, but we had no way of knowing. He'd tried to control every other part of my life, and having a phone company friend run a tap into my private line would be just like him. Ideally, my parents and I could have worked out a code the last visit I'd had with them back in December, but we never thought of it. I guess a life of stealth is something you work out piecemeal, one mistake at a time. It was too late to do anything about it now, so we settled for small talk and generalities when discussing Alex and me. It was all I could do to staunch the flow of words that begged to come, to give her hope that this weekend would be the one, and within the week she'd see us both face-to-face.

The conversation ended with my vision blurring and coming tears choking my voice, "I love you, Mom. I really love you."

"I love you, too, Kati," she replied softly. "It'll be all right. Don't worry."

Don't worry. It seemed that these days everyone was telling me that.

We entered Pachino proper late that afternoon. It looked older than I remembered. Winding, narrow streets threaded through residential areas that appeared much the same as when the Allies, under the code name "Operation Husky," invaded Sicily in 1943. A lot of the town's homes predated that explosive event by hundreds of years. In some places, huge, flat paving stones connected streets and alleyways (wide enough for only one vehicle) providing the sensation while driving of running over someone's ribcage. The piazza was wide, lovely, and peopled mostly by older gentlemen on slat benches, reading or playing cards, and young mothers out walking with their children. The pace was wonderfully slow, and I got the impression that this was one place on the island that deliberately veered away from the 20th century in preference of the old ways.

We found the dock in a little cove, a small mooring area out in the middle of nowhere, a few kilometers from Pachino. It was perfect, close enough to the town for a quick getaway, yet removed enough to allow us to maintain a low profile. The whole of it consisted of a wide cement slab easing down into the water and a few unmonitored slips, where a couple of small fishing vessels rocked lazily with the incoming tide. Temi pointed out our sail-boat, and my heart leaped. In the slanted rays of the afternoon sun, its white paint gleamed, making it look heaven-sent. And although to others, its thirty-five-foot length might seem less than impressive, to me it was a dream come to life. Equipped with a motor, it would make good time on our "Malta Run."

Temi gave the area the once-over and then pulled into the parking area close to the cement slip where the boat was moored. He pointed with his chin and smiled broadly. "There's their car. Told you."

Not another person was in sight, anywhere, either on land or topside of the few other boats there. Probably in the summer the place saw more activity; but this early, it was pretty much ours. As we approached the sailboat, I watched as it moved gently in the water, seeming to breathe, the mooring lines alternately tightening then growing slack. The only sounds were the quiet lap of little waves against the hull and the occasional creak of straining rope fibers. The whole area seemed deserted. When we were level with the deck, Judy poked her head out of the forecastle and smiled, real big, offering a happy, "Welcome aboard."

Inside, I felt like I'd walked into a homecoming party. Everybody was all smiles and easiness, and as I was introduced to the boat's pilot, burly, soft-spoken Randy, it struck me again that so far, I hadn't met a single player in this game who fit the profile of what I'd expected. I don't know . . . you'd think all these guys involved in this kind of hazardous work would look the part: faces mapped with worry lines and punctuated with hard mouths frozen into a perpetual cynic's sneer, eyes like chips of granite, hair turned prematurely gray from all the tight spots they'd been in. Again, I was proved wrong in Randy. Young and handsome, his evident professionalism was tempered by a confident, friendly manner. Although a voracious reader—his assigned area was crammed with books of every description—he had none of the standoffish manner characteristic of deep thinkers. His smile invited conversation and familiarity.

The only one missing was Ian, the final member of our exclusive club. He'd gone to fetch drinking water, Randy said, and would be back shortly.

Looking around, I was surprised at how tight the confines would be with all of us, including Alex, onboard. Furthermore, I couldn't see a single bed-down spot. I found out later that every bench could be made into a throw-together bed, using cushions that were stowed during the day. A man I assumed was Ian suddenly came aboard toting a couple of five gallon water buckets and set them on deck. He was a bit smaller than Randy, his head topped with short-clipped hair the color of a new penny. It fairly glowed in the sun. He ducked his head as he entered, and greeted me with a smile, a handshake, and a careless "How's it goin'?" which he turned out in a soft Scottish accent.

Randy and Ian had only recently been introduced in preparation for the rescue. For the time being, their main duty was simply to stay on the boat, maintaining a "Condition Orange" readiness for immediate departure for Malta, should we manage to retake Alex. It was mostly a boring job, which accounted for Randy's collection of books. Every now and then they'd had to field questions from the curious, usually other boaters, who, like American RVers, bragged about where they'd been and where they were going. Their cover story was a common one, especially for the young and footloose—fishing, sailing, and sightseeing, and nobody bothered to inquire further.

"Massimo is staying at a friend's house in Pachino," Don said. "Drink up and we're on our way."

Judy had poured me a cup of coffee, unfortunately of the Americanized, aqua di polipo strength. "What happened to you guys earlier?" I asked. "I was so worried when we couldn't get you on the walkie-talkie. We lost you a few minutes out of Palermo."

Judy snickered, "Blame that on your ex! Do you know that guy drives like a maniac? I never saw in my life a civilian take curves the way he did. Don tried hard to keep up with him, but we also wanted to get here in one piece. We lost sight of the car about an hour into the drive here, but we knew he would be in Pachino, and the town's not that big. We spent about half an hour going up and down streets until we found where he'd parked."

I grimaced, "Massimo always drives that way."

Indeed, he'd driven like that since I'd first met him. Once we were rear-ended by a bus in Palermo because of his fancy maneuvers. His fast talking turned the situation on its head, so confusing the bus driver that he ended up thinking it was his fault, and we drove away from the incident with another notch in Massimo's gloat gun and my case of whiplash that he dismissed with a flippant, "You'll be okay in a few days."

As I had lain on the bed in our apartment, with spikes of pain shooting through my neck, I cradled then infant Alex and wept softly. My baby could have been killed. In the car, I'd been holding him in my lap for the short drive home, and for a long time afterward, all I could think of was how it might have ended.

Judy squeezed in beside me. If we pulled this off, we'd be packed like sardines till we reached Malta. "We don't know yet what the setup is, how we'll get access to Alex," she said, "but if we can get him on his own, even for a minute, he's ours."

A thrill shot through me. *Ours. You mean mine.*

Her voice grew somber. "Katie, remember that you'll have to control him once he's in the car. I know we've been through this already, but just as a reminder to you. If we take him, it'll happen fast, and in the confusion he could do anything—kick, bite, scream, or even just sit there in shock because he won't realize what's going on. It'll pass quickly once he knows you're with him. Just keep talking softly to him, reassuring him. We need his cooperation to make this work."

I felt a little short of breath. "Okay. Whatever it takes."

Don stood. "Let's go take a look."

The four of us—Don, Judy, Temi, and I—sat scrunched in our tight little car, down the block and kitty-corner fronting the house where Massimo had parked. He was in there, fifty yards away, with his girlfriend Anna and with Alex. There was no way of knowing whether this was his final destination. So we waited it out, my compatriots' eyes constantly scanning the home and the street, while mine were glued to the carpet. When doing "floor duty," it was the only view I had. Surveillance was usually a disagreeable mixture of excitement and boredom. We were in the older section of Pachino. The street was scarcely more than an alleyway, paved intermittently with asphalt and those large flat stones from another era. All in a long row, the cookie-cutter homes were low, ancient, and topped with the dusty, ubiquitous red tile of old Sicily. On the outside, they were depressingly dingy, with walls blasted gray by centuries of weather and pockmarked with whiter scars where the plaster had long since peeled away. Their sepia tones were reminiscent of a tintype from a century earlier.

I was allowed only a brief glimpse every now and then because I had assumed my customary position on the floor and raised my head only enough to see but not be seen. Mostly I huddled, listening to the others talk quietly about options and possible snatch scenarios. My nerves were really on edge. We were very close to Massimo, and this ancient street was so narrow that an inquisitive pedestrian with prying eyes might make trouble. If Massimo was alerted now, it would be all over. With his professional pull, I'd be barred forever from even visiting Alex and would likely be deported. That would kill me.

In the scant quarter hour we'd been on this surveillance, no one had entered or left the building. The street itself was virtually empty. Besides Massimo's car, ours was the only other one parked there. It was the dinner hour, and most people were inside for the evening meal. The scent of spices and cooking food drifting through the auto's open windows, the occasional faint clatter of silverware and muffled voices from one home or another all offered up a feeling of almost haunting domesticity. A flurry of sparrows, their wings flashing in the last rays of pre-dusk sunlight, flitted from rooftop to rooftop, their little chipping calls loud in the stillness.

Don turned the ignition key, and the car hummed to life. "I think they're there for the night," he said. There was no way of knowing if this was Massimo's final destination or merely a stop along the way, so we planned an early morning stakeout. As we had done that day, Don and Judy would man one car, Temi and I another.

Don eased the car quietly into the street and past Massimo's car, giving both it and the house a quick once-over, taking in more detail and mentally cataloguing it for future reference. We hit one of the main drags and in no time were on our way out of town. Once on the coast road, eerily empty at this hour, we headed for an outpost of a restaurant a few miles away. It was nice to sit upright again and actually look out the window.

We rolled to a stop in a small parking area just as the last of the day's sunlight pulled back into the western sky. Like all the other buildings in the area, the restaurant was a squat, concrete structure whose overlay of whitewash had long since weathered away. Overlooking the sea, it bore without nobility the ravages of wind, sun, and rain. The paved parking area immediately adjacent gave way to a perimeter of dead weeds and heavy scrub. It was literally on the edge of nowhere, right next to the road but far from any other signs of habitation. I was genuinely surprised to see a few other cars parked out front. Like our little team, everyone else had to drive some distance just to get here, and I wondered why anyone but folks like us took the trouble when there were other eateries right in Pachino. Standing beside our car for a moment to stretch the kinks out (how I've appreciated spacious, gas-guzzling American SUVs since), we walked the few feet to the entrance and went inside.

Wow. It was all that came into my mind, and not in a cheery way. The restaurant's interior was a holdover from silent film's horror-movie days. The room was dimly lit, whether to create atmosphere or because the owner was too cheap to pay his electric bill I'll never know. The walls were of stone and very dark wood, ancient-looking and somehow forbidding, enclosing us like a cave. On each of the dozen or so tables, a small candle flickered from within a smudged glass globe, and I suspected that to save money, the flowers they illuminated had been gathered from beneath nearby headstones. I expected us to be met at the door by some Grade-B character named Igor, all bent over and clothed in a hooded tunic and Robin Hood tights. Pinning us with his one good eye and proffering a leering grin, he'd limp his way to a quiet corner table with us in tow, and leave us with menus soiled by his grave-digging fingers.

The waiter who actually showed up was a rather bored young man whose demeanor screamed that he'd rather be anywhere else. The food was excellent, and from our window the view of the dark, rolling sea was spectacular. As we ate, we laughed a lot to keep up our touristy appearance but discussed in quieter tones the next day's preparations. As I looked around the room, I felt we needn't have bothered with pretense. In this perfect atmosphere for intrigue, everyone in the dining room appeared to be doing the same thing. I'd have bet that, like us, half the people there were quietly discussing some illegalities or secretive deals, casting furtive glances our way and hoping the distance prevented our eavesdropping. Oddly, this thought gave me genuine comfort, honor among thieves and all that sort of thing.

Getting back to the boat by about ten o'clock, we crawled into our respective sleeping areas, with the men on rotating watch. Exhausted and wonderfully stuffed with seafood, I drew the blankets around me and was asleep immediately.

When I woke early the next morning, it was to the smell of coffee. Pasty sunlight came into the cabin from the windows just above me. I lay there a moment, listening to Temi move around, getting together some gear. When I sat up he smiled, and referencing the coffee said, "Better get some of this. Don and Judy are already gone, and we need to be on our way, too."

I downed a cup of coffee but was too keyed up for breakfast. Temi, though, had already put together a snack bag to take with us, and within fifteen minutes, I was ready to go. Ian and Randy wished us happy hunting, and we headed for the car.

The morning was a gray one, with low, heavy clouds all the way to the horizon, and a cool breeze coming off the water. I wondered if rain would hinder or help the operation.

We drove to Pachino and cruised back and forth through the streets as near as we could safely get to the stakeout area. I was on the car floor (where else?), so to another driver Temi appeared to be alone. Shortly, the walkie-talkie in the front seat opened up. It was Judy. "They're getting into the car, now. We're on them."

I poked my head up for a look, and even as Judy was giving radio directions, their car passed us! Temi swung our vehicle in a smooth arc and soon we were part of the motorcade. I sat up full, not too concerned now that we were heading away from town, and straining for a view of the other half of our team on the road ahead. But in the time it took for us to reverse course, we'd lost sight of them. Temi and Judy maintained a running communication, though, and in a half hour we pulled off the road at the base of a hill, moving the car unobtrusively behind a thicket of low brush where Don and Judy already waited. We exited the car in a hurry and scrambled to the top. From behind the walls of a very old, long-abandoned cement building, Don glassed the area below. Handing me a pair of binoculars, he said, "There they are. Take a look."

A quarter mile below us, Massimo's car sat in the gravel driveway next to typical country style home. Miles of dry emptiness stretched away on all sides. Massimo stood talking to another man who worked a large barbecue on wheels. Flames occasionally licked upward through the grill and clouds of smoke periodically wreathed the two men. Beside the house, a typical gray, one-story structure with tile roofing, Alex wandered through some weeds with a new friend, throwing rocks and pointing every now and then. Even as we watched, other cars began to arrive, each disgorging an amazing number of people. Don mentioned that besides Alex, Massimo's girlfriend, Anna, had come, as well as another man and his young son, all in the same little car. Sicilians take carpooling to an extreme. It is just their way to pile into a vehicle with the enthusiasm of a mob of college kids squeezing into a phone booth and shutting the doors. I've ridden in these compact models where people were crammed literally two deep, sitting on each other's laps, and alternately crushing one person then another as the vehicle made sharp left and right turns.

In the end, about twenty or thirty people showed up for the picnic, going in and out through the home's open doorway, mingling outside and taking food cooked on the barbecue into the home. It seemed that's where the feasting would take place, possibly because of the threat of rain.

Don apologized for not being able to take Alex while the group was still at the house in Pachino. "We thought about it," he said apologetically, "but there were just too many people getting into Massimo's car. It would have been a bad move."

Certainly I understood. I was hopeful we'd have our chance later.

We watched the crowd below for a long time, each of us with our own pair of field glasses, standing or crouched down in our preferred spot, pressed against the decayed concrete of our abandoned house. There was no real danger of being spotted from here, and the sky's overcast shielded the binocular lenses from any giveaway glint of hard, reflective sunlight. This was a curious place, this house or whatever it had been, and once, I looked through the dingy windows to peer inside. There were a couple of empty rooms, strewn with old trash and a few splintered two-by-fours. Stringers of old cobweb hung limply from the plaster ceiling. The only door was padlocked and the place had a sad, disused feeling about it. It was probably used at one time or another more as a storage unit than a living quarters. The bare knob atop was just as forlorn. Even scrub refused to grow there, just a few scattered clumps of yellowed weeds still clinging in death to the parched ground.

We discussed back and forth our limited options. For the raid to be a success, Alex would somehow have to be lured from the cordon of guests and taken with as little fanfare as possible. As a child, he could actually be missing for some time, the others

Killing time with Temi while waiting for "the right moment"

quite naturally assuming he was outside playing or roaming the empty land with friends, and that could offer us quite a good head start on getting to the boat and weighing anchor.

Conversation eventually tapered off, and we all watched awhile silently. Through the binoculars, I could see Alex. He looked so close as he played soccer with a friend. His laughter and the "thump" of their feet against the ball carried faintly to me. My heart ached. *Oh, Baby. You don't know I'm watching. Please look up so I can pretend you see me here.*

One at a time and in small groups, the people drifted into the house till the barbecue was left by itself, still huffing wisps of smoke from chunks of meat that had fallen through the grill onto still hot coals. The wind picked up, cool and insistent, and then a sprinkle of rain fell from a heavy sky. I turned up the collar of my jacket and continued to glass the house, hoping to catch a glimpse of Alex, thinking that, even from this distance, I might hear his voice from the open doorway.

It began to rain in earnest, and we all moved into the car. By that time, we had been there most of the day. Earlier, I had distractedly munched some of the snack food Temi had brought, but I was too adrenaline-pumped to really get hungry. Now, as I sat in the back seat and listened to the steady drumbeat of rain on the roof, my stomach gurgled, but I was too disappointed to eat. We all knew by this time that the mission was likely a bust. It would soon be dark. After the rain let up a bit, we moved again to the top of the hill to watch and wait, and it wasn't long before Massimo, Alex, and the others came out of the house, gave their goodbyes all around, and got into their car. The vehicle made a U-turn in the wide area in front of the house, skirted the other vehicles lined up on the driveway, and made for the road to Pachino.

My heart sank. The others were disappointed as well. Getting into our respective cars, I watched Don and Judy head out in order to pick up Massimo's car and follow him back to Pachino, while Temi and I drove silently back to the sailboat.

With all my heart I had hoped, almost believed, this would be the time, that tomorrow we'd land in Malta and I could call my parents with the good news that Alex and I were reunited and on our way home. My frustration level was reaching critical mass. Alex had been so close, all hands were mustered, and now I was growing impatient. I would have to wait a little longer—or a lot longer—and I only hoped I could hold out. Too much of this back-and-forth stress was ripping my heart to shreds.

About an hour after Temi and I got back to the sailboat, Don and Judy came aboard. With Ian and Randy, we all sat crunched together in that little decks area below, mulling over the day. Don tried to bring some perspective, "I don't see where we could have done any different," he said somberly, "It just wasn't the right time."

Early the next morning, Don and Judy drove to Pachino while the rest of us stayed on the boat and ate breakfast. They came back less than an hour later, with the news that Massimo and Alex had already left for Palermo. Scrub this operation. As I slung my overnight bag from my shoulder, I didn't bother to hide my disappointment. At the same time, I realistically assessed our chances in hindsight. A lot of things mitigated a successful mission—the crowd of people at the picnic, having to make an unrehearsed getaway through the streets of a strange town, trying to get Alex alone. It had been one of those grit-your-teeth-and-try-again scenarios, and I knew it. Knowing didn't lessen the heartbreak, but it helped bring some perspective.

The drive back to Palermo, with Temi trailing Don and Judy's car, was a bit less subdued. A veteran of these missions, he was used to the occasional setback and wasted no time in conveying to me his optimism for a near-future rescue. After a while, I opened up, and we began discussing some other possible means of getting Alex. By the time we were on the outskirts of Palermo, I was a bit more comforted and ready to explore other avenues. This was only strike two, and in this business, they'd swing as long as they were at bat. As long as their cover wasn't blown, they'd be able to keep trying.

But now, a gnawing anxiety was replacing my disappointment. The day was growing late, and I'd promised Mom I'd call before she went into surgery. At a six-hour time zone difference, I had to hurry or I'd miss her.

"Temi," I said urgently, "could we look for a pay phone? I really need to talk to my mom. She's going into surgery tonight, and I promised I'd call."

He nodded, pressed the accelerator, and moved our car level with Don's on the multilane. Tapping the glass, he rolled down his window, and Don did likewise. "Katie needs to call the States," he shouted out, and Don gave the "okay" signal. Temi pulled ahead, and we kept our eyes peeled for a booth.

In our final approach to the city, we entered a heavier traffic flow. Palermo's huddle of downtown buildings, glowing softly in the late afternoon sunlight, stood against a sky washed deep blue from the previous night's rain. Flapping in the breeze, laundry hung from a thousand clotheslines strung on apartment balconies gave the city an almost homey appearance.

We took an exit ramp and wound through a dozen streets looking for a phone stand. This was no easy task. In Palermo, locating one near enough to a parking area took near military planning.

"There!" I leaned over the headrest of the empty seat in front of me and pointed eleven o'clock. Temi swung the car sharply to the curb and braked, with Don and Judy's vehicle pulling in right behind him. Jumping out of the back seat, I ran the few steps to the phone and, using my phone card, tried to place the call. The line was dead. I sprinted back to the car, and we looked for another one. We made a second stop at a phone with the cable neatly cut. Four other times we tried, getting nearer and nearer to Mondello, and with each stop, the frustration level built with not a single working phone!

By the time we reached Mondello, I was frantic. A block from my apartment, both cars swung into a parking area, and I was pushing the door open before ours came to a complete stop.

"I'll see you tomorrow," I told Temi over my shoulder, slung the overnight bag on my shoulder and ran to the little street where I lived. As I hurried there, I fumbled in my purse for the gate key. Unlocking the gate, I pushed it open and in one quick motion I was through and shoving it closed behind me. My quickened footsteps were sharp in the twilight stillness, echoing from the driveway walls that enclosed me from both sides. Getting to my apartment, I unlocked the door, went inside, threw the overnight bag on the floor, and grabbed the phone from beside my bed. I quickly dialed, and a woman's voice at the other end surprised me.

"Mom?"

"Kati, I was beginning to think you wouldn't call."

My emotions were a whirl of relief and concern. "You wouldn't believe what I went through to try to get hold of you. I'm so sorry! A half-dozen public phones in this lousy city that don't work, and I've been on them all. Wires cut, phone lines dead, you name it. What are you still doing there? Shouldn't you be in prep at the hospital by now?"

Mom laughed softly. "I don't have to be there for another hour. I'm so glad you called. I was just getting ready to leave. Any news?"

I knew what she meant, of course, but couldn't answer directly, just in case someone else was listening, "Pretty much the same here. No change. The weather's been nice but nothing special going on, same old."

She sighed, "I understand. Well . . . I really need to leave if I'm going to get there on time. Big day today, you know. Your dad will call when I'm out of surgery. Don't worry. Everything will be okay." She was reluctant to let me go, and her voice, making her sound so near over the phone, couldn't close the real miles between us. "I love you, Kati," she said, and my throat went dry.

"I love you, too, Mom."

A hard silence followed the "click" at the other end. I sat there a long moment, a little worried about her and suddenly very, very tired. I lay down and that quick, I was asleep.

12

The Snatch

Chi ha salute e libertà, è ricco e non lo sa.
Who has health and freedom, is rich
and doesn't know it.

I was awakened by an insistent jangling inside my head—no, beside my head. From the fog of exhaustion, I swatted blindly, aiming for the alarm clock before realizing that the phone was the culprit. My eyelids flickered open and registered darkness. A seeping quiet came through the open windows: no traffic, sirens, voices of pedestrians, no morning radio programs sounding from the other apartments. I felt as if I had slept only a few minutes.

Bringing the phone to my ear, I groaned into the mouthpiece the traditional Italian greeting, "Pronto . . ."

The trembling voice at the other end startled me awake, "Katie, this is Apuka."

Suddenly chilled through, I sat bolt upright in bed, cradling the phone in both hands, "Dad? What is it . . . ?"

"Kati, your mom had her surgery, and we lost her."

I felt like someone slapped me. "What?! We what?"

Dad's voice choked, and trailed off like the last echo in a cave, "We lost her . . . lost her . . ."

I didn't hear what he said immediately after that. Numbness swept over me, and I sat rigid as wood, the phone having slipped away from my ear and caught in both hands just below my chin.

Other voices came from the receiver, little buzzing insect sounds, and after a moment, I mechanically raised the earpiece.

"Katie, Katie?" It was my sister-in-law Karen, "Are you there?"

My voice was flat, a dead monotone in the dark, "I'm here. Tell me what happened."

Karen was struggling, "We don't know. They removed the tumor and she started hemorrhaging. They revived her twice, then . . . she was just . . . gone . . . I don't know what . . ."

Everything was moving in slow motion. I sensed my lips moving but felt my speech slurred, "How is Dad?"

Stupid question.

The tragedy made Karen blunt. "He fainted when the surgeon told him. We had to catch him before he hit the floor. They hooked him up to IVs, and he's come around, but he's, you know, still in shock. We all are."

The surgeon had also taken it hard, Karen told me. It was the first time in his twenty-year career that he'd lost a patient, and to have it be a longtime friend was almost more than he could bear. Dad actually began consoling him awhile. Later I found out that he stayed up three consecutive nights, going over every move of the surgery, wondering aloud what he could have done differently.

"Katie, are you all right?"

"No," I murmured without thinking, "I'm not." Then the tears came with sobs that strangled my voice, "I need to call Don and Judy . . ."

Switching on the bedroom light, I reached for the phone book and thumbed through the pages, brushing away the tears so I could see to dial. Karen stayed on the phone with me till I located the number. "Here it is," I rasped, "Look, I gotta go."

"Okay, Katie. I'm so sorry. We'll call you later?"

I said through sobs, "Okay," then heard Karen pass the phone to someone else. "Katie, Katie are you still there?"

It was Dad, and at the sound of his trembling voice I fell apart, "Apuka, how could this happen? What are we going to do now? We'll have to stop everything. I have to come home . . ."

A determination I didn't know he possessed swept across the dark ocean and grabbed me by the heart, "Kati, you listen to me. No matter what, you have to keep going. Do you hear what I'm saying? Your mother wanted this more than anything else in the world. To stop now would be the worst thing you could do. You have to be strong. Kati, are you listening?"

His words had an immediate calming effect. For a brief moment I felt myself in a sheltered spot while gale winds raged around me, "Okay, Apuka," I quietly said, "I won't quit."

I heard some of the tension leave him, "I know you have to go. I'll call later. I love you, Kati."

"Me, too."

The "click" on the other end of the line propelled me back into the storm, and my fingers raced across the phone's dial pad. One ring, two. A sleepy voice responded with the American "Hello?"

"Judy," I said, in sudden panic, "Judy, my dad just called, and my mother died during surgery."

"No!" It was a shout, a rage, "Stay there, Katie. We're on our way."

I sat staring at the phone book in my lap and wept.

A half hour later, as I still sat on the bed, a buzzer sounded suddenly in the room. The dresser clock read 4:30 a.m. I moved from the bed to the wall by the front door, depressing the little white button that would unlock the outside gate to the apartment complex. A moment later a car pulled up out front. Then there came the rapid opening and closing of two car doors, hurried footsteps across the paving, and the quiet, insistent knock at the front door. Judy entered first, and instinctively I fell into her, sobbing wildly. Don closed the door behind him, and we all hustled to sit on the bed together, while Judy held onto me and cried. Between gasps, I rambled like a crazy woman, jumping from one subject involving my mom to another, "How could this happen? I had spoken with her just last night . . . Judy, she died, she died . . . Oh, she really liked you guys . . . Dad, too . . . we have to finish this . . ."

Caring as they were, they just let me go on until I was pretty well cried out, adding only occasionally their sentiments about my parents, and how glad they were that Dad had determined we needed to go on with the plan. With one on either side, they enfolded and gently rocked me, soothing with soft words and reassurances, encouraging me to be strong.

At one point, Don broached a subject that was untouchable up to that point. His voice was gentle, but firm. "Katie, now, you know you're going to have to keep up the playacting with Massimo's family. We can't let them suspect anything's changed. They find out your mother's gone, they'll lock up Alex and throw away the key. They'll know you'd try to get him."

"I don't know how you're gonna do it," he somberly added, "but you have to put up a good front. You can't let them suspect anything."

Of course, he was right. I had to be the consummate actress. He was also right in that neither he nor I knew how I was going to pull it off. I had a visit scheduled with Alex that very day. With my heart dragging on the ground, was I supposed to be happy and attentive to the games we played, the books we read together? At the moment, I was a straightjacket candidate. All I really wanted to do was collapse onto the floor and cry like a baby.

By the time they left for their hotel, the sun had been up for a couple of hours, and noise from the street and my neighbors had been long coming in through windows that Don had shuttered as a precaution. He hadn't wanted anyone looking in. With the day just starting, they planned a quick shower and breakfast and would come back later to check on me.

Opening the door, they turned back one more time to smile encouragement. I was apologetic. "I broke the rules," I said meekly, "I'm sorry."

Judy touched my arm. "Don't worry about it," she reassured me and regarded me with great tenderness, "You're going to make it, Katie. We all are. You'll see. Keep looking ahead."

They had no sooner driven off when I broke the rules again and called Fabio. I needed him to know. "I'm coming over," was his instant response, and it threw me into a panic.

"No, you can't! It's not a good . . ."

Fabio was curt. "Katie, I'm coming. You stay there." And with that, he hung up, giving me no chance to rebut.

In the end, I was glad he did. He'd phoned his work and told them an emergency had come up and he'd be going in late or not at all. We sat together for hours, him holding me while I cried and held him back, and he let me talk aimlessly while he murmured little bits of encouragement. It wasn't his words that were most important but the fact that he'd come, dropped everything and was there, just for me. He knew the implications of my mother's passing, that it would impact "the plans" he sensed intuitively but never openly mentioned. And there he was, risking his personal safety with involvement, even peripherally, in something that could earn him a jail sentence. I learned a lot about his character that day.

When I'd cried myself out for the second time that day, I insisted he leave, hinting that I had an "engagement" later in the day. As he stood to go, a knock sounded at the door, and Judy's voice came from outside. I was stricken with dread and was sure I inhaled sharply as my hand flew to my mouth. Throwing a quick, fearful glance at Fabio, who stood calm as a Renaissance sculpture, I went to the door, opened it and with a dumb expression lamely said, "Hi," and waved the two of them inside.

Oh, this was crazy. Of all the things that could go wrong! A careless someone must have left the gate open, because the two hadn't buzzed to be let in. It wouldn't have made any difference. Fabio was wise to what was going on and knew the two of them, from my conversations, by name. But instead of the splash of cold water I'd expected on the scene, a warm summer breeze blew into the room instead. Don and Judy were all smiles and friendliness. "Fabio, I'm so glad we finally meet! I've heard so much about you . . ." Shaking hands all around, Fabio returned the greetings, and they all stood conversing like old friends. Finally, Fabio excused himself on the grounds of going to work, and we all saw him to the door.

As he drove off, I stood with my back pressed against the door, swamped with embarrassment. "I'm so sorry," I said in a little girl's voice. "That wasn't supposed to happen."

Don shrugged, and unaccountably chuckled. Judy grinned. "Oh, well," was all she managed.

"He won't say anything," I assured them.

"He knows anyway," Don said, not without a certain wry humor. "If he was going to spill it, he would have already done so. I think we're good."

"So," Judy cut in, "let's make a few plans for this afternoon."

At a prearranged point, I met them later in the day, and as I got into the car, I noticed an addition to our crew: Carlo was a spare-framed, quiet young man who, I was told, fished for a living and in the off-season picked up a few odd jobs to keep his bachelor lifestyle solvent. Through a contact Judy knew there, he'd been recruited on the island of Pantelleria, about 60 nautical miles from Sicily. It was a tiny place, small enough to drive around entirely in an hour and far enough off the beaten track that once Carlo performed his narrowly defined task, he could return and take up where he left off, with no one the wiser.

The drive to a restaurant some distance out of town was a quiet one. Both Carlo and Temi knew of my mom's passing, and aside from their offering quiet condolences, the only sounds were the hum of the car's engine and the occasional shift of gears. We pulled into the parking lot of a small place, active then with the midday meal, and went inside. Don encouraged me to order something and keep up my strength; though I did so to please him, when my pasta arrived, I merely stirred it with my fork and after a few experimental bites pushed the plate away. Depression and anxiety always had its way with me through killing my appetite. Three years of living like that, coupled with my daily dosage of either alcohol or sedatives, had pared me down to a dangerously thin build. This latest blow threatened to be a killer. If we didn't resolve this rescue soon, I'd literally waste away.

Carlo was the only one of the group to show any animation. He was constantly looking around, taking in the sights, and obviously enjoying his food. For him this seemed to be a lark. As he was being paid well and all expenses were taken care of, for the time being he lived like a king. His main drawback was that he couldn't speak a word of English, so I had to constantly translate. With a background in Spanish, Temi could sometimes make him out because of the similarity of Spanish and Italian words. The two of them seemed to hit it off, in fact, and shared a room at the hotel.

Marina in Mondello

Some half-hearted discussion about "plans" moved around the table, but for the most part it was a no-go. Zombie-like, I stared out the restaurant window and drifted to other places, reliving past incidents, hearing my mom's voice greet or scold me, reminding me to get ready for dinner. It was gone, all of it. Not a full day earlier I'd spoken with her, neither of us knowing it would be for the last time. It struck me that there was poignancy to life, a profound sorrow that edges even our happy times. People really do die; they are loved ones who you'd never thought of doing without. They are parts of you that live on in memory long after the grass carpets the gravesite. And stuck here three thousand rotten miles away, I couldn't even stand weeping with my dad as they laid her to rest.

We eventually left the restaurant, and they dropped me off a couple of blocks from my apartment so I could get ready for the Alex visit. At 4:00 p.m., I stood at the stop near the Mondello piazza, waiting for the bus to Palermo and wondering how I was going to do this.

About twenty minutes later, I stepped down from the bus and dragged myself across the street to Giovanni's apartment building. On the way, I rehearsed facial expressions and mentally ran through a couple of innocuous remarks that I hoped would detour suspicion that something was amiss. On the other hand, the family might mistake my depression for my supposed surrender to their terms. Who knew? I could only try.

Greeting the doorman with as breezy a *buongiorno* as I could muster, I brushed past him and went to the elevator. A knock at Giovanni's brought Nonna to the door, and with a greeting and a smile, she let me in. Alex came rushing from his room and threw his arms about me, jabbering about one thing or another and leading me by the hand into the day room. There, warm sunlight fell in great splashes across the floor, and a soft breeze wafted in from the open doors leading to the balcony. Alex's friend, Antonio, sat on a bean bag watching TV. He turned and grinned as I came into the room. The scene itself seemed so homey and genteel, as if I should be glad to be part of it. It felt instead like a mockery.

Immediately they ganged up on me and begged to play "Cops and Robbers," like kids have done everywhere. Apparently, the game was best with at least a threesome, and I guessed they'd discussed it prior to my arrival that day. Normally, I didn't like the idea of Alex playing with even toy guns and us pretending to shoot one another, but the game was an intense one, and distraction was the one thing I needed at the moment. So we leapfrogged around the house with "guns" in hand, hiding behind first one piece of furniture then another, taking imaginary potshots till the apartment was fairly riddled with imaginary bullet holes. We laughed a lot, and they might have heard us through the whole building as we mouthed the repeated "Boom!" of pistols and the "Zing!" of ricocheting lead. I think in the end I "got it," but I might have taken one of them with me.

No one suspected a thing, and I left Alex that evening with a hug and smile, and a polite goodbye to the grandparents.

A special moment alone, taken by Alex's friend Antonio with my camera, unbeknownst to Alex and me

Once outside the building, though, that all changed. Standing across the street at the bus stop, I was consumed by rage. Visiting my own child as one visits a friend, never alone with him, begging to have a special outing, and that chaperoned . . . and now I couldn't even share my grief with him. His grandma gone, and he didn't even know. Standing on that street corner with traffic whizzing by, I stared at the apartment building across the street and hated.

Upon arriving home, I phoned Don and Judy at their hotel and arranged a meeting. A half hour later, they picked me up a block from home, and along with Temi and Carlo, we drove to a restaurant for the evening meal. Earlier, I couldn't eat, but anger had by then whetted my appetite. On the way, Don relayed condolences from Randy and Ian who had by that time sailed the boat back to its mooring at Licata.

After dinner, they took me back to their motel. I had brought along a change of clothes because Judy had insisted I spend the night with them. I was very grateful for the invitation. I remembered how it was just after Alex had been kidnapped. I loathed being alone in my California apartment. Everything reminded me of him. Friends would stop by and spend an inordinate amount of time filling the vacuum left by Alex.

That night, Don slept on the couch while I shared the bed with Judy. Comforted by their presence, I slept peacefully.

An interesting subject came up in conversation with Alex a few days later. He had been overeating and knew it—mostly sweets, which were routinely supplied by an over-indulgent Nonno, despite my earlier protestations—and he was beginning to feel the unintended consequences. He was getting a little pudgy, and some of the kids at school were beginning to notice—as they do at that age—and making it a special point of teasing. Alex had had enough. He wanted to get in shape. Would I help him?

He mentioned specifically the stadium a couple of blocks from Giovanni's apartment. The Stadio delle Palme or "Stadium of the Palms" was a massive, beautiful place, surrounded by palm trees and used during season for soccer matches. Italians are a soccer-fanatic lot, supporting their respective teams with a near military fervor. An Italian lottery, in which participants bet on teams, routinely netted a lot of money for those with an eye for the match winners. Especially on Sundays, the flow of traffic and pedestrians was phenomenal. Runners and walkers used the track beside it all the time in the off-season, and in fact, the area was a gathering place for sports enthusiasts of all kinds, from basketball players to gymnasts. Alex asked, with hope in his eyes, "Could we go jogging there one day soon?"

A great big light went on in my head. I knew the place well. It was perfectly situated, and with enough pedestrian activity to cover our retaking of Alex. We had to get permission from Giovanni for Alex to go, of course, but maybe that wouldn't be too hard since the effects of all that candy were obvious. I could almost envision the old man poking Alex's rounded tummy and saying with a grin, "Why not? A little exercise would do the boy good."

Even so, he would send along a chaperone or two to keep an eye on me, but I knew that "the gang" had dealt with those kinds of hindrances before.

With a strained nonchalance, I told Alex, "Go ahead. Ask your Nonno." Then added with a wink and a conspiratorial whisper, "But don't let him know I put you up to it. Tell me tomorrow what he said."

As my rigidly enforced time at the apartment was up for the evening, I wrapped Alex in a tight hug and kissed him, "See you tomorrow, kiddo. Love you."

Upon returning home, I met with the crew and, driving around, we discussed this newest opportunity. Right away, Don took off with it. "Perfect!" he exploded. "What a setup. All we have to do is make sure you get him to an exit where we'll be waiting with the car. Katie, this could be it!"

I was pretty jazzed myself, not just because of Don's irrepressible enthusiasm, but also because I was anxious to redirect their energies to what I thought would be a safer procedure. For the last couple of days, they had been discussing a previous idea—just going into the apartment in a lightning raid, past the grandparents, and taking Alex in one fell swoop. I nearly choked when I heard that. When options run out, these military folks have a tendency to shrug and plow through obstacles. They figured, quite simply, that they weren't about to go home without getting Alex for me. I was all for that, but I didn't want half the country after us because of how we went about it.

On the following visit to Alex, I asked whether he had queried Giovanni about a jog at the stadium. Yes, he told me, but hadn't received a definite answer. I clenched my jaw. "Okay," I said firmly, "Let's go ask him right now."

We marched into the dining room where Giovanni sat at the kitchen table reading a book, rigid as one of Michelangelo's masterpieces. In all the years I'd known the man, even during the times Massimo and I lived with them prior to my divorce, he'd preferred these straight-backed chairs to anything more luxurious, as if this borderline asceticism was good grooming for a more studious nature. He did look quite studious as his eyes skimmed across the book's pages and the intensity of the subject matter made him either oblivious or indifferent to our entrance. We stood there only a moment, then as a "Go ahead," I poked Alex in the back.

"Nonno," Alex said decisively, "Have you been thinking about what I asked you yesterday? Can we go to the stadium for a jog?"

His gaze lifted from the book. "Well, I guess it would be all right to go one of these afternoons," he replied distractedly.

Alex's face lit up. "Mamma, too?"

"Sure," he was being magnanimous and knew it.

Alex spun and gave me a hug. My heart raced, and I felt a little lightheaded. A slight grin creased Giovanni's face. Surely he would come along to keep an eye on us—he or Massimo, or

The stadium in Palermo

both—but that was to be expected. The important, crucial point was that he agreed.

Now, another, entirely different set of dominoes had been lined up. And the first one silently fell.

Normally, I hated leaving Alex but this time I could scarcely wait to get out of there so I could "make my report" to the rescue crew. Enthusiasm spread like wildfire, and I discovered that Don had already done some reconnaissance around the stadium and the adjoining areas. Outfitted in a new jogging suit and blessed with classical Italian looks, he blended in perfectly with other runners and sportsmen who frequented the stadium. By car, both he and Judy had also scouted out possible escape routes.

The following morning we all went to the stadium area for a look around. Arriving in two separate cars to deter suspicion, we canvassed the grounds, the running track, and the wall of bleachers that ringed it, carefully examining every exit and, with one eye on individuals or groups who passed us in their early morning routines, guardedly discussed our rescue and escape. Don told me to pay particular attention to the second exit, and as we swung past on our "tour," he outlined the plan.

Once on the track, I was to jog with Alex and whoever was to accompany us, and eventually try to pull ahead and get lost in the crowd. The second time around the track, and once safely out of sight among the other runners, I'd pretend to see Fabio's car outside the second exit in the parking lot and prompt Alex to go with me to check it out. Fabio, of course, would not be there. Instead, Don would be waiting for us to approach the vehicle in which Temi would be behind the wheel and Judy in the back seat. At the right moment, Judy would pop open the door and quickly slide over as I lifted Alex bodily and whisked him into the half-empty back seat. Then I'd jump in, wedging him between Judy and myself, and hopefully calming him down immediately.

The plan had a good chance of success because of the strong relationship between Fabio and Alex. It was cemented by, of all things, Fabio's Santa Claus impersonation two years earlier.

Though rather retiring in nature, one Christmas season, Fabio had overcome his shyness long enough to don the outlandish outfit requisitioned from a friend, and pay an impromptu visit to Giovanni's apartment during one of my daily visits with Alex. Nonna was a bit nonplussed when she opened the door and Fabio "ho-ho-hoed" his way inside, but what could she do—give Santa the boot? So Fabio played it to the hilt, and Alex was nearly delirious with joy at the visitation. Alex also had known that Fabio and I had been seeing each other for some time, and in his mind, this only strengthened the ties between us all.

Two days earlier, I had purchased a few little items for Alex in anticipation of the "snatch." At one of the outdoor markets, I bought some of the simple things I hadn't bought him for three years as a mother: a toothbrush, underwear, a couple of shirts, and a pair of pants. These I crammed into my overnight bag, along with a few of my own clothes and toiletries, plus my and Alex's passports. I stared at the bag before committing it to Judy's custody, thinking how pitifully small my life had become.

I could fit the whole shebang into a two-foot long fabric cylinder. Everything else would be left behind.

We all met the next morning and went over the plans thoroughly. Don had me translate Carlo's specific instructions; he was to be in a rental car parked at a predetermined place outside the city. After our escape with Alex, we would drive there and hurriedly switch vehicles, whereupon Carlo would leave an anonymous phone message with the rental agency, revealing the car's location. Afterward, he was to avoid the airport, and immediately take a boat back to Pantelleria. If he did as he was told, he'd be back home that night, with money in his pockets and no one the wiser. I repeated the instructions several times, asking him if he had questions or if anything needed clarifying. He vigorously affirmed his understanding, and I took that at face value. He left us then to drive to the switchover point.

That afternoon, we all went over the plan one last time before I left for my visit with Alex. Strangely, the fear in my heart had ebbed, and taking its place was a feeling of confidence bolstered by a suddenly iron will. Not knowing if this would be the day, I nonetheless prepared myself to play my part in the rescue. Everything would be in place. If it turned out to be a no-go, well, that's just the way it was, and we'd plan some more. But until I knew for sure, I determined to be ready to take my kid and run.

A short while later, I stepped off the bus at the stop across from Giovanni's apartment. It was an absolutely gorgeous Saturday afternoon, a perfect day for running off some excess poundage in the fresh air and sunshine. With my purse slung over my shoulder, I crossed the street, walked up the concrete steps to the entrance, and greeted the doorman in passing. While in the elevator, my nervousness returned, devilishly pricking holes in my nonchalant veneer. My mind raced: *What if Giovanni's changed his mind about letting Alex go with me? What if he's suddenly suspicious? Could he have found out about Mom? What if the whole family goes along, and we can't pull away from them, or if they've taken the precaution of having all the exits guarded? What if . . . what if . . . what if . . .*

Let into the flat by Nonna, I walked past Giovanni and went into Alex's room where he was setting some schoolbooks to one side for later homework. Immediately, and trying to keep the tension out of my voice, I asked him, "Well, are we going jogging today?"

Alex beamed, "Nonno said 'Yes!'" He grabbed my hand and squeezed it, "I'm going to run like crazy."

Keeping my breathing even, I smiled, "Oh, that's great, Sweetie. When can we go?"

Massimo's voice came from the other side of the doorway, "I'm coming."

He walked into the bedroom and stood there a moment, as if he expected a response, but I disappointed him. Frankly, I didn't trust myself to speak. I noticed that both he and Alex were rather overdressed for a jog, Massimo in his business suit and shiny shoes and Alex in his good school shirt and pants. *Surely, they're not going running like that*, I thought, but then I reasoned that maybe the grandparents hadn't expected Alex to take the outing seriously and actually run for any considerable distance. Maybe they thought he'd stroll around the track once or twice without breaking a sweat and then decide it wasn't enough fun. In the end it really didn't matter anyway, because if the team grabbed him, he wouldn't be doing any running anyway.

From the other room, Giovanni yelled out, "Are we going or not?" Alex grinned wide and pulled me to the door. Anna, Massimo's girlfriend, moved suddenly into the doorway. Startled, I pulled up short. Alex's friend, Antonio, suddenly appeared beside her, ducking under her arm and coming to stand beside Alex. "Come on!" he said, and we all filed out the open door. With Giovanni in the lead, we headed for the stairs at Alex's insistence to "get more exercise."

I couldn't believe this. The whole family was going along! How in the world was I going to get Alex away from the lot of them? The crew was already stationed in the parking lot and at the second exit. Would they call it off, I wondered, when they saw the odds swing dramatically against them? Conversely, I also thought that maybe that would be the last time I ever saw the inside of that apartment building.

Out in the bright sunlight, we crossed the busy intersection and walked quickstep the two city blocks to the stadium. To passersby, we looked like the typical Sicilian family on a Saturday outing. It was a lovely day for it. The palm trees all around the stadium and adjoining grounds swayed gently in the warm ocean breeze, and, hazy in the afternoon sun, the steep, green mountains formed a nearly idyllic backdrop. Inside the running track, off to one side of the stadium itself, the gaiety and abandon of the runners, gymnasts, and soccer players gave the place an almost carnival atmosphere. Had I indeed been happily married, surrounded by a warm and welcoming family, this could have been just the place to enjoy the afternoon.

In contrast, however, at night the mood around the stadium altered dramatically, taking on darker tones, especially around the parking lot and the bus stop immediately adjacent. Not realizing this when I first came to Sicily, I waited at this very bus stop while men cruised slowly past in fancy cars, eyeing me and making lewd comments. Revolted, and unable to understand, I moved away from the area to the stop across the street. Come to find out that the stadium area was unofficially the "pick-up spot" for local prostitutes. I was horrified, but counted myself fortunate that nothing went amiss my one time there. It could have ended very badly.

This day, we stood as a group just outside of the flood of runners flowing in a smooth, unbroken line around the track. Massimo paused to light up a big, fat cigar. That was one point in our favor. I thought something to the effect that a heavy smoker in dress shoes, who also hates exercise, shouldn't be too hard to lose. Also, Anna would keep pace with Massimo, not us. That's two down. Giovanni was in good shape, but about seventy years old. That, too, should count for something. Having Alex's little friend along as a jogging partner would be another issue entirely, but I couldn't stop to think too much about it. I reasoned that if this was indeed going down, it would all happen so fast that he wouldn't be a major problem. We all entered the running stream and took off.

Almost instantly, we lost Giovanni. He just disappeared. I thought maybe he had met a friend and stopped to talk. With a huge (fake) smile, I urged the boys into a faster pace. "Come on, you slowpokes! Can't you go any faster than that?"

Now they had to prove me wrong, and they kicked into high gear. The adrenaline was coursing through my system, so I had no trouble keeping up. I could have outsprinted anyone in that stadium at that point.

The first time around I spotted Don. He stood at the second exit in his running clothes, surrounded by a milling crowd and looking for the entire world like a jogger just taking a breather. Funny, how to me he stood out from the mob ebbing and flowing around him; it was as if he wore a great big flashing sign: "Keep back! Kidnapping in progress!" Surely, someone must have taken note of him and informed the police, who were even now closing in. They were watching me, too, I felt, Massimo's henchmen, maybe from the bleachers. Fear gnawed my stomach, and I suddenly wanted out of there, real bad, just to grab Alex and plow through the crowd to Don, and the waiting car.

I deliberately controlled my breathing to head off a panic attack and kept pace with the crowd, listening to the drumbeat of a thousand pairs of feet. So many people could be a good or bad thing: good if we could blend in with so many; bad because of so many potential witnesses of what they would naturally assume was a kidnapping. Don's eyes glanced off me, lingering just long enough to let me know he'd seen me. His presence imbued me with a sudden calm. Okay, Katie. Keep focused. Still not knowing if this was going to play out the way we rehearsed, I pressed on: weaving in and out of the fluid crowd, snatching a quick look over my shoulder every now and then to make sure Massimo wasn't close. Thankfully, he was nowhere to be seen.

An eternity later, it seemed, we approached our personal home stretch, our second time around the track. This was it. The second exit loomed into view. There was Don, and this time his eyes bore into me. I saw him back out of the exit into the parking lot. My heart was pounding, and I was afraid my voice would crack. "Hey," I blurted out, "isn't that Fabio's car over there?"

I pointed at the second exit, even as we bounced up and down in tandem. Alex's eyes lit up and he shouted excitedly, "Where?!"

"Over there, by the exit," I responded. "I really think it's him. Let's go see!"

Breaking from the crowd, the two boys and I trotted to the exit. I immediately noticed a middle-aged man in a jogging suit standing to one side, watching me intently. From his ears protruded two little white buds, and clipped on his pants pocket was a small dark walkman . . . or communication device. A panicked little thought whispered, *Oh, boy. They have their own people here.* Despite the heat, a chill snaked up my spine. I pointedly avoided looking at him and continued past him till just outside the exit. *They know*, I thought frantically, *they're all over the place. They've been watching us the whole time.* I stopped at the edge of the parking lot for a second and leaned over, as if to catch my breath, but it was a hesitance borne of fear. As I decided to bluff it out, the guy moved away from the exit and strode purposefully toward me. I nearly fainted. This is it. It's all over.

"*Mi scusi*," he said, and pointed to one side. "*Lo sa di chi e' questa moto?*"

My knees nearly buckled, and I felt like laughing out loud. I was so relieved I could have kissed him!

"No," I answered in Italian, "I don't know who owns that motorbike. Sorry."

With the key in the scooter's ignition, it was a prime target for theft. This Good Samaritan was just looking out for the other guy.

The kids and I hustled into the parking lot. There it was—the getaway car. It had been backed into the lot, facing the street. From behind the wheel, Temi stared fixedly at me. I could see Judy in the backseat, also watching. Don stood leaning against another vehicle within arm's reach of our own, appearing nonchalant as groups of runners swept past him both coming and going.

I don't ever remember actually getting to the car; we were suddenly just there. As Alex asked, "Where's Fabio?" The passenger's door flew open, and I leaned down to put my arm around Alex's waist. Don beat me to it. Like a coiled spring, he shot forward and swept Alex into the air and in one deft motion slid him into the backseat beside Judy. I literally jumped in after him and slammed the car door as Don jerked open his own door. The car was moving before he was completely inside.

"Go, go, go!" Don commanded, and the car roared to life.

Alex was crying, and I cradled his head and rocked him. The pitch of my voice sounded high. "We're going home to America, Sweetie. Don't worry. It's all right. We're going home. Your grandpa's waiting to see you."

It all took place so fast, so intensely that I don't even remember what happened to Alex's little friend who was running with us. Later, I learned he was questioned by police about the snatch.

As we sped away, Judy exclaimed, "Look!." She pointed out the windshield to a young woman in a red sweater taking down our license plate number. Temi punched the accelerator, and we rocketed forward. We hadn't gone a hundred feet when the car squealed to a sharp stop, throwing us all violently forward. Another vehicle had pulled, broadside, directly in front of it. We all said it at once—"No!"—thinking that it was an unmarked police car that had been assigned to bar our way of escape. Coming out of nowhere, having to weave professionally in and out of the crowd, it seemed the whole thing had been a setup. But that quick, the car gunned it and veered off into traffic. Just another crazy Sicilian driver!

Temi punched it, and we sped into traffic, skimming from one lane to the other, per Sicilian custom, and screeched to another abrupt halt, this time behind several cars stopped for a red light. Don kicked open the car door and shot into the street, racing from one car to the next, slamming on the hood of each and shouting, "Emergenci-a! Emergenci-a!"

The cars in front parted immediately, and Don dashed back inside. Temi hit the gas, and we were on our way again.

The dramatic mood swings caused by an adrenaline surge seem crazy to anyone who hasn't experienced them. The emotions somehow need to get out, often inanely. Don had no sooner gotten back into the car when the tension broke with chuckling and nervous jibes. What Don had meant to say was "Emergenza!" but instead had kicked into the American habit of adding an "a" to the end of the word, ridiculously hoping to improve his faux-Italian dialect.

"Nice accent, Don," Judy kidded.

Temi chimed in, "Yeah, cool. I like-a the way-a you-a talk-a."

Don threw up his hands, "Well, I didn't know how to say it!"

About twenty minutes of high-speed driving later, we reached the second car, and Carlo. He hadn't known whether we'd be there today or not, and on seeing us he launched himself out of the car, standing beside it as we pulled to a smooth, sudden stop. With barely a word, Temi and Carlo exchanged keys, and we all piled inside, this time with Don at the wheel. He put it into gear, and we lit out again at Sicilian speed.

Poor Carlo. We later found out that he had disregarded his part of the rescue plan and hung around Sicily a few days, living it up with his part of the payoff. I could have slapped him. He had been repeatedly warned to adhere to the three most important rules of bit playing in this kind of operation—follow orders, follow orders, *follow orders*! It didn't take long for the police to nab him. I heard they gave him a pretty rough time, and he spilled all he knew. He spent some time in jail.

After switching cars, Alex had stopped crying but was exhibiting symptoms of mild shock. I kept soothing him with words about home, hotdogs, movies, and of course, his grandparents. A few days earlier, Judy had taken the precaution of buying a Game Boy, knowing Alex would need some distracting until he got used to the idea of his sudden liberation. Granted, it was a rough way to be set free since there had been no way to prepare him. He fingered the Game Boy and made some tentative plays on it, but emotionally drifted in and out awhile. All the time, I reiterated that these were all friends, helping us be together, to get home safely. I know he understood, but with his emotions all in a whirl, it was still very hard for him. He didn't really begin to come out of it until, at one point, Don and Temi had pulled over for a moment to look at a map and quickly discuss the best route out of there. Alex looked up and said suddenly, "I know this place."

It was the first time he'd spoken, and his voice broke some of the tension. Both men turned around and Don, smiling, gave him a closer look at the map. "So, you recognize it, huh?"

Alex nodded, leaning close and pointing at one specific spot on the map. "We went to the beach here once."

He seemed to feel a little better about the situation after that, sometimes even joining the conversation and offering suggestions.

He always retreated again into himself, however, and for the most part remained quiet.

Poor little kid. I wished there had been a cleaner way to do this, an easier transition. Thoroughly confused, he was glad to be with Mom but scared in the company of these wild, friendly strangers who had stormed into his well-ordered world. He had long been accustomed to the idea that he would be spending the rest of his life in Sicily, that Italian would be his primary language, and that the customs and religion of this land were his. Indeed, though he had flashbacks of good times in the U.S., he showed every sign of becoming completely assimilated into Sicilian society. He was rapidly becoming a native son. For all of us to sweep in like a Mediterranean cyclone and sever him from all he'd become accustomed to in the past three years, no doubt, seemed unnecessarily painful. I consoled myself with the idea that although he didn't fully understand at the moment, he would soon. The important thing was to get him off the island. As long as we were stuck here, the bonds would continue to exert their influence on him. All I could do then was hold him close, whisper assurances, and trust the professionals.

We stayed off the main roads, rightly fearing that, by now, police had mobilized and roadblocks and/or checkpoints would be set up at strategic points. With the sailboat waiting in Licata, this diversion threw a monkey wrench into our plans. There was no real way of determining a time factor. With all of the minor back-country roads we found ourselves on in the past few hours, our arrival at the dock would be put off. Ian and Randy had already been alerted, so they'd be prepared to cast off at moment's notice. The problem lay in getting there.

At one point, we discovered that our paved road, heading inland from the coast, turned suddenly to gravel, then to nothing at all. It simply dead-ended. We were lost. While unforeseen, it was totally understandable. Like everywhere else that had huge tracts of farmland and backcountry, networks of roads known only to locals never appeared in detail on maps of any kind.

Assuming they'd always actually lead somewhere, even if going in our generally plotted direction, proved a mistake. Backtracking a few miles, we wound up on a hill overlooking a sea of low brush. Don pulled the car to a gentle stop and turned off the engine. Throwing one arm over the back of the driver's seat and turning to look at us, he sighed, "Okay, this is it for now. We keep driving, we're gonna wind up going in circles. Let's go over the map carefully, and stay put till dark. It's far too dangerous to keep on like this while it's still daylight."

Alex sat quietly, his mouth a firm, tight line. Judy fished in her purse and turned to him, smiled, and held out a candy bar. It was one of his favorites. He politely but guardedly refused. "Come on," she coaxed, "let's see that million dollar smile."

Unaccountably, something clicked, and he gave her one of those big, beautiful grins that had always thrown sunshine into my dark world. The car's interior fairly lit up, and he dug into that candy like it was the last one on the planet. The smell of chocolate, the sounds of munching, and the back-and-forth of unimportant chatter did a lot to lighten the oppression of being hunted.

The waiting was the worst part. Between Don's staring at the sky and murmuring "Come on, come on!" to a waning sun, and all the while keeping my own anxiety in check, the minutes just dragged. As the men studied the map and quietly discussed our next move, Judy, Alex, and I all took turns going out into the bushes to relieve ourselves while the others stood guard. There wasn't much to guard against, honestly, but it was better than doing nothing at all.

It seemed like hours, but eventually twilight eased across the cloudless sky, muting the green of the brush and blurring the land's contours. We lingered awhile longer till the shadows deepened, then drove to the highway below us. Once on the blacktop, the road was ours alone. A route had been decided upon, and from that point on we drove mostly in silence. While the professionals scanned the road and kept their ears open for pursuing police, I luxuriated in my son's presence. Sitting in the back seat, listening idly to the hum of the car's motor, I don't think my arms ever left Alex for a full minute. I cradled him, leaned my head on his own, and kissed his cheek. He was mine now. Just let them try to take him back. This time I'd fight.

A half hour later, we entered a village that, on the map, seemed sleepy and uninteresting, a perfect portal to pass right through without incident. We picked the wrong day for that to happen. Once within the village perimeter, we were literally swarmed with people, a carefree, slowly moving mob of hundreds that eddied around our little car and hemmed us in. Many were eating ice cream or other snacks bought from street vendors, and it seemed as if we'd just missed a big event, a parade or something. We later surmised that the celebration was in honor of a patron saint. As there was no room for our car to maneuver or turn around, Don just smiled and waved, slowly bulling his way through.

I lay nearly prostrate on the floor with Alex who, by that time, had in heart joined our little cadre and was doing his part willingly. Judy nearly splayed out on top of us, as much as possible shielding us from view with the lower part of her body. I risked a peek now and then and drew my breath in sharply. They were all around us, passing by the window above me just a handbreadth away. I could hear what seemed like a million voices, filling the night with laughter and idle conversation. My main concern was that nobody would get peeved enough to call the local cops on the only driver anywhere in sight. Looking around a bit too late, we spotted the moveable barriers that indicated the road had been closed to vehicular traffic, so we were clearly in violation. We all hoped that Sicilians' casual disregard for traffic laws would extend to us in this situation.

It did. As soon as we escaped the human tide, we hit the road that led out of there to Licata. An hour's drive took us to our next big juncture, which I believe was Agrigento. A major city, it contained lots of people, lots of police. Don pulled over into a wide spot, and we all sat silently for a moment, staring at

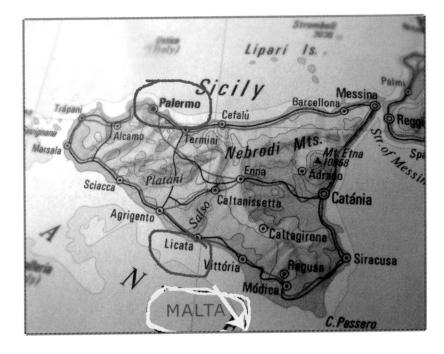

the string of street lamps that lit the way across a bridge leading into the city. In the backseat, Judy studied the map.

"Any way we can get around it and still get to Licata?" Don asked.

Judy shook her head. Her voice was somber. "Not that I can tell. There's only one road straight through, and we're on it."

Don grimaced, took a deep breath, and moved the car forward. There was no way of telling whether a checkpoint barred our route or even if the police had been put on alert this far from Palermo. We were by that time a considerable distance from Palermo, and with no way of knowing our planned route, the law would be kept reasonably busy scouting out possible departure points. For all they knew, we were still in the city, holed up somewhere in a safe house till the heat was off. Or we could have launched out by small boat from any one of a hundred spots along the coast or boarded a private floatplane huddled in an isolated cove. Plus, they had no idea how many conspirators had actually been involved in the rescue and whether they were friends or hired professionals.

Through Sarah, I later learned that the first place they checked was my apartment in Mondello. Escorted by the police, Massimo pounded on my door and screamed in Italian, "Come on out, Katie! We know you're in there! You're not going to get away with this. Open up!"

Some of my shocked neighbors stood on their balconies and craned to see the commotion, while others hurriedly filed into the little courtyard to inquire directly of the police. As the officers explained that I was a kidnapper, one of my neighbors snorted loudly in disgust. "Ha!" she yelled, pointing at Massimo, "He's the kidnapper! Don't you know that he took Katie's child illegally from the United States?"

I was told that at that point, the officers became silent, turned, and glowered at Massimo. Obviously that was the first time they'd been told the flip side to this story.

During the drive through Agrigento, Alex and I took our assigned places on the floor of the car, while Judy slid over as much as possible to make it look as if she occupied the space. Keeping our heads down the whole time, we could only make out the incessant flash of streetlamps or the headlights of oncoming vehicles and hear the usual clamor of traffic as we entered the city. Everyone in the car fell silent. Don slipped easily into the traffic stream and kept up a fast, steady drive for the ten or so minutes it took to get through Agrigento. When the cacophony of traffic sounds died away, I lifted my head and peered out the window, watching the city peel away behind.

About an hour later, we began seeing road signs alerting us of our approach to Licata. My heart thumped wildly as we entered the town, and I involuntarily tightened my hug around Alex. Everyone grew quiet. I didn't know exactly where the sailboat was moored, but had been told by Judy that Ian and Randy had been put on alert just prior to Alex's rescue. They'd be ready to shove off at a moment's notice. There had been no communication with the two of them since. For all they knew, the raid had been aborted, or we'd been captured, or delayed through having to skirt multiple checkpoints. Or for that matter, we might still be on the road or holed up in some impromptu safe house till pursuit died down. Though Ian and Randy had already been through multiple rescue operations, each time was different, with logistics sometimes varying from moment to moment. The longer we delayed, the higher the tension would rise. Their eyes would be glued to the road leading to the docks.

Our car slowed as we began passing scattered groups of people. Abruptly, we were swarmed again, nearly engulfed in a crowd of partiers eating ice cream, laughing, gesticulating in fluent Sicilian. Another celebration, a big one! This was incredible. All I wanted was to pass quietly through town, get to the boat, and get out of there. Again, this could mean thousands of witnesses or a chance to get lost in the crowd. I only hoped the police weren't out in force to maintain order.

The city docks were right ahead. I could see our sailboat—that beautiful, sleek, gleaming white sea bird waiting to swoop us away—sitting motionless, tied up at a slip by itself, for a quick getaway. Ian and Randy stood lounging on the dock beside the boat, and when they spotted us, they immediately scrambled into action, one aboard to start the engine and one by the cleats to loosen the mooring lines as soon as we boarded. Don pulled smoothly into the parking lot and the car disgorged the lot of us almost before a full stop. Judy shoved my small overnight bag into my hand and motioned for Alex and me to follow. None of us spoke. Over the cacophony of the mob of celebrants, our hurried footsteps on the concrete sounded loud and hollow. Don drove a short distance away to park the car, leaving the keys in the ignition. If Carlo did his job, the auto rental agency would be contacted anonymously tomorrow and informed of the location of both vehicles. Don raced over to us and in one lithe movement leaped onboard.

The boat's engine was already humming. As we eased smoothly away from the dock and out into the dark Mediterranean, Judy grabbed my arm and nearly breathlessly said, "Katie, look!"

From the stern of the boat, we watched as the land receded, the sky above us now aflame with the most spectacular fireworks display I'd ever seen. Chills ran up my spine. It seemed so propitious, as if God Himself were giving us a sign of His good favor. I nearly cried right there. With a huge smile, Judy, still looking skyward along with me, said, "Katie, this is for us. It's our farewell."

Farewell indeed. Goodbye, Sicily, and good riddance. If I never saw that island of pain again, it would suit me fine. As the boat picked up speed, I faced forward into the gathering wind and stared at a sea no longer dark, but red, gold, and celestial blue. It was a good sign. At that moment, a joy flooded me, and I felt that I really was free.

None of us could have known that the hunter had already begun a chase that would cross continents.

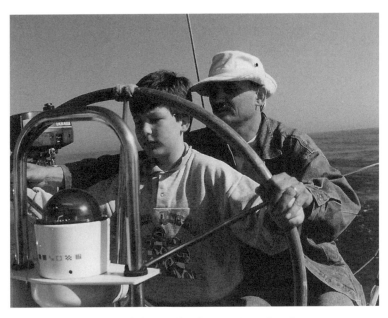

Sailing to Gozo and then Malta the morning after the escape—
Don with Alex here

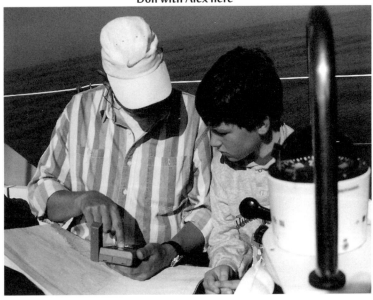

Ian showing Alex the GPS and where we are

13

Hopscotch

**Scappari d'un cozzu di cuteddu.
To barely escape. (lit. To escape by the
thickness of a knife's edge.)**

$\mathcal{I}$ awoke the next morning to the sounds of muted conversation and footsteps on the wooden deck directly overhead. Warm sunlight flooded the cramped sleeping quarters, and I could feel the sailboat buoyed along on rhythmic swells that seemed much like the soft, relaxed breathing of the child beside me. My child. Smiling to myself, I gently tightened my embrace on Alex and lay without moving, relishing the sensation of uninterrupted motherhood.

How long I had wanted to do this! It's impossible to overstate the significance of that moment. For three horrendous years unable to provide the least things required of me, as a mother, I now had the opportunity to actually put my arms around Alex and go to sleep with him beside me, and no one could forbid it. The joy was almost more than I could bear. Last night, before crawling into this tight little space, really only big enough for one, Alex had brushed his teeth with—yes!—a toothbrush that I'd bought for him. I hadn't been allowed that luxury since he'd been kidnapped. Massimo and his parents had provided Alex with all the necessities, I suppose, to prevent what they had considered inconvenient emotional attachments between Alex and me. Now, on the run, he literally had nothing but the clothes on his back, and all that I alone could provide for him. I felt restored and vindicated, heroic, almost.

Alex stirred, smiled, hugged me, and then got up to use the bathroom. After my turn, we went topside where the men had stood watch in shifts all night long. Judy stood with Don, leaning against a rail, and grinned real big when she saw us.

"How'd you sleep?"

I smiled. "Like a rock." Glancing down at my rumpled clothes, I halfheartedly tried to smooth out some of the creases. I must have looked a mess, but my appearance seemed so unimportant right then. Down below, I'd run a comb quickly through my hair and call it good, wanting only two things—a cup of coffee and the sight of land. The quicker we got to Malta, the sooner we'd be shooting toward Cairo, then home.

After Alex was introduced all around—he was immediately accepted as "one of the gang"—Ian showed him the little GPS unit he was using to fix our position. Always curious and now feeling he belonged, he explored the boat bow to stern and asked a flurry of questions. Reading the map and helping plot course, taking a turn at the wheel with Don helping guide his hand, and scanning the sea ahead for any sign of land all sent him happily spinning away into every boy's dream. The whole ordeal had suddenly become the adventure of a lifetime.

I sat watching him for quite a while, listening to the sound of his voice and drinking in his presence. At the moment, the situation seemed more like a family outing than anything else. The sky domed above in a flawless blue, with only a few streamers of brilliant white cloud skirting the horizon. The wonderfully placid Mediterranean hugged our little boat to its blue-green waters, and nothing, nothing in the world seemed amiss. If we hadn't been on the run, I could have gone on like that forever.

Then I remembered Mom, and the knife again cut deep. I couldn't keep Alex in the dark about it. He'd be expecting Gramma when we arrived in the States, and it wasn't fair to hide this from him. Taking him aside, I sat him down, and stroking his hair while his eyes searched mine, my heart broke. "Sweetie," I said gently, "I know it's been a lot for you to go through, but

I have to tell you something. It's not good news." Alex became very serious, saying nothing, watching intently.

Taking a deep breath, I squeezed his shoulder and said, "Grandma died a few days ago, while having the surgery I told you about. I didn't want to say anything the day it happened or days after because of our situation. I'm so sorry, Honey."

The look on his face I'll never forget. His whole demeanor crumpled, and the joy of only a moment earlier fled away. Holding him a long moment, I fought back the tears I hadn't been allowed to publicly shed over her passing. Alex leaned onto me as we sat there, swaying with the sea's rhythm while the warm breeze played over us.

"Hey, I know this place!"

Hours had passed since our talk, and the crew, knowing our sadness, had not intervened awhile. Alex took a solitary turn around the boat, working through his own personal grief journey. Silent for a time, he suddenly piped up when he saw the island.

"That's Gozo! We learned about it in school!"

Sure enough, Gozo loomed directly ahead, and it was a mere hop from there to Malta, then a plane trip to Cairo, then home.

While some of the crew chimed in with "Good job, Alex!," Don suggested we go ashore and find a pay phone. It would be good, he said, to find out what was happening in Sicily.

"Who do I call?" I asked, my anxiety suddenly spiking.

Don shrugged. "Who are you close to? Who can you trust not to give you away?"

Immediately I thought of Sarah. She would give me the scoop on the police mobilization over our "kidnapping." With the sailboat as close to the island as possible, Don and I launched out in the little fiberglass dinghy, which had been lashed to the sailboat's flank. A few minutes later, we hit the pebbled shore and pulled the tiny craft onto the beach. Directly ahead was what appeared to be a restaurant, closed for Sunday, and to one side of it, a pay phone. As soon as Don made fast the dinghy, we sprinted across the beach to the phone. Standing beside me and prepping me with questions to ask, Don craned his head as close to the phone as he could while I dialed. After a long pause, a man's voice answered.

I swallowed hard, "Hi, Stefano. It's me, Katie." I felt ridiculous, like I should have said, *How's everything going? We're all having a great time. Sun's out, sea's calm. Alex? Oh, you know Alex—made it through the kidnapping just fine . . .*

Stefano's booming voice jolted me back to reality. "Katie! What have you done? Do you know half the Sicilian police force is combing the island for you and your friends?"

Taken aback at his tone, I let the anger seep into my own voice. "Hold on. Alex is mine, remember."

"Katie, you have to come back. It'll be better that way. But you have to do it now!"

Incredulous, I shot back, "You're kidding, right? No way. I've got my son, and I'm keeping him."

"Where are you now?"

I pinched my lips together and fumed.

"Katie, tell me where you are . . ."

I slammed the phone down. I simply couldn't believe it that Stefano had spoken to me that way. What was with all the inane accusations? He knew the situation from day one and had been a stalwart compatriot through the past three years. Boy, was I hot. Some friend! I angrily relayed to Don what he hadn't been able to hear for himself. He drew in his breath sharply, "Okay, let's go. Their phone might've been tapped."

Scrambling back to the dinghy, we shoved off and once aboard, the crew gunned the engine.

A short while later, the sailboat eased into the marina and pulled up to an empty slip. Don barked orders as Ian and Randy leaped from the deck to tie her fast. The rest of us hustled off the boat and put as much distance as we could from the rescue vessel. Judy had selected a hotel nearby, and we booked in for a day. In the room, she urged me to call my dad and tell him the good news.

With the phone pressed against my face, I broke down as soon as he answered and half sobbing said, "Apuka . . . we got him. We got him."

Before he could say anything, his composure broke. I could hear him weeping freely over the other end. His sobs spurred mine afresh, and for a moment, we wept together for both the success of the mission and over the loss of his beloved wife and my mother. Our reunion on American soil, I knew, would be bittersweet. Oh, how I wish Mom had lived to hear this news!

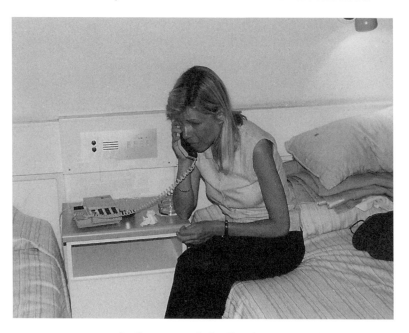

Crying and talking to my dad, telling him we got Alex

I handed Alex the phone and for a few brief moments he and his grandpa talked—Alex of his invigorating experience and happiness at being with his mom, and Dad of his eagerness to see us both again and hold us to himself. We talked about fifteen minutes. We might have to leave at a moment's notice, and

I couldn't afford to be in the middle of a long-distance phone call. Afterward, the three of us took turns showering, then settled down to wait.

Three scary hours passed before the men showed. They'd had to clean the boat thoroughly, Don explained, and then waited around while the owners inspected their vessel. Then he dropped the bombshell, "The family knows we're here."

My blood froze.

"How do you know?" Judy prompted. She was alarmed, but threw up a shield over her emotions.

Heaving a sigh, Don slid his gaze from one of us to the other, while Temi, Ian, and Randy stood looking on. "I'm not sure, except that the two guys who rented us the boat were asking all sorts of questions—who was on the boat besides us, where had we gone, that kind of thing. Too suspicious to be coincidence. Plus, I made a few inquiries of my own."

He leveled a calm but firm look at me. "I'd had a hunch that your friends' phone was tapped. I was right. The family knows where we are now."

My voice was drawn taut as piano wire, "We have to get out of here."

Judy came to sit beside me and draped a comforting arm over my shoulder. Don half grinned, a fleeting gesture. "We need to sit tight. We've got plane reservations, and by midnight, we'll be on our way to Cairo. Let them find us there, if they can."

It was a challenge, but not a very firm one. Even if they didn't track us down before our flight left, it would be a simple matter for them to check departure records and follow us, or worse, have us detained by the authorities once we landed. My fear of spending time in an Egyptian jail nearly brought on a wave of nausea. Our time aboard ship came back with a vengeance. It had been so idyllic on the water, as if we could sail into eternity on placid seas, under a warm morning sun. For a few fleeting hours everything had been perfect, so perfect that I'd forgotten the danger. No, we had not escaped yet; we'd only been in the eye of the storm.

During this kind of wild, covert operation, a good many things remain hidden. The whole picture comes together later when the dust settles. While on the run, we only saw bits and pieces of things outside our immediate sphere. At the time, we had no way of knowing that since their phone line had been tapped, neither Stefano nor Sarah could risk giving encouragement when I had called. What had seemed a betrayal was merely playacting. And as I would realize while pondering the whole escapade years later, everyone involved played a part, became characters in their own right, sometimes reading from their own hastily written scripts.

When night fell, we all ventured out to eat dinner and killed the remaining time before our flight. Busy as usual, Don had made some more discreet inquiries and found the search for us was still going full bore. None of his Malta contacts could offer any new information as to the whereabouts of Massimo's family or if any of them had yet arrived.

Also, we were unsure where the Maltese authorities stood. My first time on the island, three years earlier, the woman at the American embassy had informed me of the local police's reluctance to become involved in what they considered a domestic affair. Since according to the Italian courts, I was still technically

Massimo's wife, my retaking Alex could be considered, by Maltese law, to be a private situation, and they might declare an official hands-off. We could only hope.

Dinner that night was quite the affair. Instead of being over-burdened with the seriousness of the situation, the whole crew ate, laughed, and chattered away like they hadn't a care in the world. We were the typical group of tourists again, carefree and big spenders, and none of the other patrons gave us a second glance. Alex did himself proud. In honor of his impending trip back to the country of his birth, he ordered a footlong hot dog. The lot of us guffawed and poked him when the waiter laid the prodigious sandwich before him, and Alex dug in like a true American. Although he came up a bit short, he managed to polish off most of the dog and sat back in his seat with a Cheshire-cat grin. He then turned to me and asked if we could go for a walk, just the two of us.

I looked at Judy and she nodded, cautioning us to stay close. As the restaurant faced the waterfront, the group had a clear view of us coming and going and would be able to run interference in a heartbeat if the moment warranted it. Although quite anxious, I didn't want to betray my fears to Alex, so I took him by the hand, and we strolled out into the warm Malta night.

It was a lovely few minutes alone, together. Boats bobbed languidly in the dark sea, and the gently moving reflection of the streetlights on the water was mesmerizing. The air was rich with the scent of cliffs and sea.

We talked about simple things, in quiet tones, walking slowly. I realized that for Alex, it was beginning to sink in, really, and that he was thinking ahead to his return to the States. It was not an easy thing, this uprooting from his adopted home. He loved Sicily, in a boyhood way, but he had been rudely thrust into a man's role and was coming to grips with the challenge. Things would never be the same for him, and he knew it.

We did not go far, and on our return, we saw the crew filing out of the restaurant and heading our way. We all met and commenced the short walk back to the hotel.

Once there, for the most part Alex and I just watched the others. They naturally had a whole lot more gear to pack than either of us. One small denim carry bag with a shoulder strap did it for the two of us. I couldn't help thinking again how little a person's life must be to pack it all into something that could fit into a plane's overhead compartment. I also wondered, with a certain fear, if this would reflect our coming life in the States. I didn't waste time kidding myself. Massimo had powerful connections, and his ruthless insistence on getting his own way might well translate into having us followed all the way home. No one who's never lived in Sicily as a working person can really grasp the intricacies of power, politics, and connections. There, enough money can buy virtually anything one might desire, legal or otherwise, and the tendrils of this dark network reached a long way. It would be a simple matter for Massimo to hire a tail, an agent of his own who could go where he himself could not, and make it difficult for us to live a normal life.

While waiting for the others, Alex fell asleep on the bed. I lay quietly down beside him, studying every line of his young face, softly stroking his hair. For Temi, Randy, and Ian, this would be goodbye; they had flight reservations to London at the same time as our departure to Cairo. There was sadness to this separation that I hadn't anticipated. In the two months we'd been together, I'd grown to love them all and see them as my heroes. I'd watched them closely, been an intricate part of their planning, and relished their camaraderie in this dangerous game of subterfuge. Along with Don and Judy, they'd been a wonderful stabilizing influence in my life when I'd needed it most. Now, with them heading in another direction, I couldn't help feeling as if our "family" was breaking up. What would I do without them?

A little after eleven o'clock, Don phoned for a taxi, which met us at the hotel entrance. Oddly, it was an open jeep, with barely room for all of us plus our luggage. We all piled in and held on for dear life while the driver, a silent, intense guy, veered wildly through winding streets like a 1920s bootlegger trying to shake a Fed off his tail. I kept waiting for some of the luggage (or one of us!) to spill over the side with each two-wheeler around sharp corners. We made it to the airport after only a few minutes' drive, hurriedly got out of the taxi and paid the driver off with a generous tip. With our adrenaline levels going through the roof, we stood a brief moment and looked at each other. Here it was—split-up time. Don, Judy, Alex, and I would go on to Cairo, while the rest of my heroes would head to other compass points. We hugged, exchanged well wishes, and I kissed every one of them on their stubbled cheeks. Then they were gone, luggage in hand, vanishing into the airport complex.

The remaining four of us walked to the entrance. When we reached the "In" ramp, the doors slid open by themselves, and the sudden, gaping hole seemed more like a portal to some alternate universe. It was my gateway out of an abusive, hellish three years.

Inside, our footsteps loudly echoed from the hard, polished floor. With the exception of a few idling airport personnel, the place was dead. I wasn't sure if this was a blessing or not. We'd

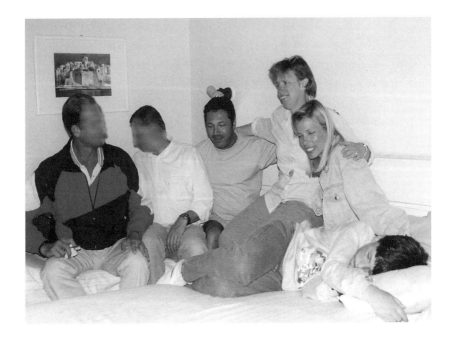

been so accustomed to having our movements masked by melting into the crowds that I felt the sudden emptiness of our surroundings made us stick out like the fugitives we were. I kept trying to swallow, but my throat was dry. My heart was pounding so hard I was sure that, by itself, it would attract attention to us. Doing my best to look like a carefree tourist with her son, I followed Don and Judy to the first checkpoint.

As agreed upon beforehand, Don held all passports and airline tickets. With nerves of steel, he and Judy stood unconcernedly while the guards perused our papers. We had less than an hour till departure time. If we were held here for any reason, even for a short while, we'd miss the flight and have to figure out another quick way off the island. Inside I was screaming; outside I was holding my breath. I needn't have worried. With a rather bored look, the guards handed back our papers and waved us through, and without incident, we made it to the boarding area. When the plane finally taxied to the gate, I believed I'd never seen such a lovely sight. Big, beautiful, and sleek, it was our deliverance to another life. Getting aboard and settling into our seats, we all sat rigid and barely breathing till the engines roared and the world tilted below us. Tension eased away like air escaping from a pricked balloon. I cranked the seat into a recline position, eased my head back and, still holding Alex's hand, slid into a contented sleep.

Cairo was unlike any city I'd ever seen. Noisy, dirty, and frenetic, it was a confusing jumble of bumper-to-bumper traffic leading through both wide, people-choked avenues and streets skinny enough to spit across. Women in hijabs and men in long cotton shirts that fell past the knees, street vendors hawking their various wares, and everywhere the staccato of Arabic all combined to wash over me in an unexpected culture shock. Dawn light was just beginning to gild the tops of the highest buildings as our taxi driver navigated his official jalopy, alternating his chatting with us and pointing out landmarks with the occasional angry shout at other drivers and fist shake out the open driver's window. He seemed to have perfected his alarming driving style in Sicily.

Fifteen minutes later we pulled up at our hotel, a five-star establishment a stone's throw from the Nile River. Judy had mentioned beforehand that in the Middle East, it is best to stay in hotels that afford very good, if not luxury, accommodations. To set up in some Egyptian dive is just looking for trouble. Such an obvious move is expected of fugitives, and lower rate quarters come with their own dangers from opportunistic locals. A five-star setup gave our group an air of respectability, completing the tourist veneer we hoped would thwart any questions from the wrong sources. At any rate, we wouldn't be there long, just a few hours then on to the border. Once we crossed into Israel, Don thought, we'd be pretty much home free. Massimo wouldn't dare follow us into Israeli territory.

We checked in and took the elevator to our room, a nice setup with a double bed and a couple of cots. What we needed most was sleep. At that point, I could have zonked out on my feet. But there was no rest for Don. He immediately left to ferret out some information.

The professionalism of these people is astounding. Where they get the energy, nerve, smarts, I'll never know. The whole thing has always been beyond me, how, even when all the details haven't been worked out and they are winging it, as a team they possess an eel-like maneuverability that enables them to evade danger or pursue quarry clear to the other side of the globe. Plus, they seem to have an encyclopedic knowledge of tricks and techniques for dealing with everything from avoiding detection to engaging in effective counter-surveillance. Judy one time showed me a simple yet effective method for "tenting" documents (such as a coded or private message) that needed to be quickly burned to ashes to keep it out of the wrong hands. I don't think I'll ever need to use that one, but on thinking back, it's still very cool that I could do it if I had to.

After a couple hours' nap, the three of us woke and showered, wanting to be refreshed for the drive to the border. About the time the last of us got out of the shower, Don entered the hotel room. His expression was haggard, and his eyes bloodshot from lack of sleep. There apparently was no bad news because only three things were on his mind at the time—a hot shower, a good meal, and a soft bed. It was quite late (or early, depending on how you look at it!), so after Don's shower we all crashed.

The next morning, Don disappeared again while the rest of us sat down in the hotel restaurant for breakfast. "I'm gonna check things out," he said quickly. "I'll be back shortly."

When he returned, he mentioned that he had touched base with some of his contacts in Cairo, and we'd have to wait for some feedback. He had an inkling that Massimo would send someone from the consulate here or maybe the police, but so far, it was a no-show. We'd be moving on tomorrow anyway, but a lot could happen in twenty-four hours. I knew Massimo well. He was enraged that we'd pulled a fast one and his pride wouldn't let him call it quits just because we'd left Sicily. At this moment, he was busy hunting the lot of us, and if he could find out we were in Cairo, he'd be here like a shot.

Don and Judy were a bit more relaxed, however. After breakfast, we mostly hung around the hotel lounge area, talked, and watched Alex cavorting in the pool. We later went on a short walk beside the Nile River (which was close to the hotel), then back to our temporary home base to lounge around some more. The hotel food certainly helped ease away the hours. Such an assortment of cakes, pies, and pastries! Who'd have thought Egyptians were so big on sweets? Complemented with the ritzy setting, I could have closed my eyes and imagined myself a jetsetter on the French Riviera. I'd never known running from the law could be so much fun!

Because Don had yet to hear any new information from his contacts, he suggested we do the tourist thing and take in the pyramids after lunch. Yes! The image of that outdated book Fabio used to read aloud to me as a sedative flashed into my mind, followed swiftly by an image of Fabio himself. Sweet, protective Fabio . . . I wondered briefly if we'd meet again. He had been such strength to me, and I owed him, big time.

Under the warm Egyptian sun, we played "tourist" to the hilt—camel rides around the pyramids and the Sphinx, a fascinating trip deep into the close confines of a pharaoh's tomb, strolling on desert sands that had known the sandaled feet of both king and slave. For a history buff like me, it was an incredible experience. Coupled with Alex's sudden liberation and my own from our island-prison, the giddy whir of joy had me spinning emotionally upward into the hot blue sky.

I'd wanted to stay to see the sunset over the pyramids, but we had to get back. We were still on the run, after all. Don absented himself while we rested in our hotel room, but he was back within an hour. His face was taut.

"We gotta roll," he said with urgency. "My people tell me that Massimo's right here in Cairo, with some other guy—who, I don't know—and they're checking the hotels as I speak. It's only a matter of time till they check here."

Shocked, I literally felt my jaw drop. Instinctively I reached out and drew Alex to me. I had expected determination from Massimo, but nothing quite so drastic. My voice trembled, incredulous, "How did they find us?"

"He was only an hour behind us when we left Malta. It wasn't too hard to figure out where we'd gone from there. I guess he hired a chopper and pilot and came here express."

Judy was already stuffing her travel bag, and I hurried to stow what few items we had brought out for our overnighter. We exited the room in two minutes flat.

Once in the lobby, Don told us to stay together while he located a taxi driver. Standing to one side of the lobby with Judy, I felt like I glowed neon, like everyone in the building could tell I was a fugitive. Instinctively, I tried to shield Alex from view, in case Massimo strode through the hotel doorway breathing fire. I was truly terrified, and only Judy's gentle grip on my arm bulwarked me against a panic attack.

"Where are we going?" I whispered, my eyes darting around the room. There was a scattering of people of varying nationalities in the lobby, but no one seemed to notice us.

Me, Judy, and Alex—In the lobby in the Cairo hotel before our quick getaway to crossing the border into Israel. I was very nervous here standing in the lobby, knowing that Massimo and his guys were in Cairo looking for us. We were waiting for our driver to come pick us up.

Judy's voice was calm, a salve to my raw nerves. "We're going to make for the border," she said quietly, "Once in Israel, they won't touch us."

What frightened me as well was this mystery man who came along with Massimo. Who was he? Somebody important, no doubt, and probably with some pull with the Egyptian authorities. My mind raced ahead to Dad's home in the States. *Surely we'll be safe there*, I thought . . . *he wouldn't follow us all the way . . . ?*

It was a moot thought. Right then we were a long, long way from the States.

We later discovered that the Sicilian newspapers were making sensationalist fodder out of the rescue and subsequent pursuit by the authorities. "Ritrovato in Egitto" (Found in Egypt) proclaimed the May 9, 1995 edition of *Giornale di Sicilia*. The "account" of our capture by swarms of police, as we rested peacefully in our Cairo hotel room, came as quite a surprise, especially since we were informed of the supposed event long after we left Egypt. When the furor died down, our "arrest" was quite the topic of joking among us.

Don hustled back and motioned to the door, and we hefted our sparse luggage and left the hotel.

In the taxi, I constantly threw quick glances at Don and Judy, gathering a little encouragement from their stoicism. They chatted with the driver, with each other, and joked occasionally with Alex. They kept up the "tourist" deception beautifully. For me, I faked a few smiles and mentally ordered my rigid limbs to relax.

Once we left the clogged streets of Cairo, the desert road stretched out almost invitingly before us. The drive took a seeming eternity, and had it really been part of a vacation, it would have been fascinating. Passing through a myriad of small villages, we saw up close the often primitive way of life of a people that up until then, I'd only read about. Robe-clad villagers led pack donkeys and even the occasional camel down dusty streets, and in front of the mud-brick homes, old men lounged, following us with their eyes but not waving. The children often greeted the taxi with enthusiasm, running barefoot on the parched, hard-packed earth.

By the time we reached the border, it had been dark for some time. Jumping out of the cab before it rolled to a complete stop, Don woke up the disheveled border guards and explained that we wanted to cross, right then. We were in for another shock. The border was closed for a Muslim holy day—Mohammed's birthday, I think—and we'd have to return after midnight the next day.

Don shot our taxi driver a stern look. We suspected he'd known all along that we'd be turned away, but hungered for the huge fare the trip would garner.

We pulled an about face and headed back the way we'd come, and wound up in a classy hotel on the shore of the Red Sea. White sand beaches, luxury accommodations, a huge pool, and all the tourist trimmings didn't take the edge off our predicament. Acid was grinding up the inside of my stomach, and I fought off a round or two of panic attacks. Outwardly, Don and Judy were more accepting of the situation, and they spent a lot of time calming me down. I still had a role to play, they reminded me, and an American tourist sporting a deer-in-the-headlights look could possibly garner some unwanted attention. We didn't want people remembering us specifically. The idea was to blend, just be another happy face in the crowd.

Still, uppermost in my mind was the knowledge that our pursuers were virtually breathing down our necks. My thoughts ran wild. I just knew Massimo was even then on his way here, and I found myself tossing repeated glances skyward and listening for the approaching *Whump, whump!* of rotor blades. He had to know where we were by then, and likely his important friend had already arranged for a contingent of Egyptian police or military to converge on the resort. I felt the longer we stayed in one place, the easier it would be for him to snare us. The mood gave new meaning to those old movies where the convict escapes from a southern jail and plows through swamps and thickets, while the sound of baying hounds echoes through the woods. Only this was no movie. This was real life.

In hindsight, it's rather amazing how being on the run affected me. It was as if my whole body had become one big sensory organ. I found myself covertly studying faces in a crowd (to gauge possible dangerous intent), deliberately listening in on other people's conversations (to detect any comments about me), mentally mapping out exits and entrances of each building we entered, and gearing up to fight—physically, viciously—if cornered. Alex was mine, now, and they (whoever "they" turned out to be) would have to kill me to separate us again.

The downside of that kind of readiness was that my mind, although becoming honed for survival, also imagined all sorts of scenarios that could not reasonably take place. When we'd found that Massimo had tracked us to Cairo, to me he grew to nearly Homeric proportions. It's foolish, of course, but I began to think that there was nothing he couldn't do. No matter where we went, he'd find us. He had money, power, connections, and the iron will to hunt us down. These thoughts drove me nearly to the breaking point, and during that twenty-four hour period, I was just a hairsbreadth from running and screaming into the desert.

We killed a lot of time the next day along the beach, and lounging by the hotel pool while the hours dragged by. The Egyptian night finally settled on the sea, and at about 10:00 we crammed into another taxi for the two-hour trip to the border. It was as if we hurtled through a long, dark tunnel; the night closed in around us, and our headlights flashed past occasional signs in Arabic and English that blared: "Warning! Do Not Stray from Roadway. Buried Mines in Desert." It felt like one more nail in the coffin, because surely after the frenzied flight across international lines with our pursuers burning up the road behind us, I didn't dare feel any confidence that we'd actually make it all the way to freedom.

Spasmodically, I scanned the roadway for the headlights coming up behind us. If they caught up with us now, that would finish it.

As the driver pulled away and disappeared into the night, we seemed to draw one huge, collective breath and entered the compound. A clear sky stretched overhead, shot through with brilliant stars. The evening was beautiful as only those of the desert could be, and in other circumstances it could have been awe-inspiring. But once past the creaking metal gate the air was heavy, thick with tension. Here was where the rubber would meet the road, the last great obstacle to freedom. Enclosed by what seemed miles of fencing topped with erratically strung barbed wire, the compound had both the appearance and feeling of death-in-waiting, a dark, smothering atmosphere reminiscent of those old Depression-era films where the con walks haltingly to that little room at the end of the hallway. It wouldn't have been hard for us to feel that we, too, had our own special appointment to keep with "The Chair."

When we arrived, the same two guards "greeted" us, making no attempt at officiousness. Hatless, unshaven, and with dark, rumpled uniforms, they were immersed in their own boredom, a boredom tinged, perhaps, with a bit of irritation that anyone would have either the temerity or inanity to cross in the middle of the night. But this time, they let us in. In staccato English they beckoned us to follow them across the compound to one of two low, flat-roofed buildings, whose façades had long since been weather-stripped. It was probably typical of a hundred forgotten offices that straddled Middle East borders. I'm only guessing, of course, since this was my first fugitive run in Arab territory.

Everything seemed to move in slow motion, the same feeling one gets when trapped in a chase nightmare, when the feet seem stuck in molasses as the fearsome pursuer quickly gains ground. We knew Massimo's hounds pursued, although we had no concrete proof they'd tracked us into the desert itself.

The pace all the way from Malta, where our pursuers were only an hour behind, was exhausting. Coupled with the strain of heightened awareness, our nerves were pulled taut. The last week of flying under the radar was taking its toll. All activities blurred into one another at that point. We half-expected to have been placed on some kind of detainment list; and there in that suffocating enclosure, I frantically cast about in my mind for a viable "Plan B" in case we were placed under arrest. A panic attack swept over me, covering my mouth with an invisible hand, choking off both breath and speech.

Into this emotional melee, a young German girl came, outfitted with a rucksack and possessed of an extraordinarily blasé attitude. Sauntering out from the desert, this young blond, attractive, and totally alone girl wore the expression of a bored socialite doing her weekly jewelry shopping. What really alarmed me was that I'd seen no car headlights, no indication she'd hitched a ride. She was suddenly...there, showing no fatigue, hatless and wearing the most outlandish pair of plaid slacks I'd ever seen. Her accent gave away her nationality, as she spoke briefly with one of the guards. My mind, already on hyper-drive, was trying to process this new arrival, as she joined our little team for escort. Who in the world was she? Was she a plant or perhaps part of an "advance guard" hired by Massimo?

The small building's interior matched its outside shabbiness. It was meagerly furnished with one desk and chair, a lamp, and a filing cabinet. In retrospect it's odd I didn't notice a phone or radio of any kind, but I think now that they must have had some way of communicating with the outside world. Perhaps the other building was a communications hut. I'd never know. Inside this one, the walls were dirty, and the floor, which for some reason I recall as tiled, was atrocious, chipped, filthy, scarred with drag marks and sand abrasion.

I cast furtive glances at Don. Always our point man, good old, rock solid Delta Force Don appeared unfazed as he showed his passport. A consummate actor, he afterward mentioned his stomach had been tied in knots. With little mastery of English, the one guard examining our papers engaged in some stifled communication with Don, decided it wasn't worth the effort, then proceeded to the other passports. It must have been for only seconds that he looked at each one, but time hung in the stale air. After a moment, an eternity, he handed back both my and Alex's passports without a word. No questions, nothing.

The guard beckoned silently, leading us to an old bus parked at the far end of the compound. He pointed and all of us—including the strange German loner—stepped up into the bus and sat down on old cushioned seats that squeaked under our weight. Then we waited some more.

Fifteen minutes or a half hour later, another unshaven, disinterested guard appeared, stepped up into the bus, and plopped down heavily in the driver's seat. He keyed the ignition and without bothering to shut the door propelled the bus slowly forward through a narrow enclosure into another fenced area. The place looked like a war zone. The guard dismounted, left the bus, and was immediately replaced by one whom we assumed was an Israeli who, also without speaking, geared up, drove the remaining few feet onto the Israel side, and parked.

As we sat there, a plainclothes Israeli policeman entered the bus, scanned our faces, and smiled broadly. At that precise moment, I felt he looked like an angel, and his presence seemed to fill the dark bus with sunlight.

"Good morning, everyone," he said in perfect English. "Welcome to Israel. I hope you have not had to wait long and that your trip so far has been pleasant. You are now in the Gaza Strip, and those proceeding to Tel Aviv should arrange for a taxi. Do not remain at the border. I wish you all a very warm welcome. Enjoy your stay here!"

The little crowd of us gathered our stuff and descended the few steps to the ground. As simple as that, we were on Israeli soil. The bus pulled away, leaving the four of us standing in the still night. The strange German girl disappeared into the darkness, leaving as mysteriously as she had arrived.

Instantly, it was as if a veil had lifted, and the air that was heavy and oppressive on the Egyptian side became dramatically lighter, clearer. Even the heavy silence of the Egyptian night contrasted sharply with the Israeli side. Here, little birds called to one another from the shadowed brush surrounding us. It is no exaggeration to say that it was as if we had crossed some spiritual demarcation.

Don hailed the policeman who was getting into his vehicle. They talked quietly for a minute or two, then they walked off together. A few minutes later the cop drove off while Don strode back to where we yet stood. "Nice guy," Don said, "he helped me get in touch with a taxi service, but we have to walk up the road a ways to wait."

I stared hopefully from Don to Judy, both of whom wore the biggest grins I'd seen so far. "Then that's it? We're . . . we're here . . . ?"

Don chuckled. "It's done. You're safe, Katie. Nobody'll follow you across that border."

I wanted to scream, dance, and collapse all at the same time. High on adrenaline for the last few days and utterly exhausted from too little sleep, I opted for "collapse" but there was nowhere to do it. According to the policeman, there was a bench a little distance up the dark road. A walk was fine with me. The further I got from that border, the better I'd like it.

Ten minutes later, we came upon a bench right beside the road. Turned out we'd have an hour wait till pickup. I really couldn't care less. For the first time in days, I could genuinely relax, and the thought of having absolutely nothing pressing for immediate attention was something akin to wonderful. There in the warm Israeli night, I eased back into the wooden slats and let the tension ease away.

As if by some unheard cue, Alex burst into song, dancing happily before us, as we laughed and watched him from the bench, clapping and urging him on. I can't recall the nature of his happy song. But in later years, I would learn of Moses leading the children of Israel out of Egyptian captivity with Miriam leading a song of rejoicing to the Lord for their miraculous deliverance.

Funny, but that day, Miriam's song had become ours as well.

We had been delivered.

14

The Long Journey Home

Diu chiudi 'na porta e grapi un purticatu.
God closes a door and opens a portico.

As fascinating as it was, being deep in the heart of that Egyptian pyramid was also a bit frightening. The air was close, thick with a kind of smothering stuffiness. For all its history, the place was a crypt; the stone walls hemmed us in, and the grit of millennia in our teeth spurred a craving for escape to again breathe in the open.

Israel was that first breath of fresh air.

For the first time in years, I felt I could shed the fears that had nagged me into near insanity and just enjoy the moment. Don and Judy assured me that Massimo wouldn't think of pursuing us into Israel, as he'd have no opportunity to retake Alex. Even if he and his important friend could elude the elite Israeli security forces and the ubiquitous military personnel, the average citizen was used to being on the alert, and many went about their daily business armed. Should something separate me or Alex from our protectors, one cry for help from either of us would bring a veritable citizen's army to our aid. And it didn't hurt that when people learned we were Americans, the smiles widened, hands extended, and a familiarity like that of old friends blossomed.

While the food generally was wonderful, the seafood was simply out of this world. We literally feasted, as if someone had thrown us a party. At one point, Don excused himself to check things out with his Israeli contacts (that man knew people everywhere!) and when he returned, he assured us we'd be safe should our immediate plans somehow go awry. Later, we went shopping with the little money we had left, and Alex was quite taken with a monstrously oversized "Coca-Cola" (written in Hebrew) sweatshirt that he grew into quite handsomely. He has it to this day.

We spent the night in a decent hotel, then went to the airport the next day. After examining our passports, one of the security people began questioning us in fluent English. "You came across the border from Egypt—by car?" he asked with a surprised inflection.

We all nodded, me hoping I didn't have to actually say anything. I didn't trust myself to speak, struggling just to keep my breathing even. Don and Judy smiled, but the officer eyed us suspiciously. "Why?" he asked, his dark eyes probing. "Why by car? That seems a bit out of the ordinary. Why not take a plane directly to Tel Aviv?"

Don explained, "We're tourists, and wanted to see the country, up close. We've taken taxis all over. That's how we travel."

The officer wasn't buying it. Gesturing to a female guard a short distance away, he pressed us. Something was not right, and he knew it. Speaking rapidly in Hebrew to his companion, he then turned and pointed at Don and Judy. "You," he said politely but firmly, "come with me."

They split us up. The guards left with Don and Judy in tow, drawing them off to one side but just out of earshot. Alex and I stood there watching until it was our turn. Both guards came toward us very officiously and posed the same questions:

"Where have you come from?"

"Why were you in Cairo?"

"Why did you cross the Egyptian border in the middle of the night?"

"Who are you running from?"

After all we'd been through, we faced yet another challenge, but I felt more ready for this one. I stuck to the story we'd rehearsed innumerable times, answering the same questions over and over. Fortunately, by then Alex had grown into his role, and mostly remained silent. His big, imploring eyes no doubt had the desired, "Please let me be" effect on the guards, and while favoring him with the occasional smile, they basically left him alone.

The whole grilling took about a half hour, and by the end of it, the male guard was mildly frustrated. "Your stories don't match," he said, without going into detail, "and I'm wondering what you've got to hide."

For a silent moment, he fixed us with his penetrating gaze, then resignedly heaved a little sigh. "But . . . since I have no real reason to detain you . . ."

He handed over our passports and waved us on. Although I craved a backward glance, I resisted the urge. I could feel their eyes boring into my back, and I just wanted out of there.

Once on the plane, which would prove to be a "red-eye special," Judy nudged me and with a smile said, "There's a surprise waiting for you when we get off at JFK. I phoned one of the local television news stations. We're going public."

The jet taxied onto the runway, the engines roared, and we were airborne. Looking out the window as the earth slid past below, I bid an acid goodbye to Massimo and the three years he had stolen from me.

It was a fitful night's sleep on the plane. It seemed we hung in the air forever, and my mind wouldn't shut off. I kept waking to check that Alex was still beside me, to touch him, to smile at him, to assure myself that this past week hadn't all been a dream. Intermingled with the joy and utter exhaustion was the unrelenting heartache of my mother's passing. It had been a hammer blow that threatened to wreck everything, and now, as I looked ahead to a reunion with Dad, I knew our separate griefs would blend and we'd walk through this thing together. The first thing we would do after getting settled would be to visit where they'd laid Mom to rest. To see the place with my

Flying home to America . . . together and free at last

own eyes would be a door closing on that part of my life, but it desperately needed doing if I was to know any peace.

As I gazed at my son, sitting beside me without a "chaperone" and in turns sleeping or chattering away happily five miles above a turbulent world, I comforted myself with the thought that at least this part of it was over. Surely, it was over . . .

At 5:30 the next morning, at the JKF airport a FOX News affiliate filmed our deplaning. As we walked quickly through the concourse, the reporter peppered us with questions about the kidnapping, rescue, and escape, while the cameraman filmed. I opened up, big time. This news thing was a good strategy. Though only a few minutes long (I was anxious to get to Dad's house), the interview offered me a televised vindication.

With our permission, the reporter and camera crew followed us to Dad's New Brunswick home and filmed our reception there. Dad met us outside, along with my brother John and his wife,

Karen, who lived close by in Edison. When I saw Dad for the first time since Christmas, I fell against him while he held me. Both of us broke down completely. We felt the same things—tremendous relief that the ordeal was finally over and deep heartbreak that Mom hadn't lived to see it.

Inside, things were somewhat lighter. The FOX crew followed us around and filmed Alex getting acclimated to his "new" surroundings and being lavished with attention and chocolate doughnuts. With his Italian accent showing, he hammed it up for the camera, openly glad to be home.

The news guys were just super. Seated around the kitchen table, they listened as I explained the past three years and our recent escape. Their sympathies stirred, they recommended we go more than local with the story. The injustice of it would spur righteous outrage among viewers and could solidify my position as the rightly aggrieved party. We kicked the idea around for a few minutes.

"I don't think it's a good idea," John said slowly. "You're home after all, and this thing should pretty much be over."

I agreed. "Local is fine," I said to the reporter, "I don't want to do any more than that. I just want to get on with my life."

The crew understood completely and wished us the best. They filmed a bit more outside the home with closing comments, thanked us for inviting them into our lives, and left. Don and Judy also left that day. They had put their lives and family on hold for two months in order to pull this off, and now their end of it was fulfilled. Dad and I couldn't thank them enough. We hugged and I cried, so grateful that the ordeal was in its final stage. The two of them had been more than rescuers, more than friends, really. They had become family, so integral to our lives that I found it hard to imagine now a day without them right there. As they drove away, a piece of my heart went with them.

How does one "get on with normal life" after something like this? During the next few days, Alex and I went for walks, ate at fast-food joints, laughed and talked happily, and went on drives with his grandpa; but the specter of what had happened sometimes shadowed our time together. After something like this, all the feeling, the emotion, and even the fear doesn't simply evaporate. I felt much like I'd imagine a soldier does after a hard tour. He doesn't just leave the "line" behind and go blithely on his way. Sometimes, flashbacks of specific battles fly out of the blue, and he maintains awhile a continued heightened alertness, a preparedness for the next deployment. For all my dreaming of how wonderful it would be to have Alex again—and it was, certainly—I was still on edge. Alcohol and tranqs were still a real support mechanism. I'd kept up the regimen throughout the last few years, through the planning and rescue, and continued when I got to Dad's house. I didn't tell him, of course. He would have been mortified. But I couldn't quit; they were old friends helping me through the daily routine and keeping the fear at bay. The blessings of having Alex, notwithstanding, I felt what I can now only describe as post-traumatic stress. After all, Massimo was still out there, and I found myself thinking that perhaps it would never really be over.

It wasn't.

Less than a week after we returned to the States, Dad came to talk to me. He was upset and began to explain what had transpired just outside.

As he was pulling into the driveway, he noticed a car parked a half block away. A man in street clothes sat behind the wheel, alone in the front seat, seeming to read a book or study something by the console. Something clicked in Dad's head, and he remembered the vehicle from before . . . several times before. As sharp as he is, it all fell together immediately, and he was outraged. Somebody—guess who?—had put a tail on us. Slamming his car into "park," Dad got out and stormed off down the sidewalk. The man looked up, pretended not to notice, then looked away again. Coming broadside, Dad shoved his finger aggressively forward and fairly shouted, "I know who you are and what you're up to! Get going!"

The man offered some half-hearted protest, but Dad would have none of it. "I'm telling you right now," he said with rising anger, "leave us alone!"

Without a word, the detective keyed the ignition and pulled away from the curb. Dad stood watching until the car disappeared around a corner.

This turn of events completely flipped me out. It had only taken a few days (days!) for Massimo to set the dogs on us again. As Dad related the incident, I hugged Alex to me and fought down the panic. He'd never let us go. I'd always be looking over my shoulder, waiting for some faceless stranger to burst into our lives and take Alex away from me again. Alex looked up at me, comforting and worried at the same time. This poor kid. I kept thinking, *What kind of life can I give him if we're always looking behind us?*

I looked at Dad and barely choked out, "We can't stay here. He knows where we are. He won't give up."

Dad sighed heavily and nodded. "I'll call Don and Judy," he quietly said. "I don't know what else to do."

When he got off the phone a couple of minutes later, he looked at us sadly. His voice was subdued, "Judy'll leave today to meet us in D.C. You'll go back to North Carolina to stay at their house."

His heart was breaking. He'd waited till I got back with Alex to have the memorial service for Mom, and even this he wasn't able to pull off. I wouldn't even be there to grieve with him.

Dad and my brother John's father-in-law drove us to Washington. There was an urgency about the trip that cut off idle conversation, and I guess John's in-law was there to ride shotgun, in case. We met Judy and her son at a prearranged spot just outside the city, and I gave Dad one last lingering hug. There were tears in his eyes. He leaned down and hugged Alex to himself, hard, kissing the hair of his head several times. I could barely speak. We switched cars, and as we drove away, I looked out the back windshield. Dad stood by his car, staring after us. I cried while Alex hugged me.

The Feeney's three-bedroom, two-story home stood in a quiet suburban neighborhood of Fayetteville, North Carolina. The neighborhood was of the genre I'd always envisioned for Alex and me: tree-lined sidewalks, spacious front porches, and enclosed back yards. Our arrival would prove something of an inconvenience for the at-home family—which, at that time, consisted of Judy, her two teenage sons, and a few dogs. Don was away tending to CTU business out of state. As Judy's daughter had recently moved out, Alex and I were assigned her bedroom. I was glad not to be forcing one of the kids out to the living room couch, but even had this been necessary, I was assured that my undetermined stay was not a peculiar event. The Feeney's was a safe house that had harbored its share of parents who found it necessary to disappear after their children's rescue from an abusive or non-custodial spouse. When someone needed to disappear, this was where they went. Alex and I were only the latest in a long line of clients who had taken shelter there until legal issues were rectified or they needed to go deeper underground.

Much of the following month was a study in boredom. The popular idea of continuous excitement while being on the run is more myth than reality. The truth is, hiding out is dull. There's only so much reading or watching TV one can do before the urge to get out into the real world sets the teeth on edge. The feeling must be akin to holing up in an Alaska cabin for weeks on end while the winter rages outside. Cabin fever, here I come. Judy encouraged us to go out for neighborhood walks or have picnics in the area park. Alex and I brainstormed about the things we could do with the little money I still possessed. Walking the Feeney's many dogs made for a good exercise routine. Judy also loaned us her minivan, and we'd go on library forays. Sure, it was still reading, but it was also an escape to someplace different. Even a change of location alleviated some of the daily tedium.

It was on one of our library visits that Alex realized how little he actually knew about American history.

"Mom," he said, with a youthful alarm in his eyes, "I have to start studying about this stuff. When I go to school in September, I'm going to be so far behind everyone else, I'll be embarrassed."

On our return to Judy's house that day, Alex and I carried armloads of books he felt he'd need to master before attending school. Alex put his nose in those books, and do you know he memorized every American president—in order!? I was so proud of him.

Sometimes a change of scenery, much as we craved it, was ill advised. Alex and I really didn't know the area, and we were in some ways quite naïve. We once took a long walk to the nearest mall, not to spend money we didn't have, but to enjoy window shopping and the charged atmosphere of buying and selling. It wasn't on par with the Sicilian open-air markets, but it would do in a pinch. We shared a soda while there and had a great time talking and browsing. On our way back, Judy's son pulled up alongside us, staring incredulously from behind the wheel, "Katie, you two shouldn't be on this street. Do you know how dangerous this place is?"

Looking around, I didn't think the neighborhood particularly seedy, but I took his word for it. We got in the car and listened attentively as he read us the riot act on the way back home. Really, I was touched by his protectiveness. I felt cared for, a part of the Feeney family.

An incident did occur, however, that could have led to much graver consequences. On one of the rare days when Alex and I were home completely alone, two young men in tee shirts pulled up into the driveway and sat quietly talking. Peeking at them from behind the living room curtains, I was certain they'd been sent by Massimo. My heart thumped as I strained to hear their conversation, but they spoke too softly. They remained for quite some time, talking. I knew the garage door was open and led right to the door to the kitchen. Briefly, I considered calling the police, but disregarded the idea. There would be paperwork involved and a lot of questions I really didn't want to answer. I opted for calling Judy. Ducking as I slid past the window, I made for the nearest phone and called her office. My voice was low, but strident with fear. "Judy, there're two guys sitting out in your driveway."

I could tell she was instantly alert. "What are they doing?"

"Just sitting there. Do you think the family sent them?"

"I don't know; it's possible. Do you want me to come home?"

I didn't answer right away, not knowing what to do. Alex came wandering into the room at that time. He gave me a quizzical look and asked, "What are you doing, Mom?"

"Please stay away from the window, Alex," I said, a little too quickly. I didn't want him alarmed but had to tell him something. Calling him over, I said quietly, "Honey, there are two men out in the driveway. You just go back and watch TV. It'll be okay."

Amazingly, he sauntered back into the other room, and I noticed at that moment the car backed out of the driveway. I let go a long-held breath.

Mulling it over later that evening, I decided that they were probably opportunistic thugs who considered robbing the house or taking something from the open garage, and thought better of it. This consideration came as something of a relief. In my convoluted thinking, it was better to be fighting off robbers than having to take on Massimo's emissaries, whoever they might be.

My fear of Massimo unfortunately bled over into my relationship with Alex. He was only then beginning to understand what had happened to him in Sicily, and the anxiety stirred by the possibility of another kidnapping—should Massimo find us—moved him to keep very close to me at all times. We never slept in separate rooms, and though we had individual beds, Alex moved his across the floor to join with mine. He'd often move into my own twin bed, sleeping so close that I'd wake up with a strained back or numbed arms from the cramped positions in which I'd slept. We rarely discussed his kidnapping or subsequent rescue, but the threat of discovery and another enforced separation shadowed us both.

This circumstance was merely one of what I had been forewarned to expect. A child's rescue was only the first step toward a strong re-bonding with the rightful parent. Periodically, Judy reminded me that the emotional damage could be long-lasting or permanent, depending on how long the child had been away in a foreign land, how much he had assimilated, and what falsehoods had been told him. Some even later moved back to the land from which they'd been rescued. "He might become resentful, at first, so you'll need to be patient," Judy had said gently. "You might have a lot of rebuilding to do with him."

This terrified me. What would I do if, after all I'd gone through to get him back, he should simmer inside and one day turn his back on me?

Fortunately, none of that ever happened. Aside from the fear of being retaken by Massimo, Alex moved right back into his American heritage. He was young but savvy; he knew who had wronged him and determined not to be separated again.

I did, though, have my own transitional difficulties. I sorely missed my daily cappuccinos and certain Sicilian foods, and sometimes forgot simple things every American takes for granted. For instance, I'd sometimes dream in Italian. And once, when planning a trip to the store, I couldn't remember if, as in Sicily, the shops closed every day for a few hours. *Do they have a "siesta" time here?* I wondered. Also, I'd forgotten some common words, and when stumped, I'd turn to Alex and ask in Italian, "What is the English word for . . . ?"

It was frustrating because I didn't even want to hear the word "Sicily" at that time. That country had claimed enough of me, and I wanted to shed it like a moth-eaten sweater.

About two weeks into our underground routine, an unexpected opportunity presented itself in the form of a phone call from quite a startling source. Two Italian newsmen, Francesco Ballo and Carlo La Corte, living in the U.S. and working for the state-run Italian television service, contacted Judy's office. They jointly inquired, persuasively, if they might be allowed an interview with Alex and me. Cautious, but sensing an opportunity to have our side of the story televised in "enemy territory," Judy okayed it, but with one stipulation: the reporters were honor-bound not to reveal our location. They enthusiastically agreed, and the interview was on.

They arrived at the Feeney home one bright summer morning, two lively men in their forties, fluent in English and all smiles and handshakes. Accompanied by an American camera crew, they set up first in the living room and peppered us with the usual rescue questions, filming all the while and conducting the interview half in Italian and half in English. They and Alex really hit it off. Good-naturedly engaging in some on-camera banter, one of them asked Alex if he knew any good jokes in Italian. Alex began in English well enough, but the English interpretation got him tongue-tied. "Well, just say it in Italian then," they coaxed, and when Alex finished they roared. They'd no doubt heard it before, but they were so taken with this happy little boy with the nonstop grin, they couldn't help themselves.

The Italian reporters, Don and Judy, and Alex and I

We eventually moved to the backyard where they continued filming. I knew the footage of Alex and me kicking around a soccer ball and laughing away would go over well with the intended audience. Italians love their kids, and for a while, Alex was one of their own. To actually see him having a good time, looking healthy, well fed and active, would serve to reinforce my contention that I wanted the best for him and could provide it if only we were left to live in peace.

Afterward, they were so pleased with the interview and by then apparently on our side that they took the lot of us to a steak lunch. When the dessert tray was brought around and Alex couldn't decide, Mr. Ballo said with a flamboyant wave of his hand, "Leave the tray. We'll take the whole thing!"

When they left us that afternoon, we felt we'd won a couple of converts to our cause.

Ladies Home Journal also wrangled a phone interview with me and later sent a photographer for some photos of Alex and me together. The story, spotlighting the Feeney's rescue work and featuring other child rescues, appeared in the October 1995 issue under the title "The Baby Savers."

As one day moved into the next, boredom ground away at my nerves. It's one thing to be moving somewhere, even if you're looking over your shoulder at your pursuer. It's quite another to be anchored to the same place, the same unending routine. We had no idea how long we'd be there, especially since Judy had made some inquiries and discovered that we, along with the Feeneys, had made Italy's "fugitives" list. The Italian authorities knew by then we were in the States, and I thought it likely they were pressing for extradition through channels. But only Dad knew where we were, and no matter what happened, he'd never talk. Officially, we had disappeared. But "disappearing" means you keep your head down and don't attract attention. In a way I felt I was still on the floor of that rental car in Palermo, keeping out of sight of the law.

It's shameful to put it this way, but the boredom got so bad that when Judy invited me to a church service one Sunday, I accepted. I hadn't been to church since I was a kid, anyway, and I thought also that it wouldn't do Alex any harm. They had a children's church he could attend while I stayed with Judy.

The people were warm and welcoming. Judy, not being overly concerned about suspicion, introduced me to a few by name. Judy was well known for having all sorts of visitors, at every season of the year, it seemed, so no one took any notice of one more she had brought along. For my part, I was generally at ease and glad to be out of the house.

Something happened, though, that was entirely unexpected. I actually began to listen to the Scriptures being read, and like Mary, Jesus' mother, "kept all these things and pondered them in her [my] heart." For the first time in my life, I heard about Jesus and what was called "the plan of salvation." God had a plan? This was news to me. My life to that point had seemed a haphazard assemblage of crises, and I couldn't imagine a God who took a personal interest. If He was like what they said, why was I such a mess? Why had I been hurt so many times, emotionally abused by my husband, had my child stolen from my arms, been forced to live for three years like a slave in an enemy camp? I genuinely had more questions than answers.

We all attended a couple more services (there was always something going on there), and though I liked the place well enough, the message and the peace it alluded to, remained just out of reach. Alex was happy with children's church, so I didn't have to twist his arm to come along. The change of scene was nice, and I'd always liked learning new things. A week of revival meetings was announced to commence in just a couple of days. We'd go to those too, I was told, if Judy had the time to take us.

The first day of revival meetings, I was feeling particularly low. I sat in a chair way in back, steeped in my personal misery. Dad had held off Mom's memorial service long enough. There had to be closure. That very day the service had been held, and I couldn't be there, couldn't share his grief and bid my own mother goodbye. I felt robbed, cheated, and abandoned. Plus, my life was a torturous collage of panic attacks, pill-popping sleepless nights, and fear of the future. Even though I had finally gotten Alex, I was still clawing at the edges of some dark pit, trying to climb out. Though I wanted it badly, I didn't even know what "normal" was anymore.

Then, sitting there waiting for the service to begin, I suddenly sensed God speaking to my heart. I realized that all the negative things God had allowed to happen in my life and all the good things He had orchestrated, He was now using to get my attention and to draw me to Himself.

As I realized at that moment how real He truly was and that He cared enough about me to bring me to this place to hear His Word and answer His call (for it was as if God was calling me by name), it felt like a ton of bricks had fallen on me. I saw now that God had allowed me to come to this place of complete brokenness so that I could "see" and finally realize how desperately I needed Him. Yes, I thought. *Of course. It all makes perfect sense now.*

A peace I'd never known washed over me, and as I sat in that wonderful solitude of heart, it was as if the rest of the world—the church, the people, everything—just vanished, and I sat alone . . . with God. God had spoken to me, not in an audible voice, but one that rang clearly, gently, unmistakably, in my heart. There really was a plan for my life! All the Scriptures that had been preached in the past few services came back to me in a rush. I didn't necessarily remember the exact words, but the meanings were very clear. I needed Jesus Christ. He would save me forever if I would accept His free gift of salvation.

This was it! The pieces suddenly all came together. I'd always had a terror of dying because I knew the grave was not the end. No one needed to tell me I was a sinner. I'd known it all my life but just hadn't given it much thought, probably because my recognizing the reality of my own personal (and many) sins would lead to the inevitable conclusion that I was doomed to an eternal hell. *That* much I had believed, even before coming to Christ this day. Growing up in church, I knew that Jesus was the Son of

God, that He died for my sins and rose again from the dead, but I never knew what it all meant. What in the world did that have to do with me, personally? Until that moment, Christ had been a mysterious Deity, a far-off God who wasn't personally interested in me, my life, my problems. He was Judge, but I'd never been told that He was also Savior, my Savior, if I'd only receive Him by faith. As if struck by lightning, I was hit with the burning desire to be saved from my sins.

I sat completely enthralled as the night's sermon was preached, and when they gave the altar call, I ached to go up front. But I just couldn't do it. For the first time in my life, I realized the full import of being a sinner bound for hell and that God was calling me to Himself, but in so realizing, I refused to take my part in it lightly. I felt that if I answered that altar call, I'd be bound to do "my part" and live for Christ; I honestly didn't think I could do that. I would not accept Jesus publicly then fail Him. What I had yet to understand is that God saves us as we are when we put our trust in Christ, then fashions us into faithful disciples of Christ and continues to forgive our sins when (not if) we stumble (Ephesians 2:8-10).

A middle-aged lady beside me that first night sat studying my face. Her lips parted in a gentle smile, and very sweetly she asked, "Honey, do you want to go up front? I'll go with you . . ."

But I declined by gently shaking my head. When the service was over, I went home with Judy and thought deeply, at the same time both troubled and ecstatic.

All throughout that week, as I sat in those back row seats, I longed to go forward and proclaim Christ publicly, but held back. Absurdly, I kept thinking, *I have to go through the ceremony, or it's not official.* I heard and read so many times that week in John 3:16 that "God so loved the world, that He gave His only begotten Son, that whosoever believeth in Him should not perish, but have everlasting life." But how could I accept that love and forgiveness and then later disappoint Him—after all He did for me? In my heart, I had already accepted Jesus as Savior. But I continued to struggle. I had to be sure I'd be able to keep my commitment to Him.

On the last day of the revival, I reached a crisis point. No matter what, this time I was going up front. In the company of many others, I repeated aloud the "sinner's prayer," savoring every word. What happened at that moment is indescribably wonderful. The weight of my sins fell away, and I knew that I had been born again. The old Katie was dead, and a completely new one stood at the altar. I was so overwhelmed, I nearly shouted for joy. I was saved! No more wallowing in fear, afraid of God's punishment. Jesus had taken it all. More than that, I had settled it in my heart that what God had started in my life, He was strong enough to finish. Even if I failed miserably, and I was sure I would, I rested in the knowledge that He would help me and keep me eternally for Himself.

From that night on, my faith took wings. Judy was so very happy for me, but we had little time together after the revival due to her pressing work schedule. Also, no one at church really took me under his or her wing so, while I knew very little of the Bible, I was determined I would learn by digging into it on my own. After each service, I'd go over every Scripture quoted in the sermon and then study the Bible in private. It was like pouring cool water on parched ground. I just drank it all up, memorizing what I could and always keeping my Bible close. God's Word had become a part of me. Prayer became as necessary as breathing and was incredibly refreshing. How had I lasted all those years without it?

Strange and wonderful things began to happen during this time. One day soon afterward, as I stood in the open bathroom doorway prying the cap from a new bottle of tranquilizers, Judy came down the hall, saw me, and shook her head. "What are you doing, Katie?" she asked with a bit of exasperation. "You don't need those."

Her words made a little light go on, and I realized she was right. I looked at the bottle one last time and threw it in the waste basket. My desire for alcohol simply disappeared too. From that moment on, the panic attacks subsided dramatically and were gone altogether within a couple of weeks. I finally had assurance of eternal life, and that made all the difference. With assurance of salvation came peace, and with peace . . . well, drug use became suddenly obsolete.

During this time, Fabio had been keeping in touch with me through Dad. I learned that the day we rescued Alex, Fabio had been taken to police headquarters and grilled for information about the rescue team. They had obviously learned that Fabio and I were close. Fabio was honestly able to deny to the police any knowledge of the rescue. At the same time he was being interrogated by the police, the Carabinieri (separate from the local police and more powerful many times over) got wind of what had happened and that Fabio had been taken in. They went to Fabio's father's house in the middle of the night (while Fabio was still at the police station) and said it was a good idea if his father would give them Fabio's passport to hold onto for safe keeping because the police might take it away from him. They were protecting Fabio because he was a former Carabinieri, and they knew him well. Fabio's father gave them the passport. Fabio was released by the police a few hours after questioning, and as promised, the Carabinieri returned Fabio's passport to him within a few days.

Fabio's continued information relay with Dad eventually culminated in a letter smuggled to me. As I sat reading it, the import literally stunned me. Fabio declared—not asked, mind you—that he was coming to the United States, expressly to be with me. Not only that, but our previous relationship would no longer suffice. He was coming to marry me, and that was that. My hand flew to my mouth. What in the world was he thinking? My life is in complete disarray, I have no job prospects, we can't even live together openly, but he wants to tie the knot? He must have taken leave of his senses . . . or I had, because I didn't try to forbid him. It wouldn't have worked anyway since Fabio, as gentle as he is, is possessed of a steely determination when he sets his mind on something. The way he looked at it right then was that our marriage was a done deal, and I had just better get used to the idea.

The only stipulation I would have, when next contacting him, was for him not to (yet) tell my father. There was just too much up in the air right then to lay this on him as well.

As I sat with the letter in my folded hands, I mentally racked up all the hurdles he'd have to clear—immigration with its mounds of paperwork, finding a permanent place for all three of us, securing a steady job . . . the whole thing seemed crazy. Still, the up side was that he was a kind and gentle man, the very antithesis of Massimo, and he and Alex already liked each other a lot. And I had to face it, now that it was forced upon me, that I really did love the guy. His loving and gentlemanly demeanor had won my heart long ago.

Oh, the irony! I'd had precious little time over the past three years to consider falling in love, and now that I finally opened the door, I was hiding out four thousand miles from my future husband. Even he didn't know exactly where I was!

The lawyer who had handled my original California custody hearing also managed to contact me again through Dad. We spoke briefly over the phone, and he was very excited we'd rescued Alex. In an interview with a Santa Cruz newspaper, he detailed the route we took from Sicily back to the States and refused to divulge my whereabouts even as he defended my actions.

Just when the drama of it all seemed to taper off, Judy was informed that someone had tried to access Alex's baptismal records. There were other incidences, too, all in a row, like the odd phone calls she'd get at her office that convinced her Alex and I needed to skip town. By that time, we'd been with the Feeneys for a month. Dad set up for us to live with his sister in the Everglades town of Naples, Florida. The place was small and quiet; unless someone knew about Aunt Helen, we'd be safe there. We all took a flight to Miami where Judy rented a car and drove us the rest of the way to Naples. When we said goodbye for the second time since getting back to the States, my heart broke afresh. She had become a sister to me, and I hated to see her leave.

In Florida with my aunt and Alex

A fun moment with Grandpa

In Don and Judy's backyard

Home in the States at last, Alex was no longer the little 5-year-old he was when he left; by the time I got him home, he would soon be as tall as me.

Aunt Helen knew the full story and was happy to offer her house as a safe haven. It was there I really began to relax. I'm not really sure why, except that it seemed to be the last place on earth Massimo would think to look for us—a small town at the edge of the Everglades, near the bottom of North America. When not pitching in to help her maintain her characteristically spotless house, Alex and I took walks, had picnics, and went bike riding. Aunt Helen also loaned us her car, so we took in the surrounding countryside. It was truly lovely, warm, and laid-back, and tinged with excitement when we went to watch the spectacle of alligator wrestling! Alex also enrolled in the local YMCA day camp, and with others of his age went to the zoo, the beach, and all kinds of other outings. He loved it. It was with this group that he gained a lifelong interest and love of chess.

During this entire time, there was some behind-the-scenes legal wrangling between Massimo's family and the lawyer I had retained while in Palermo. Several compromises were forwarded by the family, including an inducement that I petition the American courts to withdraw the kidnapping warrant still in effect against Massimo. In return, the family would petition the Italian court system to withhold filing abduction charges (which it had not yet done). Dad covertly sent several of Massimo's and Giovanni's letters care of Judy. I read and discarded them, having heard all the same sentiments before: "Come back, and we won't contest you having full custody of Alex," only hardened my resolve to keep him from them. At this point, I still regarded Sicily as my one-time prison and all Sicilians—save one—as antagonists. *Come back? Yeah, right.* The past three years had worked a lot of naivety out of me.

Meanwhile, Fabio had moved to Illinois to stay with Sarah. She vacationed in the States every summer while Stefano remained abroad, so there was plenty of room for my groom-to-be. While there, he did odd jobs and wrestled with his immigration paperwork.

We didn't actually meet again until I moved back to Dad's about a month later. My Palermo attorney had by then informed me of the court ruling that finally (!) acknowledged my lawful custody of Alex, so any threatened pursuit by Massimo had been rendered legally void. Amazingly, the woman judge in the case, before whom I'd appeared several times, came out publicly in support. Her stance was a huge blow to adverse media opinion of me and did much to assuage any residual anxiety on my part. Not that I had any intention of ever traveling to Sicily again, but it was nice to know that the Italian authorities would not pursue extradition.

With the heat off, Fabio took a plane from Illinois, and we spent that day getting reacquainted. The atmosphere was tense though, and conversation stilted. Fabio was hard pressed from every side, from working his way through the immigration maze to holding down two full-time jobs in order to afford a decent apartment and furniture for the three of us. I felt terrible, watching him, but there was little I could do, other than lend him moral support. The fact that Dad still didn't know of our engagement made it all the harder to talk intimately. When Fabio left for Illinois a couple of days later, my heart went with him, but really, I still wondered if our planned marriage would see the light of day.

Through all the uncertainty of the future, within me there was an ever-rising hope. The Bible had become my lifeline, and my relationship with Christ grew into something wonderful. I knew firsthand what Jesus meant when He said, "My sheep hear My voice," because I conversed with Him daily, and He with me through His Word and His Holy Spirit. How strange to say that, but He became more real, more powerful than all the troubles that had plagued my life. When He said, "I will never leave you, nor forsake you," I believed Him, and when I needed wisdom or direction, I asked, and I received. I craved prayer like food. Although my heart rejoiced, my mind still couldn't wrap around the truth that there was Someone in my life who wouldn't let me down, who would see me through every trouble, and in the end lead me home.

Home. As a world traveler, I'd never really had one. Growing up in New Brunswick, I couldn't wait to get away, and in

California, I wanted to go to new places. Even upon returning to the States with Alex, the restlessness, the uncertainty of "settling down" had me always looking over the next horizon. It wasn't until I found the Lord that I knew my real home wasn't here on earth. Call me old-fashioned, but the knowledge that "I go to prepare a place for you" thrilled me to the core. No more running, no more fear. Even in death, I would be ready, eager, to be ushered into the place Jesus had prepared just for me.

My new faith prompted in me a desire to have Alex attend Christian school. There was a small facility a few miles from Dad's, and at my first meeting with the superintendent, I leveled with him about Alex's transcripts: we had none. But when I gave him the whys and wherefores, the man's eyes lit up, and with a few exclamations of "Praise God!" he waived the transcript portion and graciously admitted Alex for that school year. Alex proved himself a terrific student, and was, in fact, the only one of his classmates able to name every single American president up to the present! His outgoing nature helped him make many friends, and best of all, he was exposed every single day to a Christian atmosphere where the Bible was taught and faith lived out.

On a more personal note, though I attended several churches, none seemed agreeable. I didn't mean to be picky, but the ones I had tried close by lacked vibrancy and a love for teaching the Word. Having been raised from the dead and now living in Christ, I wasn't about to go back to the graveyard. I wound up listening to a lot of good Christian radio, and combined with daily prayer and Bible study, it helped fill the fellowship void. I trusted God to lead me to the right church, at the right time.

An incident occurred during the school year that—on top of all His other deliverances—vividly demonstrated God's protection in my life. One weekday afternoon, with Alex still in school and Dad on a business trip, I returned home from my day job as a medical assistant. With an armload of groceries, I passed the dining room only to notice that some jewelry from Mom's upstairs jewelry box lay on the floor. A chill ran up my spine. *Someone's been here*, I thought; immediately I set the groceries on the table and reached for the phone, planning to call 911. Suddenly, it occurred to me that whoever it was could still be in the house. I hurried to the front door, and once outside, I got in my car and for a moment sat there, staring at the house and wanting to see if anyone made an exit. Thinking that I could become a target, I put the car into gear and drove to the fire station down the street, asking one of the men to phone the police.

When the two officers arrived, I met them by the front driveway and entered the house with them, explaining that the intruder might be my ex-husband. As I gave them some of my back-story, they looked at me like I had two heads and clearly believed I was exaggerating.

In walking through the house with them, I came to realize that I'd interrupted a burglary in progress. We found the upstairs closet doors wide open with both the coats hanging up and the shoes on the floor skewed as if someone had moved them in order to stand in the closet and hide. This scared the daylights out of me. The guy had been right above me when I had come home. If I had gone upstairs for any reason . . .

It appeared the thief had entered by an unlocked kitchen door. The police took fingerprints but offered little hope of resolving the case.

That night was a long one, although I didn't tell Alex why I slept with all the house lights on. I had called Dad, but there was nothing he could do from so far away. It was good, though, to hear his voice. It made him seem closer, and that was comforting. Dad did change the locks when he got home a few days later.

All this made me realize again just how protected I had been all through my lifetime. Logically, because of all the chances I'd taken, the careless living, the drugs and alcohol, I should have been dead or a human wreckage at least. But God had other plans for me, and His thoughts toward me had been "more than the sands of the sea." He had loved me before I had even known Him, and by His grace and mercy He watched over me all of my life. I could have been assaulted that day or worse, but again I was delivered. Such love was something I couldn't understand, but only accept in faith and rejoice.

There were some things, of course, that I continued to struggle with, such as my animosity toward Massimo. He actually called on the phone once while I was yet staying with Dad. His voice was the last one I expected on the other end.

My careless "Hello?" was followed by a split second of stunned silence, then a cautious, "Katie, is that you? What are you doing there?"

My heart went stone cold, and I spat out words like ice chips, "Never mind. What do you want?"

"I want to talk to Alex."

"He's not here. He's at school right now."

"What time does he come home? Will you let me talk to him?"

"He'll be home about 4:00 our time. You can phone anytime after that."

"All right."

Click. From both of us.

It's interesting how, when you're away from someone you can't stand, you think you've dealt with the issue. But the emotion isn't gone; it only hides. I realized as I stood by the phone that all the old feeling, the rage, the . . . hatred . . . welled up in me the instant I heard Massimo's voice. As a new Christian, I knew that attitude was sin—plain and simple. After all, Jesus had forgiven me; I couldn't dishonor Him with my own unforgiveness. As quickly as the hatred resurfaced, it vanished, this time for good. In a moment of time, a miracle had happened, and I walked away from the phone a free woman. I knew I had forgiven Massimo.

At the end of Alex's school year, we left New Brunswick for Illinois. By then, by God's provision and Fabio's hard work, a decent apartment awaited the three of us. We were married in a quiet civil ceremony, and though without a ring—poor Fabio hadn't yet been able to scrape enough together for that—I happily took on the last name, Sapienza.

A few weeks into our new life, Fabio presented me with a gift, beautifully wrapped in a huge box. The initial unwrapping uncovered another, smaller box inside. Another box was fitted inside that one, and so on, till the last box was big enough to hold no more than . . . a ring. Oh, it was the most beautiful I had ever seen, a diamond set in gold, and its loveliness literally robbed me of speech. I was to discover that in order to save enough money to buy it, that dear man had worked nearly every waking hour and for months lived on little more than crackers and canned tuna fish.

As we settled into home life, we finally tied into a church that involved meaningful worship, faithful preaching of the Word, and genuine Christian fellowship. It seemed we attended every time their doors were open, and Alex especially loved children's church. One communion Sunday, not long after we began attending, Alex appeared troubled. "Mom," he said, very serious, "I want to take communion."

My heart leaped. "You know what you need to do, honey. Would you like to talk to the pastor?"

He nodded vigorously, and what followed was a few short minutes of intense discussion among the three of us. I believe Alex had already received Christ months before. His demeanor, his love for the Word and Christian fellowship all pointed to a personal relationship with Jesus. Now, he was stirred to make his commitment public, to stand before those he already considered his brothers and sisters, and declare openly his faith in Christ. At the altar call just prior to communion, he bravely stood alone as he was led in a sincere prayer of commitment to the Lord. I nearly cried for joy, and a few minutes later, for the first time in our lives, we celebrated the Lord's Supper together, not just as mom and son, but as brother and sister in Christ.

Later, Alex contrasted his education at the Catholic school in Palermo with the biblical way of salvation.

"Mom," he said with genuine amazement, "it's so easy! Before in (Catholic) catechism, I had to follow so many rules, and I never knew if I was saved or not. But Jesus really made it easy!"

Yes, He carried us when we were strangers in a far off land and lifted our hearts and made us free. And He returned to me the son who had been stolen from my arms.

> Thus saith the LORD;
> Refrain thy voice from weeping,
> And thine eyes from tears;
> For thy work shall be rewarded, saith the LORD;
> And they shall come again from the land of the enemy.
> And there is hope in thine end, saith the LORD,
> That thy children shall come again to their own border.
>
> Jeremiah 31:16-17

Epilogue—The Returning

È fattu lu beccu a l'oca.
All's well that ends well.

Twelve years can be both a lifetime and just yesterday.

The plane's shadow slid across the crystal Tyrrhenian Sea as we made our descent into Palermo. I was caught up in a whirlwind of emotion as some of the old landmarks I knew so well came into view: Isola della Femmine or Women's Island, uninhabited now but reputed to have been the site of a 16th Century women's prison; the long broken coastline where I had spent so many hours contemplating my life and the circumstances in which I found myself; the ubiquitous marinas; and off in the distance Mondello, which I couldn't quite see but which called to me from out of the early summer haze.

Touchdown onto the runway of the Aereoporto di Palermo-Punta Raisi solidified what had only moments earlier seemed like a dream. I was here, it was real, and the feeling of hard pavement beneath my feet as we deplaned afforded an incredible sense of homecoming. I couldn't quite place the feeling. All I knew was that I nearly wept for joy.

Walking beside me, Fabio smiled widely, partly because he was home, but also because he enjoyed watching my reactions. Upon takeoff from O'Hare I had cried, and a concerned Fabio had leaned close and whispered, "What is it? What's the matter?"

In that contradictory way of women, I smiled through the tears and told him, "Oh, I'm so happy. We're really going back."

On the surface, the trip was a social one. It had been some years since Fabio had visited his family, and he longed especially to see his mother living in Palermo. In between visits to his other relatives (one sister lived in the mainland village of Isola della Femmine and another in Carini), we sought out all the old places that yet held so much personal meaning—the huge flat sunbathing rocks of the Capo Gallo, favorite swimming spots, the little outdoor cafes where we'd buy those terrifically strong espressos and just talk. On our visits to Mondello, as we strolled along those white sand beaches, I felt swept back to those dark cloud times, to those hours we walked hand in hand while I endlessly intoned my Alex heartbreak, and Fabio offered comfort by few words and a strong presence. It was on these beaches, too, that I'd sit alone daily, staring out at the sea, wrapped round with the warm breezes while the seagulls wheeled just above, mewling plaintively, as I fantasized of first one then the other escape plan.

Walking the lovely little streets of Mondello, another set of remembrances rushed in—there the piazza had been flooded; over there stood the phone booth where I'd first met Judy; and finally, there, at Via Mondello, the days and nights I'd gone, lonely and depressed, to my little ground floor apartment with the huge mold stain that threatened to eat me. We stopped outside the gate, and I peered through the wrought iron bars, drinking in the scene. There yet stood the little lemon tree where Alex's giant lemon piñata hung on that ages-ago birthday. I fancied hearing the excited chatter of little Italian voices and the victory shout as Alex swung the bat and the piñata erupted with candy.

I relived other moments as well: the night of that horrible phone call and Dad's voice telling me Mom had died; calm, strong Fabio reading patiently to me from that outdated travel book; even the everyday routine of brewing morning coffee while the radio announcer went on and on about things that mattered little to me.

The echoes died away in my mind, and though feeling the heart tug, I did not go in. It seemed somehow wrong to trespass,

279

as if those reminiscences should be left undisturbed within a past that now owned them.

There is something to the idea that things come full circle. This dozen years after a wild flight across continents, I came face-to-face with the world I'd left behind, and the difference was astounding. Now, I was free to enjoy the things my "imprisonment" had kept from me. Now, I relished the hot sand under my bare feet, the rush of scented breeze, and thanks be to God, the "peace of God, which passeth all understanding" (Philippians 4:7). Sicily truly was a lover's paradise, and Fabio and I now experienced a romance once denied us on these very shores. As he held me, both of us getting lost in the grand sweep of ocean and a collage of memories, I fell deeply in love again.

In a way, I fell in love, too, with all Sicilians. The resentment was gone. This raucous, bombastic people who had so defined years of my life now cavorted in a different light. Their almost manic enthusiasm with life touched my heart, and perhaps for the first time, I really felt like one of them, chattering away in Italian and deeply inhaling the fragrance of their world. They still drove like Bedlam escapees, still reveled in street corner shouting matches, and in their minds were always right in all things. But I found myself bonding with this people. In a sense, they and I had always been so much alike—survivors just trying to make the best of things. Had I not been there under such heart-wrenching circumstances, I would not have harbored that previous cynical view toward Sicily and her people.

Yet, it was the pain I suffered while there and the swimming upstream that brought me to the end of myself and into the arms of Christ. I was reminded this day in Palermo so many years later of God's incredible mercy, of His reaching out to a poor desperate soul who needed Him so badly but took so long in realizing it. But only when my soul was ground into the dust, my existence defined by fear, drugs, and life underground, did I finally look up to Him.

In Palermo, Fabio's mom lived quite near the cold, grey stone courthouse where I'd fought such futile custody battles. It struck me that during all those horrible times when I had publicly been labeled a rotten mother and borderline psycho, I really hadn't been alone. There stood with me an unseen Advocate of whom I didn't even know, who had borne the pain of my case—both the eternal and temporal. It was nearly too much, the consideration simultaneously making my head spin and my heart rejoice.

We also visited the complex that Alex had called "home" those three years. From street level we could see the balcony of Giovanni and Lucia's apartment, and everything looked exactly the same, a bit faded, perhaps, like an old Polaroid snapshot left in the sun, but alike in every detail, as if I'd last seen it only the day before. In my mind, I could still see Giovanni in his ascetic's chair, reading the newspaper. I guessed that Lucia, the uncomplaining Sicilian housewife, was at that moment busying herself with kitchen things. I almost wanted to see a figure pass by an open window, perhaps to convince myself that they were indeed real people and not merely characters in a fiction thriller. And there, the doorman yet stood, officious, at his post, but I couldn't tell from there if he was the same one who had greeted me daily with a kind smile and sad eyes. What would all these be thinking if they knew I had been watching then from only a good stone's throw away?

Strange that standing on the corner of that busy Palermo inter-section, I couldn't summon up the old bad feelings anymore. As we stood gazing at the place, the whole setting seemed remarkable for its mediocrity. Though my prison in those earlier years, it bore no iron bars nor towers, no armed guards to mark it as such. I saw it now as it truly was, an old building of sun-washed brick, just like a thousand others in the city. There was nothing to betray the pain it had once housed. The rage, the hatred that had nearly consumed me back then was gone. Only a lingering sadness remained, like the overshadowing of something that could have been different.

A couple of blocks away, the Stadio delle Palme drew me like a magnet. The whole arena had since been enclosed in a chain link fence, causing me to wonder if it was erected due in part to Alex's rescue there. We crossed to it and stood at Exit

#2, staring into the arena but not entering. As midday crowds swarmed past, I was rooted to the spot, frozen in time, and swamped by sudden emotion. It seemed all around me everything went silent, and I was drawn forcefully into the vortex of "that day": losing Massimo in the running mob; sprinting with Alex and little Antonio to the exit; Don sweeping Alex into the waiting vehicle. In my mind, I could yet see the young gal taking down our license plate number, her sweater, like neon, glowing red against my memory. Then the screaming of tires, Don's Brooklyn imitation of a panicked Sicilian, the lot of us getting lost at twilight, and finally the shove-off into the sea with a volley of fireworks blazing at our stern.

How could it all have been real? By what stretch could I—a little miss nobody from New Brunswick, New Jersey—actually have been an international fugitive? Had I truly gone underground, learned to live like the hunted? After a span of years, it just didn't seem possible; it was as if, though standing at the spot where it all began, I was really in bed somewhere, reaching blindly for the alarm clock's snooze button while remnant dreams blended seamlessly with a waking world.

At the airport where we would soon begin our return flight to the States, I sat in an overcrowded waiting room. Fabio, sitting next to me, had dozed off. I gazed at this wonderful man who I was still as much in love with now as I was when we first got married.

Then just before boarding the plane, Fabio and I were approached by a middle-aged man who stared at me curiously, as if trying to remember something. He spoke with some hesitance.

"Aren't you Katie . . . oh, what was your last name? You got away with your son, right?"

I smiled. He had been a neighbor in Mondello. "That's me. And I remember you."

The man beamed, nodding furiously. "Ha! I knew it! And after so many years." His hands flailed the air, and then he leaned very close and said seriously, "I've always wanted to know—was it true what the papers said? There were a lot of rumors going around."

With little time before takeoff, I gave him the short version.

"I can't believe it," he said in amazement afterward, "I just can't believe it. But here you are!"

We hugged, and he turned away, looked back once and waved, then disappeared into the crowd.

Yes, there I was, by the grace of God.

Safe in the arms of Jesus,
Safe on His gentle breast;
There by His love o'ershaded,
Sweetly my soul shall rest.
Hark! 'tis the voice of angels
Borne in a song to me,
Over the fields of glory,
Over the jasper sea.

Safe in the arms of Jesus,
Safe from corroding care,
Safe from the world's temptations;
Sin cannot harm me there.
Free from the blight of sorrow,
Free from my doubts and fears;
Only a few more trials,
Only a few more tears!

Jesus, my heart's dear Refuge,
Jesus has died for me;
Firm on the Rock of Ages
Ever my trust shall be.
Here let me wait with patience,
Wait till the night is o'er;
Wait till I see the morning
Break on the golden shore.

A Word About My Husband and My Son

Fabio grew up in Palermo, Italy, living there until he came to the United States. In Italy, Fabio spent two years in a military academy, graduating with the rank of sergeant in the elite Carabinieri State and Military Corps. But the military was not Fabio's passion. Ever since he was very young, he has had a love for computer programming and network technology. After moving to the States, he enrolled in undergraduate studies and graduated with honors (not to mention straight As) with a degree in Science in Information Technology.

Alex graduated from the prestigious University of Chicago in Mathematics and has plans to attend graduate school. He works as a research associate in an international investment bank. Alex is still fluent in Italian and speaks it at home with Fabio and I. When Alex was a teenager, he began going back to Italy each year to visit Massimo, Massimo's brother, and Alex's grandparents. Today, he has a particularly close relationship with his Nonna and his uncle. Alex's paternal grandfather passed away several years ago.

As you can tell, I am very proud of my husband and my son and am so grateful to the Lord for allowing me the privilege of being part of their lives. K—

Above:
Alex and I. He has
now graduated
from university.

Right:
Fabio and I.

Credits

Photo Credits

With the exception of some scenic photos, the photos used in *Stolen From My Arms* are from Katherine Sapienza's personal collection. In photos showing members of the rescue team, permission for use was granted.

Scenic photo credits are as follows:

Page 49: City of Valletta; Carl Beddington (UK); used with permission from bigstockphoto.com.

Page 52: Map of Italy: Ruslan Olinchuk (Russia Federation); used with permission from 123rf.com.

Page 55: Siracusa in Sicily; Antje Bunke (Germany); used with permission from bigstockphoto.com.

Page 62: Apartments in Palermo; Tupungato (Poland); used with permission from bigstockphoto.com.

Page 75: Mondello Bay; Peeter Viisimaa (Estonia); used with permission from istockphoto.com.

Page 116: Capo Marketplace; by Natan (Poland); used with permission from bigstockphoto.com.

Page 207: Stadium in Palermo; Pernicum; used with permission from istockphoto.com.

Page 220: Map of Sicily; used with permission from 123rf.com; #837430.

Proverbs Credits

Thank you to the following people for providing the proverbs at the beginning of each chapter.

Chapters 1,3,6,11: Fabio Sapienza
Chapters 2,4,5,9: Piero Antonio Sapienza
Chapters 7,8,10,13,14, and Epilogue: Arthur Dieli
Chapter 12 and Prologue: Angelo and Mario Grifasi

Song on page 283: "Safe in the Arms of Jesus" by Frances Crosby, 1868.

Acknowledgements

To all of these, I offer my deepest gratitude and can only say *thank you* for what you have done.

First and foremost my Lord and Savior Jesus Christ.

My dear "American Group" in Italy who kept me uplifted and sane throughout my very dark years in Italy.

"Sara and Stefano" for taking me in and for showing me continal support.

The lawyers in the USA and Italy who tried to help me without a good outcome.

The group in Malta for all their help and support.

The two reporters, at two different times who not only wanted to get the story but did the right thing to help.

My father-in-law Piero Antonio Sapienza for the proverbs he provided.

My brother, John, his wife, Karen, and my Aunt Helen for their support.

Don and Judy and the rest of the team who put themselves at risk to retrieve my son.

My mother and father, without whom I could not have gotten Alex back.

My husband Fabio for his incredible love and support and who went through this whole ordeal with me from Italy to the USA.

My son Alex, the best son in the world, who turned out to be a wonderful young man.

All the countless others for their help, many whom I haven't mentioned.

Finally, I am eternally grateful to Zach Taylor who listened to my story and believed strongly it was God's will that it be told.

Katherine

To order additional copies of *Stolen From My Arms,* send $14.95 per book plus shipping to:

Lighthouse Trails Publishing, LLC
P.O. Box 908
Eureka, MT 59917(use this address to order free catalog of our products.)
For shipping costs, go to www.lighthousetrails.com/shippingcosts.htm
(US: $3.95/1 book; $5.20/2-3 books; $10.50/4-18 books)

You may also purchase Lighthouse Trails books from www.lighthousetrails. com. For bulk (wholesale) rates of 10 or more copies, contact Lighthouse Trails Publishing, either by phone, online, e-mail, or fax. You may also order retail or wholesale online at www.lighthousetrails.com, or for US and Canada orders, call our toll-free number: 866/876-3910. We give 40% off for 10 or more copies.

For international and all other calls: 406/297/7756; Fax: 406/297/7993. *Stolen From My Arms,* as well as other books by Lighthouse Trails Publishing, can be ordered through all major outlet stores, bookstores, online bookstores, and Christian bookstores in the U.S. Bookstores may order through: Ingram, SpringArbor or directly through Lighthouse Trails. Libraries may order through Baker & Taylor.

You may write to Katherine Sapienza care of: Lighthouse Trails Publishing, P.O. Box 908, Eureka, MT 59917

Other Biographies by Lighthouse Trails Publishing

Castles in the Sand (a novel)
by Carolyn A. Greene, $12.95

Foxe's Book of Martyrs
$14.95, illustrated

In My Father's House
by Corrie ten Boom
$13.95, illustrated, photos

Laughter Calls Me
by Catherine Brown
$12.95, Illustrated, photos

Let There Be Light
by Roger Oakland, $13.95

Stories from Indian Wigwams and Northern Campfires
by Egerton Ryerson Young, $14.95

Things We Couldn't Say
by Diet Eman, $14.95

Trapped in Hitler's Hell
by Anita Dittman with Jan Markell
$12.95, illustrated, photos